Will Kynes
My Psalm Has Turned into Weeping

Beihefte zur Zeitschrift für die alttestamentliche Wissenschaft

Herausgegeben von
John Barton · F. W. Dobbs-Allsopp
Reinhard G. Kratz · Markus Witte

Band 437

De Gruyter

Will Kynes

My Psalm Has Turned into Weeping

Job's Dialogue with the Psalms

De Gruyter

G

MIX
Papier aus verantwor-
tungsvollen Quellen
FSC
www.fsc.org
FSC® C016439

ISBN 978-3-11-029481-1
e-ISBN 978-3-11-029494-1
ISSN 0934-2575

Library of Congress Cataloging-in-Publication Data

A CIP catalog record for this book has been applied for at the Library of Congress.

Bibliographic information published by the Deutsche Nationalbibliothek

The Deutsche Nationalbibliothek lists this publication in the Deutsche
Nationalbibliografie; detailed bibliographic data are available in the Internet
at http://dnb.dnb.de.

© 2012 Walter de Gruyter GmbH & Co. KG, Berlin/Boston

Printing: Hubert & Co. GmbH & Co. KG, Göttingen
∞ Printed on acid-free paper

Printed in Germany

www.degruyter.com

Acknowledgements

This book is a slightly revised version of my PhD thesis at the University of Cambridge. I am thankful to Keble College, Oxford for welcoming me into the college's warm community and funding my research over the past year, when most of these revisions were made. Thanks also to the editors of BZAW for accepting this monograph and to the editorial staff at de Gruyter, particularly Sabina Dabrowski, for assiduous assistance in formatting the text for publication.

When writing a PhD thesis on the book of Job, it is difficult at times to resist identifying with its protagonist. The truth is, however, that in many respects my experience could not have been more different, and this is thanks in large part to the contrast between Job's supporting cast and mine. The Eliphaz in my story, my main source of guidance and support in this project, was my supervisor, Dr. Katharine Dell, and for her wisdom, consistency, and encouragement I owe a heavy debt of gratitude. She gave of her time to help me with far more than the thesis, shepherding me gently and patiently into the world of Old Testament scholarship. She was joined by numerous others, who also offered me the kindness Job's friends were unable to provide him. Prof. Manfred Oeming invited me to the University of Heidelberg and made my term-long stay there a delight. He also gave me helpful feedback on my research and the opportunity to share it at a conference at the university. Prof. David Carr and Prof. James Crenshaw both kindly sent me copies of forthcoming articles they had written. Prof. Christian Frevel gave me valuable feedback when this project was in its early stages. Dr. Scarlett Baron, Diane Hakala, and Kim Phillips all read chapters and provided useful insight. Dr. Nathan MacDonald, who supervised my M.Litt. thesis at the University of St. Andrews, taught me a great deal about how sound scholarship should be done. The insight provided by my PhD examiners, Prof. Graham Davies and Prof. John Barton, has also contributed significantly to this work. I have also benefited from countless conversations with other colleagues throughout this project, whether at the Old Testament Graduate Seminar, Tyndale House, or the Red Bull pub. Job's story would have been much different if he had had friends as generous and encouraging as these. This thesis is better and my life is richer thanks to their input; all the mistakes which remain in the thesis are my own.

Instead of abandoning me, as Job's did (19:13–19), my family has rallied around me. I am grateful to my grandparents, James and Marjorie Kynes, for providing me with a trust fund that enabled me to undertake this PhD. I hope that I have honored their memory with my efforts. My parents, William and Susan Kynes, and Cornerstone Evangelical Free Church also helped fund my studies. My mother's encouragement and my father's guidance throughout this whole process have been invaluable, as they have been throughout my life. My wife, Vanessa, played the opposite role to Job's sullen spouse. Continually supportive, she sacrificed a great deal to help me complete this project. She and our daughters Karis and Charlotte have ensured that my psalm has been sung with joy. To her I am infinitely grateful, and it is to her I dedicate this work.

לשמע־אזן שמעתיך ועתה עיני ראתך
Job 42:5

Will Kynes
Keble College, Oxford
August 2012

Table of Contents

PART I: PRAISE

PART II: SUPPLICATION

Abbreviations

ÄAT	Ägypten und Altes Testament
AB	Anchor Bible
AOTS	Augsburg Old Testament Studies
ArBib	The Aramaic Bible
ATANT	Abhandlungen zur Theologie des Alten und Neuen Testaments
ATAT	Arbeiten zu Text und Sprache im Alten Testament
ATD	Das Alte Testament Deutsch
ATDan	Acta theologica danica
BBR	*Bulletin for Biblical Research*
BCOTWP	Baker Commentary on the Old Testament Wisdom and Psalms
BETL	Bibliotheca ephemeridum theologicarum lovaniensium
BibInt	*Biblical Interpretation*
BibOr	Biblica et orientalia
BIS	Biblical Interpretation Series
BJRL	*Bulletin of the John Rylands University Library of Manchester*
BKAT	Biblischer Kommentar, Altes Testament
BTB	*Biblical Theology Bulletin*
BWANT	Beiträge zur Wissenschaft vom Alten und Neuen Testament
BZ	*Biblische Zeitschrift*
BZAW	Beihefte zur Zeitschrift für die alttestamentliche Wissenschaft
CahRB	Cahiers de la Revue biblique
CAT	Commentaire de l'Ancien Testament
CBQ	*Catholic Biblical Quarterly*
CBQMS	Catholic Biblical Quarterly Monograph Series
CBR	*Currents in Biblical Research*
CBSC	Cambridge Bible for Schools and Colleges
CFThL	Clark's Foreign Theological Library
CI	*Critical Inquiry*
CJT	*Canadian Journal of Theology*
ConBOT	Coniectanea biblica: Old Testament Series
CR	Cahiers du renouveau
CRS	Classics in Religious Studies
CSA	Copenhagen Studies in Assyriology
CTJ	*Calvin Theological Journal*
CurBS	*Currents in Research: Biblical Studies*

DSD	*Dead Sea Discoveries*
ECC	The Eerdmans Critical Commentary
EBC	The Expositor's Bible Commentary
EncJud	*Encyclopaedia Judaica*
ErFor	Erträge der Forschung
EstBib	*Estudios bíblicos*
ExB	An Exposition of the Bible
FAT	Forschungen zum Alten Testament
FC	Fathers of the Church
FF	Forschungen und Fortschritte
FOTL	Forms of the Old Testament Literature
FRLANT	Forschungen zur Religion und Literatur des Alten und Neuen Testaments
HALOT	Köhler, Ludwig et al. *The Hebrew & Aramaic Lexicon of the Old Testament.* CD-ROM ed. Leiden: Koninklijke Brill, 2000.
HAT	Handbuch zum Alten Testament
HBM	Hebrew Bible Monographs
HBS	Herders Biblische Studien
HS	*Hebrew Studies*
HTKAT	Herders theologischer Kommentar zum Alten Testament
HTR	*Harvard Theological Review*
IB	Interpreter's Bible
ICC	International Critical Commentary
Int	*Interpretation*
ISBL	Indiana Studies in Biblical Literature
ITL	International Theological Library
JAAC	*Journal of Aesthetics and Art Criticism*
JAOS	*Journal of the American Oriental Society*
JBL	*Journal of Biblical Literature*
JBQ	*Jewish Bible Quarterly*
JBTh	*Jahrbuch für Biblische Theologie*
JJS	*Journal of Jewish Studies*
JNSL	*Journal of Northwest Semitic Languages*
JR	*Journal of Religion*
JSJSup	Supplements to the Journal for the Study of Judaism
JSNTSup	Journal for the Study of the New Testament: Supplement Series
JSOT	*Journal for the Study of the Old Testament*
JSOTSup	Journal for the Study of the Old Testament: Supplement Series
KAT	Kommentar zum Alten Testament
KeH	Kurzgefasstes exegetisches Handbuch zum Alten Testament
KHC	Kurzer Hand-Commentar zum Alten Testament
LAI	Library of Ancient Israel

LBS	Library of Biblical Studies
LCBI	Literary Currents in Biblical Interpretation
LHBOTS	Library of Hebrew Bible/Old Testament Studies
MLBS	Mercer Library of Biblical Studies
NBE	Nueva Biblia Española
NCB	New Century Bible
NEchtB	Neue Echter Bibel
Neot	*Neotestamentica*
NIB	The New Interpreter's Bible
NIBCOT	New International Biblical Commentary on the Old Testament
NICOT	New International Commentary on the Old Testament
NSKAT	Neuer Stuttgarter Kommentar Altes Testament
OBO	Orbis biblicus et orientalis
OBS	Oxford Bible Series
OBT	Overtures to Biblical Theology
OEM	Oxford English Monographs
OLA	Orientalia lovaniensia analecta
OTE	*Old Testament Essays*
OTL	Old Testament Library
OtSt	Oudtestamentische Studiën
PhL	*Philosophy and Literature*
PL	Patrologia latina [= Patrologiae cursus completus: Series latina]. Edited by J.-P. Migne. 217 vols. Paris, 1844–1864
Proof	*Prooftexts: A Journal of Jewish Literary History*
PTL	*PTL: A Journal for Descriptive Poetics and Theory of Literature*
PTS	Patristische Texte und Studien
RB	*Revue biblique*
RBL	*Review of Biblical Literature*
ResQ	*Restoration Quarterly*
RP	Religious Perspectives
RSR	*Recherches de science religieuse*
RTT	Research in Text Theory
SAT	Die Schriften des Alten Testaments
SBLit	Studies in Biblical Literature
SBLDS	Society of Biblical Literature Dissertation Series
SBLEJL	Society of Biblical Literature Early Judaism and Its Literature
SBLMS	Society of Biblical Literature Monograph Series
SBS	Stuttgarter Bibelstudien
SBT	Studies in Biblical Theology
SDPI	Schriften des Deutschen Palästina-Instituts
SJT	*Scottish Journal of Theology*
SR	*Studies in Religion*

StB	Studia biblica
StJ	Studies in Judaism
StOR	Studies in Oriental Religions
SubBi	Subsidia Biblica
SVT	Scholia in Vetus Testamentum
TBü	Theologische Bücherei
THB	The Text of the Hebrew Bible
THL	Theory and History of Literature
TLZ	*Theologische Literaturzeitung*
TRu	*Theologische Rundschau*
TTFL	Theological Translation Fund Library
TZ	*Theologische Zeitschrift*
UTAS	Ugolini's Thesaurus antiquitatum sacrarum
UUÅ	*Uppsala Universitets Årsskrift*
VE	*Vox evangelica*
VeE	*Verbum et Ecclesia*
VT	*Vetus Testamentum*
VTSup	Vetus Testamentum Supplements
WBC	Word Biblical Commentary
WD	*Wort und Dienst*
WdF	Wege der Forschung
YJS	Yale Judaica Series
ZABR	*Zeitschrift für altorientalische und biblische Rechtsgeschichte*
ZAW	*Zeitschrift für die alttestamentliche Wissenschaft*
ZBK	Zürcher Bibelkommentare
ZTK	*Zeitschrift für Theologie und Kirche*

1. Hearing History:
Connections between Job and the Psalms in the History of Interpretation

For inquire now of bygone generations,
and consider what their ancestors have found ...
Will they not teach you and tell you
and utter words out of their understanding?
(Job 8:8–10).[1]

1.1. Introduction

For a century and a half, commentators have recognized the parody of Ps 8:5 in Job 7:17–18, and over time this "bitter parody"[2] has developed into a "scholarly commonplace."[3] Despite the skepticism of some toward identifying either this or any other textual parallel in Job as an allusion,[4] the repetition of the phrase מה אנוש ("What are human beings?"), the common structure of both passages, and the recurrence of the verb פקד set in a context which reverses its meaning, have led to a nearly unanimous consensus that Job is intentionally twisting the meaning

---

1   This and other biblical quotations, unless otherwise indicated, are from the NRSV.

2   Franz Delitzsch appears to be the first to note the parody (Franz Delitzsch, *Biblical Commentary on the Book of Job* [trans. Francis Bolton; 2 vols.; CFThL 10–11; Edinburgh: T&T Clark, 1866], 1:124). The phrase "bitter parody," commonly used to describe this intertextual connection, goes back to T. K. Cheyne in 1887 (T. K. Cheyne, *Job and Solomon: Or, The Wisdom of the Old Testament* [New York: T. Whittaker, 1887], 88). The close textual parallel was observed as early as the fourth century (John Chrysostom, *Kommentar zu Hiob* [ed. U. Hagedorn and D. Hagedorn; PTS 35; Berlin: de Gruyter, 1990], 86).

3   Raymond C. Van Leeuwen, "Psalm 8.5 and Job 7.17-18: A Mistaken Scholarly Commonplace?" in *The World of the Aramaeans I: Biblical Studies in Honour of Paul-Eugène Dion* (eds. P. M. Michèle Daviau et al.; JSOTSup 324; Sheffield: Sheffield Academic Press, 2001), 206.

4   For objections to regarding this parallel as an allusion and my response, see pp. 64–67. For a general skepticism toward establishing any such textual dependence in Job, see Paul-Eugène Dion, "Formulaic Language in the Book of Job: International Background and Ironical Distortions," *SR* 16 (1987): 192; Bruce Zuckerman, *Job the Silent: A Study in Historical Counterpoint* (Oxford: Oxford University Press, 1991), 91.

of the psalm from a hymn of praise for God's watchful care to a complaint against his overbearing attention.[5] Rarely, however, has the question which naturally follows been pursued: if the author of Job interacted with Psalm 8 in such a knowing and sophisticated way, suggesting that he expected his readers to be familiar with such texts,[6] what other allusions to the Psalms may likewise make significant contributions to the dialogue between Job, his friends, and God?

The intent of this study is not merely to identify other allusions to the Psalms in Job, but to interpret them by using a systematic intertextual method to focus attention on their role in this dispute. The Psalms have been used in the past as an interpretive lens for Job. Precritical interpreters,[7] for example, compared the character Job with David, who was generally considered to be speaking in the Psalms.[8] "Psalmistische Interpretationen" of Job have been a consistent, albeit secondary, feature of critical Job scholarship, focusing mainly on the resonances between the book and the lament psalms, as will be discussed below.[9] Thus, Curt Kuhl claims, based on the book's connections with psalmic laments and hymns, that Job stands as close to the Psalms as to Wisdom Literature.[10] Similarly, Ivan Engnell argues that "from many points of view, it can be said that this work

---

5   See pp. 63–71. For ease of presentation, I will often ascribe the act of alluding to Job or his friends, but, of course, the author is ultimately responsible for portraying the characters' interaction with earlier texts.

6   Raik Heckl, *Hiob: Vom Gottesfürchtigen zum Repräsentanten Israels* (FAT 70; Tübingen: Mohr Siebeck, 2010), 64.

7   I appreciate John Barton's concern that the term "precritical" may suggest the absence of critical reading of the Bible before a certain period and its ubiquity afterwards, when neither is actually true (John Barton, *The Nature of Biblical Criticism* [Louisville, Ky.: Westminster John Knox, 2007], 189). However, I use the term as helpful shorthand to describe biblical interpretation before biblical criticism came to the fore in the seventeenth and eighteenth century, as he occasionally does (e.g., 75, 77).

8   For parallels between Job and David in Jewish interpretation, see Louis Ginzberg, *The Legends of the Jews* (7 vols.; Baltimore: John Hopkins University Press, 1998), 5:390. In Christian interpretation, Ambrose (ca. 339–397) and John Calvin both repeatedly return to this comparison. See Ambrose, "The Prayer of Job and David," in *Saint Ambrose: Seven Exegetical Works* (trans. Michael P. McHugh; FC 65; Washington, D.C.: Catholic University of America Press, 1971); John Calvin, *Sermons on Job* (Edinburgh: The Banner of Truth Trust, 1993); repr. of *Sermons on Job* (trans. Arthur Golding. London: George Bishop, 1574) and Susan Elizabeth Schreiner, "'Why Do the Wicked Live?' Job and David in Calvin's Sermons on Job," in *The Voice from the Whirlwind: Interpreting the Book of Job* (eds. Leo G. Perdue and W. Clark Gilpin; Nashville: Abingdon, 1992), 130. For more on this character-based connection between the books, see Will Kynes, "Reading Job Following the Psalms," in *The Shape of the Ketuvim: History, Contoured Intertextuality, and Canon* (eds. Julius Steinberg and Tim Stone; Siphrut; Winona Lake: Eisenbrauns, forthcoming).

9   See the survey in Hans-Peter Müller, *Das Hiobproblem: Seine Stellung und Entstehung im alten Orient und im Alten Testament* (3rd ed.; ErFor 84; Darmstadt: Wissenschaftliche Buchgesellschaft, 1995), 82–91, 111–18.

10   Curt Kuhl, "Neuere Literarkritik des Buches Hiob," *TRu* 21 (1953): 311, 312.

occupies a middle position between the Psalms of Lament and the so-called Wisdom Literature," though he believes Job transcends them both.[11] By attending to the allusions to the Psalms in Job, however, I will look through this interpretive lens from the other direction by suggesting that the author of Job is interpreting the Psalms. Through allusions to specific psalms, and not only laments, the author of Job does invite its readers to understand the book through its interaction with them, but he also provides a new perspective from which to view the Psalms themselves.

I begin with a survey of the development of critical discussion of allusions between Job and the Psalms, which has seen interest move from the historical to the hermeneutical significance of this literary phenomena, leading to the current recognition that allusions in Job to the HB, including the Psalms, contribute vitally to the book's interpretation. Chapter two will then examine the intertextual approach that has inspired this insight. In that chapter I will lay out my method for identifying and interpreting allusions between Job and the Psalms, which puts "synchronic" and "diachronic" intertextualities in dialogue. I will then apply this method in the next six chapters to the particularly strong intertextual connections between Job and six psalms (1, 8, 39, 73, 107, and 139), before offering conclusions on the implications of this intertextual interplay for the interpretation of both Job and the Psalms.

1.2. Early Critical Interpretation

Interest in possible allusions between Job and the Psalms only arose with the development of critical scholarship in the seventeenth century, and when it did, it appears that, if this rhetorical technique was originally intended to contribute to the meaning of the texts, its significance had long been forgotten. This study cannot recount the likely both complex and unconscious process that caused this allusion amnesia, most of which is lost in the mists of history, beyond suggesting that it may correspond to the "forgetting" of biblical parallelism.[12] As James Kugel argues, though it happened in different ways for Jewish and Christian interpreters, an emphasis on the divine origin of the text directed interpreters away from appreciating the import of features of its human composition, such as parallelism, and, I would suggest, allusion. Thus, for rabbinic exegesis, Michael Fishbane attributes the "tendency to forget the exegetical dimensions of Scrip-

---

11   Ivan Engnell, "The Figurative Language of the Old Testament," in *Critical Essays on the Old Testament* (ed. and trans. John T. Willis; London: SPCK, 1970), 256.

12   James L. Kugel, *The Idea of Biblical Poetry: Parallelism and its History* (New Haven: Yale University Press, 1981), 96–134, 139–40.

ture" primarily to the establishment of a fixed and authoritative canon, and Moisés Silva observes that from Origen through the medieval period most Christian interpreters "tended to disregard the human (and therefore historical) aspects of the text because of their commitment to its divine character."[13]

Though precritical interpreters showed little interest in possible allusions between Job and the Psalms, preferring instead to read the Bible as a synchronic whole, they did offer to the early critical commentators who took up the issue a wealth of observed connections between the texts on which to build. The exegetical significance they drew from these verbal and thematic affinities tended to focus, not on the question of literary dependence, but on the explanation of difficult words or the elucidation of theological concepts. Thus, for example, among patristic interpreters, John Chrysostom (ca. 347–407) showed a notable interest in psalmic parallels in Job, mentioning several (e.g., Job 5:6 // Ps 90:10; Job 7:16 // Ps 39:11; Job 7:19 // Ps 12:2–3; Job 18:15–17 // Ps 37:12[14]) and occasionally using them to cast light on difficult passages in Job. Thus, in contrast to recent interpretation of the passage, he pointed to the psalmist's humble question, "What are human beings that you are mindful of them?" (Ps 8:5) to argue that in 7:17 Job is affirming that God's attention, even if it is only evident in divine testing and punishment, is proof of humanity's worth.[15] Thomas Aquinas (1225–1274), in the medieval period, often referred to the characters speaking "according" to the Psalms, which occasionally involved the characters using similar wording (e.g., Job 23:12 // Ps 119:11[16]), but more often indicated similar theological thoughts (e.g., Job 35:12 // Ps 102:17[17]). So, for him, the verbal similarity appears less important than the related theological concept it represents, which seems to be his main concern, since he used his exegesis of the book as a foundation on which to build a sophisticated Aristotelian defense of divine providence. The same tendencies are evident in Jewish interpretation. Saadiah Gaon (882–942) based his translation of עלתה as "the authors of iniquity" in Job 5:16 on "the model of" Ps 125:3, where the same word is used.[18] Rashi (1040–1105) also pri-

---

13   Michael Fishbane, "Inner-Biblical Exegesis: Types and Strategies of Interpretation in Ancient Israel," in *Midrash and Literature* (eds. Geoffrey H. Hartman and Sanford Budick; New Haven: Yale University Press, 1986), 36; Moisés Silva, *Has the Church Misread the Bible?: The History of Interpretation in the Light of Current Issues* (Leicester: Apollos, 1987), 38–41.

14   Chrysostom, *Hiob*, 70, 86, 87, 126. I have conformed verse references to Hebrew numbering throughout this chapter.

15   Chrysostom, *Hiob*, 86.

16   Thomas Aquinas, *The Literal Exposition on Job: A Scriptural Commentary Concerning Providence* (ed. Martin D. Yaffe; trans. Anthony Damico; CRS 7; Atlanta: Scholars Press, 1989), 303. Both passages refer to hiding God's words in one's heart.

17   Aquinas, *Job*, 394. Elihu claims God will not heed the cry of the prideful, whereas the psalmist affirms that God hears the prayers of the humble.

18   Saadiah Ben Joseph Al-Fayyumi, *The Book of Theodicy: Translation and Commentary on the Book of Job*

marily employed similarities between Job and the Psalms to explain linguistic difficulties. For example, to justify translating שחק in Ps 104:26 as "to sport with" and taking it to describe God's interaction with Leviathan, he refers to Job 40:29, where the same verb appears in God's description of the beast.[19]

John Calvin showed great interest in connections between Job and the Psalms in his *Sermons on Job*, in some ways still reflecting traditional ideas, yet in others anticipating the type of intertextual reading of the two texts which has only recently been explored.[20] For example, though he apparently followed the traditional view that Job was one of the oldest books in the Bible and therefore believed it was written before the Psalms,[21] his interpretation of Job 7:17 approached that of later interpreters who read Job's lament as a parody of Ps 8:5. Though the two passages involve multiple lexical similarities, Calvin remarked that Job's statement is not like the one in Psalm 8 because there "the words are set in their proper signification" as David recounts God's care for his creatures, whereas in Job "they are taken clean contrary" as Job "turns God's providence quite upside down … instead of comforting and cheering himself with it, he would prefer that God were far off."[22]

Calvin also drew the whole of Psalm 107 into his discussion of two parallel passages in Job. On Job 5:16, where the second half of the verse closely follows Ps 107:42b, he recounted the progressive logic of the Psalm, in which God's providence is demonstrated through his deliverance after punishment, as support for the shared phrase, "injustice shuts its mouth."[23] Then, he began his sermon on Job 12:17–25, a passage which involves several parallels with the psalm, including the verbatim repetition of Ps 107:40 in vv. 21, 24, with a long discussion of God's control over kings and empires, concluding, "But God ordains it in such ways, to the end that it might be better known that such changes happen

---

(ed. Lenn Evan Goodman; YJS 25; New Haven: Yale University Press, 1988), 193. He does not mention the parallel to Ps 107:42, where a nearly identical phrase to the one in Job 5:16 appears.

19 Mayer I. Gruber, *Rashi's Commentary on Psalms* (BRLJ 18; Leiden: Brill, 2004), 618.

20 For the intersection of Calvin's commitments to historico-grammatical exegesis and divine inspiration, see Randall C. Zachman, "Gathering Meaning From Context: Calvin's Exegetical Method," *JR* 82 (2002): 1–26.

21 A rabbinic tradition attributes the book's composition to Moses (*Baba Batra* 15a). Another view, which already in 1751 Charles Peters called the "old Hypothesis," posited Job himself as the author (Charles Peters, *A Critical Dissertation on the Book of Job* [London: E. Owen, 1751], 3). For a discussion of the position of these "älteren Kritiker," see August Dillmann, *Hiob* (4th ed.; KeH 2; Leipzig: S. Hirzel, 1891), xxix. Though Calvin did not discuss the book's date explicitly, he referred to Ps 145:18 and texts like it, in which God promises to be near to all those that call upon him in truth as "texts [that] were not yet written" (Calvin, *Job*, 515).

22 Calvin, *Job*, 133. In quoting from these sermons I have modernized the English from the 1574 translation.

23 Calvin, *Job*, 93.

not but for men's instruction, as it is said more fully in Ps 107," and therefore it is "not without cause that Job stands so much upon this point."[24]

Thus, Calvin's exegesis of Job thoroughly appreciated the connections with the Psalms, noting parallels between the texts and drawing exegetical significance from them, but even he did not contemplate the possibility of Job alluding to the Psalms. The assumption of Joban priority, likely influenced by the book's patriarchal setting, precluded this explanation.[25] He also apparently failed to see how such stylistic insight could lead to theological illumination, which, despite his historico-grammatical hermeneutic, was his main concern,[26] as would be fitting for a series of sermons. The early critical reading of the book will overturn the first of these obstacles but not the second.

Between the sixteenth and the nineteenth century, Job was the object of a massive amount of study. David Clines lists over 150 books from just the first three of these centuries, an average of a new book on Job every eighteen months.[27] A survey of some of the most influential commentaries on Job produced during this period reveals many of the same trends in the treatment of verbal connections between Job and the Psalms as were evident in earlier ages. Some interpreters chose not to mention them;[28] others mentioned them rarely;[29] and still others referred to them repeatedly, though generally only to explain the meaning of difficult words or elucidate theological concepts.[30] However, as critical biblical scholarship developed, finding its first systematic presentation in Baruch Spinoza's *Tractatus Theologico-Politicus* (1670),[31] exegetical interest shifted from the divine to the human authorship of the Bible. This concern for the human nature of the text became focused, at least in the interpretation of verbal

---

24   Calvin, *Job*, 224.

25   However, even when he was writing commentaries on the Psalms, he still did not explain the parallels between the texts as allusions. See John Calvin, *Commentary on the Book of Psalms* (trans. James Anderson; 5 vols.; Grand Rapids, Mich.: Baker Book House, 1993).

26   Zachman, "Gathering," 25–26.

27   David J. A. Clines, *Job* (3 vols.; WBC 17–18B; Nashville: Thomas Nelson, 1989, 2006, 2011), 1:lxix–lxxv.

28   E.g., Johannes Terentius, *Liber Ijobi Chaldaice et Latine* … (Franeker: Johann Wellens, 1663); Albert Schultens, *Opera minora, animadversiones ejus in Jobum* … (Leiden: Joh. le Mair & H. A. de Chalmot, 1769).

29   E.g., Johannes Piscator, *In Librum Jobi commentarius* … (Herborn: Officina Typographica Christophori Corvini, 1612); Johann Christoph Döderlein, *Scholia in libros Veteris Testamenti poeticos: Iobum, Psalmos et tres Salomonis* (Halle: Io.Iac. Curt, 1779); Johann August Dathe, *Jobus Proverbia Salomonis Ecclesiastes Canticum Canticorum* … (Halle: Sumtibus Orphanotrophei, 1789).

30   E.g., Didacus Zuniga, *In Job commentaria* (Rome: 1591); Ioannis de Pineda, *Commentariorum in Iob* … (Cologne: A. Hierat, 1605); Jacobus Bolducius, *Commentaria in librum Job* (2 vols.; Paris: 1637).

31   See Rudolf Smend, "Baruch Spinoza," *EncJud*, 15:282. Barton points out that the roots of biblical criticism reach back into the ancient world (Barton, *Biblical Criticism*, 117–36).

parallels between Job and the Psalms, on the text's witness to history. A new exegetical concern for the date of Job's composition developed in the seventeenth century, which put new emphasis on possible psalmic allusions in Job, but primarily as evidence for that pursuit and not for their contribution to the meaning of Job or the Psalms. The debate over the significance of these parallels for the relative dating of the two books would last several centuries, uncovering the intertextual nature of Job and identifying many of the possible allusions that will be explored in this study along the way.

One of the first commentators to address the issue of dating was Hugo Grotius in 1644. Without listing them, he appealed to the parallels between Job and both Psalms and Proverbs to date the book after David and Solomon.[32] Following Grotius, Jean Le Clerc argued that a comparison of the many parallel texts between Job and the Psalms demonstrated that the Psalms have greater beauty and naturalness, which indicates that Job is the imitator and they the originals.[33] In the next century, Francis Hare, referring primarily to the parallel between Job 12:21 and Ps 107:40, argued that dependence actually rested in the opposite direction.[34] However, William Warburton, writing around the same time, deemed arguments of this type "equivocal" since, "if the sacred writers must needs have borrowed trite moral sentences from one another: it may be as fairly said, that the authors of the Psalms borrowed from the book of Job; as that the author of Job borrowed from the book of Psalms."[35] Still in the mid-eighteenth century, Leonard Chappelow listed three parallels (Job 7:10 // Ps 103:16; Job 5:16 // Ps 107:42; Job 12:21, 24 // Ps 107:40) as the crux of the debate on dependence.[36] However, he sought to sidestep the dispute by claiming that the verbal parallels between the books were merely "part of certain sententious, proverbial instructions, preserved from one age to another by wise and understanding men."[37]

In the nineteenth century, as critical study of Job expanded, so did the number of parallels recognized between Job and not only the Psalms, but also the rest of the HB. Because, as Samuel Lee argued, the authors of those books lived after the Exodus and Job before it, Job could not be citing their work, whereas the

---

32   Hugo Grotius, *Hugonis Grotii Annotata ad Vetus Testamentum* (Paris: Sebastiani Cramoisy, Regis & Reginae Architypographi, et Gabrielis Cramoisy, 1644), 398.

33   Jean Le Clerc, *Sentimens de quelques theologiens de Hollande sur l'Histoire critique du Vieux Testament* (Amsterdam: Chez Henri Desbordes, 1685), 183.

34   Francis Hare, *Psalmorum liber: in versiculos metrice divisus* (Ugolini's Thesaurus antiquitatum sacrarum 31; Venice: 1766), 1418.

35   William Warburton, *The Divine Legation of Moses Demonstrated* (The Works of the Right Reverend William Warburton, Lord Bishop of Gloucester 5; London: John Nichols, 1765), 42.

36   Leonard Chappelow, *A Commentary on the Book of Job* (2 vols.; Cambridge: J. Bentham, 1752), x.

37   Chappelow, *Job*, 184. Thus, anticipating form criticism, he argued that the expression "What is man?" found in both Job 7:17 and Ps 8:5 was simply a proverbial saying and therefore did not reflect direct influence from one text to another (99).

converse was "extremely likely."[38] For critics like Lee, this proved not only the book's antiquity but also its canonical authority to such a degree that it became "a sort of treasury of divinity, and worthy of all acceptation at all times, ever since its first publication."[39] For Lee, the sheer number and striking nature of these parallels exceeded the limits of coincidence, which, he argued, left the following dilemma for interpreters: "either the language and sentiments of this book must have been accessible to the sacred writers ever since the times of Moses, or else the Book of Job must have been written subsequent to them all, and so have borrowed in all this abundance from them." He proceeded to declare the latter option "an opinion which the wildest of theorists would scarcely adopt."[40]

Bateson Wright, however, undeterred by Lee's strong language, suggested that Joban priority had "been too much taken for granted" and deemed it "improbable" that "Job should be the vast storehouse of Hebrew expression on philosophical and theological problems, to which all Hebrew poets and philosophers are indebted."[41] Instead, Wright argued, in many of the parallels the opposite is true. Wright was anticipated by C. Rosenmüller, who dated the book late primarily on linguistic grounds and added the following parallels to those listed by Chappelow: Job 22:19 // Ps 107:42; Job 5:10 and 37:6 // Ps 147:8; Job 38:41 // Ps 147:9.[42] For Ferdinand Hitzig, two parallels (Job 15:35 // Ps 7:15; Job 7:17 // Ps 8:5) were adequate evidence to prove that Job must have been written after the time of David.[43] A. B. Davidson came to the same conclusion on the basis of the "distorted reflection" of Ps 8 in Job 7:17, which he deemed "scarcely due to coincidence."[44]

T. K. Cheyne, who considered the "bitter parody" of Psalm 8 in Job 7 "specially important" for dating the book of Job after the exile, when he thought it "extremely probable" that the psalm was written,[45] took a more nuanced approach to the issue of dependence between Job and the Psalms. Referring to

---

38   Samuel Lee, *The Book of the Patriarch Job* (London: Duncan, 1837), 67.

39   Lee, *Job*, 67. John Mason Good similarly remarked that Job "is occasionally quoted or copied by almost every Hebrew writer who had an opportunity of referring to it, from the age of Moses to that of Malachi; especially by the Psalmist, Isaiah, Jeremiah, and Ezekiel," which leads him to affirm the book's "high origin and antiquity" (John Mason Good, *The Book of Job* [London: Black, Parry & Co., 1812], xlvii).

40   Lee, *Job*, 86. Similarly, the "enormous number of parallels to passages in other books of the Old Testament" indicated to Edward Kissane a century later that "either the writer of Job showed an intimate knowledge of the rest of Hebrew literature, or that he exerted a deep influence on subsequent writers" (Edward J. Kissane, *The Book of Job* [Dublin: Brown and Nolan Ltd., 1939], xlix).

41   G. H. Bateson Wright, *The Book of Job* (London: Williams and Norgate, 1883), 11.

42   C. Rosenmüller, *Iobus* (2nd ed.; SVT 5; Leipzig: Ioh. Ambros. Barthii, 1824), 38–42.

43   Ferdinand Hitzig, *Das Buch Hiob* (Leipzig: C.F. Winter'sche Verlagshandlung, 1874), xl.

44   A. B. Davidson, *The Book of Job* (CBSC; Cambridge: Cambridge University Press, 1889), lix.

45   Cheyne, *Wisdom*, 88.

historical criticism as his guide, he separated the parallels involving "undeniably later psalms" from those involving "the great body of psalms of disputed date."[46] The former group was composed of the following parallels:

> Ps 103:16 // Job 7:12;
> Ps 107:40 // Job 12:21, 24;
> Ps 107:41 // Job 21:11;
> Ps 107:42 // Job 22:19, 5:16;
> Ps 119:28 // Job 16:20;
> Ps 119:50 // Job 6:10;
> Ps 119:69 // Job 13:4;
> Ps 119:103 // Job 6:25.

He then proclaimed without further discussion, "There is, I think, no question that these psalm-passages were inspired by the parallels in Job." For the psalms of disputed date, Cheyne listed these parallels:

> Ps 8:5 // Job 7:17;
> Ps 39:12b // Job 4:19b;
> Ps 39:14a // Job 7:19a, 10:20;
> Ps 39:14b // Job 10:21, 22;
> Ps 72:12 // Job 29:12;
> Ps 72:16 // Job 5:25b;
> Ps 88:16b // Job 20:25;
> Ps 88:17 // Job 6:4;
> Ps 88:19 (69:9) // Job 19:14.

He then separated Psalm 88, which he considered "clearly imitative," from 8, 39, and 72, which he claimed were "known to and imitated by the authors of Job," though without further indication of how he came to these conclusions.

As in Cheyne's work, in much of the interpretation of this time, psalmic parallels played little role beyond contributing to the discussion of the date of the book, rarely spreading from the introduction into the exegesis in the commentary itself. However, Moriz Friedländer provides an exception soon after the turn of the twentieth century. He compared Job's friends to the pious in the Psalms and recounted verbal and thematic similarities between their speeches and psalmic language (e.g., Job 15:35 // Ps 7:15; Job 18:15 // Ps 11:6) to suggest that their attack of Job "ist genau nach dem Rezept der Psalmen gehalten."[47] Job's response, then, Friedländer argued, goes beyond similar complaints by the

---

46 Cheyne, *Wisdom*, 84, 88.

47 Moriz Friedländer, *Griechische Philosophie im Alten Testament: Eine Einleitung in die Psalmen- und Weisheitsliteratur: Psalmen, Proverbien, Hiob, Koheleth, Sirach, Pseudo-Salomo, und Anhang der Bücher Jona und Ruth* (Amsterdam: Philo Press, 1904), 101.

psalmist (e.g., Job 21:6–22; cf. Ps 73:2–22).[48] Thus, in his view, both sides in the debate built on psalmic precedents.

1.3. Form Criticism

With the development of form criticism in the early twentieth century, the discussion of parallels between Job and the Psalms changed, and the hermeneutical insight Friedländer attempted to draw from possible allusions was not pursued. Attention to biblical allusions decreased soon after the rise of form criticism,[49] and a causal relationship between these two phenomena seems likely, based on the way the latter approach exchanged attention to allusions between particular texts for shared general similarities.[50] In fact, Martin Buss argues that the development of the generalizing approach of form criticism was itself a reaction to the particularism of historical criticism.[51] According to Hermann Gunkel's theory, parallel phrases were not necessarily to be seen as the result of literary dependence, and thus as indicators of a text's date of composition, but as witnesses to a common form and a corresponding *Sitz im Leben*. With similar language in multiple texts now considered evidence of a common form, the investigation into possible allusions between Job and the Psalms faded. However, form-critical categories, such as the lament, provided new opportunities for interpreters to identify similarities between the two texts. Thus, form-critical studies on Job, though employing the method in different ways, continued to demonstrate the essential contribution the Psalms make to interpreting Job.[52]

---

48   Friedländer, *Griechische Philosophie*, 111–14.

49   The lists of possible allusions in Job, which often appeared in commentary introductions up to the 1920s, eventually disappear. The last are Samuel Rolles Driver and George Buchanan Gray, *A Critical and Exegetical Commentary on the Book of Job* (ICC; Edinburgh: T&T Clark, 1921), lxvii–lxviii; Edouard Dhorme, *A Commentary on the Book of Job* (trans. Harold Knight; London: Thomas Nelson and Sons, 1967); trans. of *Le livre de Job* (Paris: V. Lecoffre, 1926), clix–clxviii.

50   James Muilenburg criticizes form criticism for this tendency (James Muilenburg, "Form Criticism and Beyond," *JBL* 88 [1969]: 5).

51   He observes, "Particularist approaches arose gradually [after the High Middle Ages] and came to play a major role in nineteenth-century historical criticism. Toward the end of that century, when many voices were raised against unbridled individualism, interest in general literary types reemerged in biblical studies." Gunkel, he claims, was "reacting against a purely particularist way of looking at texts" (Martin J. Buss, *The Changing Shape of Form Criticism: A Relational Approach* [HBM 18; Sheffield: Sheffield Phoenix Press, 2010], 101). See also Martin J. Buss, *Biblical Form Criticism in its Context* (JSOTSup 274; Sheffield: Sheffield Academic Press, 1999), 209–15.

52   Klaus Seybold, "Psalmen im Buch Hiob," in *Studien zur Psalmenauslegung* (ed. Klaus Seybold; Stuttgart: Kohlhammer, 1998), 272. Taking a form-critical approach, Seybold also explores the contribution Job interpretation can offer Psalms exegesis, concluding that Job's disputational use of various types of lament indicates the forensic role of the prayers of the accused (287).

Friedrich Baumgärtel, using form-critical categories to attempt to return the dialogue to its purported original form as a pure disputation speech, excised sections which correspond with other forms, such as the hymns in Job 5:9–16 and 12:13–25, which sound remarkably similar to Psalm 107 and even share several verbal parallels (e.g., 5:16 // Ps 107:42b; 12:21a, 24b // Ps 107:40).[53] Similarly, he argued that Job 7 was not original because the lament in Psalm 88 could just as easily fit in its place.[54] This approach resulted in his theory of an original dialogue consisting of a fraction of the current text,[55] which, Baumgärtel concluded, does not address a theoretical question like the meaning of suffering or the problem of theodicy, but instead presents the cry of a pious man in his despair as he wrestles with God.[56] This conclusion was somewhat paradoxical, given that he had excised the sections of the dialogue that are similar to the lament.[57]

Characterizing the message of the book in much the same way,[58] Claus Westermann, however, drew the opposite conclusion from the formal similarities between Job and the Psalms, particularly the laments. Instead of using form criticism as a tool for redaction criticism and expunging the sections of Job which correspond with the lament form as secondary additions, Westermann employed the approach more constructively to claim that this recurrent aspect of the text defines the book as a whole.[59] Following Aage Bentzen, he characterized Job as a "dramatization" of the psalm of lamentation, in which Job, the friends, and God correspond to the individual, the enemies, and God in the lament.[60] According to Westermann, the Job poet, standing within his tradition, "cannot express himself in other than already formed linguistic structures," and thus "dramatizes the

---

53   Friedrich Baumgärtel, *Der Hiobdialog: Aufriss und Deutung* (BWANT 61; Stuttgart: W. Kohlhammer, 1933), 18–19. See ch. 4 below.

54   Baumgärtel, *Hiobdialog*, 28–29.

55   The only remaining "original" passages appear in chs. 4, 5, 6, 8, 9, 11, 13, 16, 19, 23, and 31 (Baumgärtel, *Hiobdialog*, 189).

56   Baumgärtel, *Hiobdialog*, 187–88.

57   See Claus Westermann, *The Structure of the Book of Job: A Form-Critical Analysis* (trans. Charles A. Muenchow; Philadelphia: Fortress Press, 1981), 34.

58   Westermann, *Structure*, 1–2, 59 n. 4. Paul Volz preceded both these interpreters in this characterization of the book's message, and Fohrer follows them. See Paul Volz, *Weisheit: (das Buch Hiob, Sprüche und Jesus Sirach, Prediger)* (SAT; Göttingen: Vandenhoeck & Ruprecht, 1911), 25–26; Georg Fohrer, *Das Buch Hiob* (KAT 16; Gütersloh: Gütersloher Verlagshaus Gerd Mohn, 1963), 549. Recently, Raik Heckl has made a similar argument (Heckl, *Hiob*, 205, 215).

59   Westermann, *Structure*, 34–35.

60   Westermann, *Structure*, 8. See Aage Bentzen, *Introduction to the Old Testament* (2 vols.; Copenhagen: G. E. C. Gad, 1948–1949), 1:182. For a similar comparison of Job and the implicit voices in the lament from a dialogical perspective, see Carleen Mandolfo, "A Generic Renegade: A Dialogic Reading of Job and Lament Psalms," in *Diachronic and Synchronic: Reading the Psalms in Real Time* (ed. Joel S. Burnett, W. H. Bellinger, and W. Dennis Tucker; New York: T&T Clark, 2007), 45–63.

lament by weaving together the basic motifs of lamentation, motifs which were already ancient."[61] And yet, Westermann's form-critical perspective led him to eschew attempts to investigate allusions to actual Psalms because, he argued, the Psalms only preserve a small portion of the laments voiced in ancient Israel, so conclusions would be uncertain.[62] Even so, he claimed that Job 7:17 "is quite obviously an ironic citation from Psalm 8,"[63] and this confident assertion raises the question of further possible allusions in Job.

Georg Fohrer criticized Westermann's work for being too one-sided in its definition of the book by a single form.[64] Instead, taking a broader approach to form criticism, Fohrer argued that the book, deeply rooted in the traditional material and motifs of the HB, takes up and uses traditions from across the canon to such a degree that only a few verses in the whole text lack reference to them.[65] According to Fohrer, the Job poet mixes forms throughout the speeches, often for purposes different from their original function.[66] The most commonly used forms are sapiential, psalmic, and legal, with laments and hymns appearing most frequently.[67] In the section on formal elements at the beginning of his commentary on each speech, Fohrer often noted formal similarities between Job and the Psalms, but this emphasis seems to preclude attention to possible psalmic allusions. Thus, he referred to Job 7:17 as an ironic use, not of a particular text, but of the hymnic motif in Ps 8:5 and Ps 144:3, and though he observed several similarities between Job 12:12–25 and Psalm 107, he, like Baumgärtel, considered the hymnic passage a later addition to the book.[68]

Developing Fohrer's insight into the Job poet's extensive use of traditional forms and emphasizing their oral prehistory, Katharine Dell argued that often the forms are "misused," and that as a whole this contributes to the skeptical nature of the book. This pattern of "misuse" may be illustrated by comparing the form in Job with the same form as it appears elsewhere in the HB, and she catalogued a series of misused forms across the dialogue, the majority coming from the Psalms.[69] For Dell, therefore, the form is something separate from the text in which it appears, and the author of Job may employ that form without necessarily

61 Westermann, *Structure*, 32.
62 Westermann, *Structure*, 33.
63 Westermann, *Structure*, 72.
64 Georg Fohrer, review of Claus Westermann, *Der Aufbau Des Buches Hiob, VT* 7 (1957): 111.
65 Fohrer, *Hiob*, 48.
66 Fohrer, *Hiob*, 49–50; Georg Fohrer, "Form und Funktion in der Hiobdichtung," in *Studien zum Buche Hiob (1956–1979)* (BZAW 159; Berlin: de Gruyter, 1983), 60–77.
67 Fohrer, *Hiob*, 50–51.
68 Fohrer, *Hiob*, 167, 245.
69 Katharine J. Dell, *The Book of Job as Sceptical Literature* (BZAW 197; Berlin: de Gruyter, 1991), 125–36.

engaging any particular text. Consistent with this understanding, Dell carefully avoided asserting that these misuses involve direct reference to particular texts. With the exception of the "parody" of Psalm 8 in Job 7 and again in 14:1–12,[70] she mentions Psalm references only as examples of a certain form. For example, she referred to Job 10:2–12, not as a parody of Psalm 139, but as "a misuse of the kind of form found in Psalm 139."[71] Similarly, she described Job 23:8–9 as "a clear parody of a hymn such as Psalm 23."[72]

1.4. Intertextuality

In the past quarter century, a growing number of biblical scholars have turned their attention from generalized connections between forms to lexically specific allusions.[73] Instead of using shared forms to suggest a common *Sitz im Leben*, this new literary approach seeks to decipher the deeper meaning given to a work through its interaction with other texts. This hermeneutical method reignited the interest in textual specificity from the early critical period that form criticism had overshadowed, but instead of treating purported allusions primarily as historical data, it applied insight from literary studies to investigate their hermeneutical significance, leading to a growing appreciation for the interaction of not just forms but actual texts. Michael Fishbane may be credited with injecting this intertextual approach, which I will describe in greater depth in the next chapter, into the study of the HB with his influential book *Biblical Interpretation in Ancient Israel*. In this work, he traces later biblical tradents' use of earlier texts and argues that their form of "inner-biblical exegesis" anticipates early Jewish interpretation.[74]

---

70   Dell, *Sceptical*, 126, 129.

71   Dell, *Sceptical*, 127. For the connections between Job 10 and Psalm 139, see pp. 108–112 below.

72   Dell, *Sceptical*, 132. I will argue this passage is actually a parody of Psalm 139. See pp. 115–117 below. Dell's later work reflects the intertextual turn in HB studies as she pursues textual "echoes" of specific texts in the book of Proverbs in Katharine J. Dell, *The Book of Proverbs in Social and Theological Context* (Cambridge: Cambridge University Press, 2006), e.g., 2, 181–84.

73   Anthony Campbell has incisively characterized form criticism's fall from favor this way: "Above all … the focus away from the present text into a surmised past accessible to a scholarly few was too burdened with subjectivity to survive in a generation focused on the present reality of what was possessed in the final text" (Anthony F. Campbell, "Form Criticism's Future," in *The Changing Face of Form Criticism for the Twenty-First Century* [eds. Marvin A. Sweeney and Ehud Ben Zvi; Grand Rapids, Mich.: Eerdmans, 2003], 22).

74   Michael Fishbane, *Biblical Interpretation in Ancient Israel* (Oxford: Clarendon Press, 1985), 527. As Fishbane acknowledges (2 n. 5), his work was not without its precursors, which may be found particularly in the attempts to identify inner-biblical midrash. See, e.g., Renée Bloch, "Midrash," in vol. 5 of *Supplément au Dictionnaire de la Bible* (eds. H. Cazelles and A. Feuillet; Paris: Le Touzey, 1950), 1263–81; I. L. Seeligmann, "Voraussetzungen der Midraschexegese," in *Congress Volume. Copenhagen 1953* (eds. G. W. Anderson et al.; VTSup 1; Leiden: Brill, 1953), 150–81.

1.4.1. Job and the Hebrew Bible

Recent scholarship on Job testifies to this intertextual turn. Thus, whereas Fohrer focused on the Job poet's use of *forms* that appear across the HB, Tryggve Mettinger speaks of intertextual allusion to both texts and genres, as the book "draws on *literary material* from a very wide range of backgrounds: wisdom, law, cult, psalmody, etc."[75] John Hartley suggests that the intimate knowledge of the HB possessed by the author of Job is evident in the many parallels between the book and other HB texts.[76] According to Melanie Köhlmoos, "Der hauptsächliche kontextuelle und intertextuelle Hintergrund des Hiobbuches ist das Alte Testament."[77] Demonstrating how the later date for Job suggested by critical scholarship has influenced the recognition of allusions in Job, she grounds this statement in the book's historical setting, claiming that the high literary output of the second century of Persian rule, where she places the book, was marked by intertextual dialogue with earlier texts in the HB.[78] Though she does not go into great depth on the intertextual connections in Job, she recognizes the significance of references to Psalms 8 and 104 in the meaning of the book as a whole.[79] Further, Yohan Pyeon argues that "the speeches in Job show a deliberate attempt to employ references to biblical texts, both from Job and from other books."[80] Finally, Leslie Wilson, who dates Job to the second century B.C.E., claims that its author was "intimately familiar with all of [the HB]."[81] Whether or not the book can be dated that late and the author's knowledge of the HB can be considered

---

75   Tryggve N. D. Mettinger, "Intertextuality: Allusion and Vertical Context Systems in Some Job Passages," in *Of Prophets' Visions and the Wisdom of Sages* (eds. Heather A. McKay and D. J. A. Clines; JSOTSup 162; Sheffield: JSOT Press, 1993), 274. Emphasis added.

76   He provides a chart of some of these parallels. See John E. Hartley, *The Book of Job* (NICOT; Grand Rapids, Mich.: Eerdmans, 1988), 11–12.

77   Melanie Köhlmoos, *Das Auge Gottes: Textstrategie im Hiobbuch* (FAT 25; Tübingen: Mohr Siebeck, 1999), 15. See also Konrad Schmid's argument that Job refers to the Torah, Prophets, and Psalms (Konrad Schmid, "Innerbiblische Schriftdiskussion im Hiobbuch," in *Das Buch Hiob und seine Interpretationen: Beiträge zum Hiob-Symposium auf dem Monte Verità vom 14.–19. August 2005* [eds. Thomas Krüger et al.; ATANT 88; Zürich: Theologisher Verlag Zürich, 2007], 241–61).

78   Köhlmoos, *Textstrategie*, 1–3. Similarly, Victoria Hoffer asserts that Job displays the proclivity of Israelites in exile and diaspora to find nourishment in their literary heritage, as that literature is "playfully articulated" in Job (Victoria Hoffer, "Illusion, Allusion, and Literary Artifice in the Frame Narrative of Job," in *The Whirlwind: Essays on Job, Hermeneutics and Theology in Memory of Jane Morse* [eds. Stephen L. Cook et al.; JSOTSup 336; London: Sheffield Academic Press, 2001], 99).

79   Köhlmoos, *Textstrategie*, 362.

80   Yohan Pyeon, *You Have Not Spoken What Is Right About Me: Intertextuality and the Book of Job* (SBLit 45; New York: Lang, 2003), 66.

81   Leslie S. Wilson, *The Book of Job: Judaism in the 2nd Century BCE: An Intertextual Reading* (StJ; Lanham, Md.: University Press of America, 2006), 4. For his linguistic and socio-religious reasons for this uncharacteristically late date, see 14–15, 244.

that exhaustive, interaction with a developing HB is seen increasingly to be a vital aspect of the method and meaning of the book of Job.

1.4.2. Job and the Psalms

The Psalms often contribute to these intertextual readings of Job. Fishbane himself mentions the parody of Psalm 8 in Job 7:17–18 as an example of inner-biblical exegesis.[82] This intertext has dominated the discussion of possible psalmic allusions in Job. Even though, as noted earlier, the similarity between the two texts was observed as early as Chrysostom, the likelihood of literary dependence in these passages had been used to date the book in the early critical period, and Job's use of the psalm has been characterized as a parody for more than a century, only recently has the exegetical significance of this intertext been widely discussed. However, commentators disagree on its meaning. For some, Job's parody of the psalm indicates the skeptical nature of the book, while for others, the psalm acts throughout as a paradigm to which Job appeals.[83]

The discussion of Job's use of Psalm 8 gives an indication of the broader interpretive significance allusions to the Psalms may have in the book, but little has been done to address this issue. Several scholars have pursued intertextual readings of Job and other psalms, such as 22, 23, and 139,[84] as well as 104 and 147,[85] but these studies put little emphasis on the question of allusion.[86] Others have made general statements about the importance of psalmic intertexts for the understanding of the book. For example, Carol Newsom claims that Job's parodies render the psalm of lament "literally and figuratively unspeakable," and that he exposes repressed aspects of the psalms of supplication through fragmenting and recombining their motifs,[87] and Christian Frevel argues that the Psalms,

---

82 Fishbane, *Interpretation*, 285–86.

83 See pp. 69–71.

84 Michaela Bauks, *Die Feinde des Psalmisten und die Freunde Ijobs: Untersuchungen zur Freund-Klage im Alten Testament am Beispiel von Ps 22* (SBS 203; Stuttgart: Katholisches Bibelwerk, 2004); Douglas J. Green, "The Good, the Bad and the Better: Psalm 23 and Job," in *The Whirlwind: Essays on Job, Hermeneutics and Theology in Memory of Jane Morse* (eds. Stephen L. Cook et al.; JSOTSup 336; London: Sheffield Academic Press, 2001), 69–83; William P. Brown, "*Creatio Corporis* and the Rhetoric of Defense in Job 10 and Psalm 139," in *God Who Creates: Essays in Honor of Sibley Turner* (eds. William P. Brown and S. Dean McBride, Jr.; Grand Rapids, Mich.: Eerdmans, 2000), 107–24.

85 D. W. Jamieson-Drake, "Literary Structure, Genre and Interpretation in Job 38," in *The Listening Heart: Essays in Wisdom and Psalms in Honor of Roland E. Murphy* (eds. Kenneth G. Hoglund et al.; JSOTSup 85; Sheffield: JSOT Press, 1987), 217–35.

86 In fact, Jamieson-Drake, who discusses similarities between Job 38 and Psalms 104 and 147, states that direct dependence is unlikely (Jamieson-Drake, "Job 38," 225).

87 Carol A. Newsom, *The Book of Job: A Contest of Moral Imaginations* (Oxford: Oxford University Press, 2003), 163, 131.

which repeatedly appear as reference texts, serve as a paradigm throughout the book.[88] However, no one has combined a thorough and extensive investigation of the use of the Psalms in Job with an attempt to understand their broader role in the book.

1.5. Conclusion

Thus, after the precritical "forgetting" of allusions to the Psalms in Job, the early critical focus on their historical significance for dating the texts, the form-critical emphasis on generalized connections between texts, and the intertextual return to textually specific allusions, now with an eye to their hermeneutical value, the time is ripe to investigate these allusions anew. Though no study has been solely dedicated to this phenomenon in recent scholarship, the peripheral treatments of the issue in works on other aspects of the book, the studies of specific psalmic intertexts and the references to various psalms strewn throughout Job commentaries all suggest that a more comprehensive treatment of the issue is needed, and this I intend to supply here. Recent work on these connections has produced fresh insight into both Job and the Psalms, but most of this work has been *ad hoc*, neither built on nor leading to a coherent formulation of the use of the Psalms in Job, nor drawing wider conclusions about the impact of these allusions on the interpretation of Job. Because of the various hermeneutical interests that have driven biblical interpretation over its history, as Frevel opines, too little attention has been paid to allusions to the Psalms in Job.[89] However, in my view, intertextuality provides a means to rectify this, and in the next chapter I will shape this interpretive tool to prize open the significance of these allusions.

---

88   Christian Frevel, "'Eine kleine Theologie der Menschenwürde': Ps 8 und seine Rezeption im Buch Ijob," in *Das Manna fällt auch heute noch: Beiträge zur Geschichte und Theologie des Alten, Ersten Testaments* (eds. Frank-Lothar Hossfeld and Ludger Schwienhorst-Schönberger; HBS 44; Freiburg: Herder, 2004), 257, 262.

89   Frevel, "Menschenwürde," 257.

2. Between Times, Between Texts: Intertextualities in Dialogue

There are no texts, but only relationships between texts.[1]

2.1. Introduction

The basic premise of intertextuality, that texts incorporate aspects of their precursors, is as old as texts themselves. The term "intertextuality," however, did not appear until the late 1960s,[2] and since then, its meaning has been embroiled in conflict. This debate is well documented,[3] as is the discussion over the appropriate application of the concept to biblical studies.[4] The disputants fit into three broad camps: among those who embrace the term, the traditionalists and the progressives, and opposing both, the anti-intertextualists.[5] On the traditional side are those who understand intertextuality as an "enlargement" of older studies on the influence of earlier texts on later ones and attend to authors' intended references to their literary sources, while the progressive conception of intertextuality conceives of the method as a "substitution" for influence studies, in which these concerns recede into the background since texts are considered part of an infinite web of meaning to be untangled by the reader.[6] The anti-intertextualists attack

---

1   Harold Bloom, *A Map of Misreading* (Oxford: Oxford University Press, 1975), 3. Emphasis original.

2   See p. 21 n. 20.

3   See, e.g., Jonathan Culler, "Presupposition and Intertextuality," in *The Pursuit of Signs: Semiotics, Literature, Deconstruction* (London: Routledge & Kegan Paul, 1981), 100–118; Jay Clayton and Eric Rothstein, "Figures in the Corpus: Theories of Influence and Intertextuality," in *Influence and Intertextuality in Literary History* (eds. Jay Clayton and Eric Rothstein; Madison: University of Wisconsin Press, 1991), 3–36; Mary Orr, *Intertextuality: Debates and Contexts* (Cambridge: Polity, 2003).

4   See, e.g., George Aichele and Gary A. Philips, "Exegesis, Eisegesis, Intergesis," *Semeia* 69/70 (1995): 7–18; Thomas R. Hatina, "Intertextuality and Historical Criticism in New Testament Studies: Is There a Relationship?" *BibInt* 7 (1999): 28–43; Patricia K. Tull, "Intertextuality and the Hebrew Scriptures," *CurBS* 9 (2000): 59–90.

5   Heinrich F. Plett, "Intertextualities," in *Intertextuality* (ed. Heinrich F. Plett; New York: de Gruyter, 1991), 3.

6   Clayton and Rothstein, "Figures," 3–4.

both sides, charging the progressives with being impractical and even incomprehensible and the traditionalists with merely putting old wine into new bottles.[7]

This internecine dispute between the traditionalists and progressives is often characterized as a contest between "diachronic" and "synchronic" approaches, respectively, particularly in biblical scholarship.[8] Like "intertextuality," these terms have expanded with widespread use, straying from their original meaning in the semiotic theory of Ferdinand de Saussure, who used "diachronic" to describe the development of a language over time and "synchronic" for the language in a given moment of time.[9] However, their prevalence in this discussion makes them unavoidable. Often "synchronic" is simply used as a synonym for "literary" and "diachronic" for "historical," which shows just how far they have diverged from Saussure's usage, and is an unhelpful distinction, as well, since literary sensitivity can contribute significantly to historical investigation and vice versa. Thinking of diachronic as author-oriented and synchronic as reader-oriented better represents the difference between the two approaches,[10] but it transfers Saussure's terms to a new plane, which causes conflicts between these meanings of the words and those he intended, such as in reception history, which is both reader-oriented and diachronic, tracing the reception of texts over time. Therefore, I understand "diachronic" as a *sequential* way of reading connections between texts, in which the relative dates of texts are important because one author is referring to the work of another, and "synchronic" as a *simultaneous* interpretive approach, in which readers may read texts "all at one time" and pursue textual resonances irrespective of direct historical relationships between them, because, to quote one progressive intertextualist, "the reader is the space on which all the quotations that make up a writing are inscribed without any of them being lost; a text's unity lies not in its origin but its destination."[11]

---

7   Plett, "Intertextualities," 5. Thus, William Irwin claims, "The term *intertextuality* is at best a rhetorical flourish intended to impress, at worst it is the signifier of an illogical position" (William Irwin, "Against Intertextuality," *PhL* 28 [2004]: 240).

8   E.g., Sommer, *Prophet*, 8; Hatina, "Intertextuality," 41; Patricia K. Tull, "Rhetorical Criticism and Intertextuality," in *To Each Its Own Meaning: An Introduction to Biblical Criticisms and Their Application* (eds. Steven L. McKenzie and Stephen R. Haynes; Louisville, Ky.: Westminster John Knox, 1999), 159. In his recent survey, Geoffrey Miller divides intertextual study of the HB along these lines (Geoffrey D. Miller, "Intertextuality in Old Testament Research," *CBR* 9 [2011]: 283–309).

9   Ferdinand de Saussure, *Course in General Linguistics* (trans. Roy Harris; London: Duckworth, 1983), 79–98.

10 See Miller, "Intertextuality," 286.

11 Roland Barthes, "The Death of the Author," in *Image-Music-Text* (trans. Stephen Heath; New York: Hill and Wang, 1977), 148. Thus, Daniel Boyarin states, "Sources and influences are comparable to the historical reconstructions of diachronic linguistics, while intertextuality is a function of the semiotic system of relations and differences present in the literary and linguistic system at a given moment" (Daniel Boyarin, *Intertextuality and the Reading of Midrash* [ISBL; Bloomington: Indiana University Press, 1990], 135 n. 2).

The dispute between these two intertextual approaches overlaps with another more fundamental debate over whether intertextuality should be considered a method for interpreting texts at all. According to John Barton, to use intertextuality to attempt to elucidate the meaning of a text is a "soft" understanding of the concept, "simply adding another method to the toolbox of the biblical critic." However, he claims, "the original idea is a 'hard' one: a theory about texts in general, and indeed about how human beings understand the world as a whole, for which intertextual 'readings' of specific texts are merely evidence or illustration."[12] Though progressive intertextuality draws more directly on the poststructuralist and high "Theory" ideas of which the "hard" version of intertextuality is a forebear, and may therefore be closely associated with it (as will be evident in the discussion below), as long as it is directed to the interpretation of texts, it is just an alternative "soft" version of intertextuality along with the traditional approach. Stephen Moore and Yvonne Sherwood appeal to the widespread "domesticating" of Theory, intertextuality included, into practical method in biblical studies as evidence of the field's "susceptibility to methodolatry and methodone addiction."[13] Therefore, Barton warns that, as a result, biblical scholars who use the term risk misunderstanding or even perceptions of naivety and inconsequentiality from non-biblical scholars who may think that their methodological use of the term "is meant to relate to areas of literary theory of which it is in fact innocent."[14]

Misunderstanding is a danger in any interdisciplinary dialogue, but, as I have demonstrated elsewhere,[15] the most recent literary criticism often employs intertextuality in "soft" methodological and even diachronic ways. A recent study of the "response" of James Joyce "to his precursor" Gustave Flaubert, complete with discussion of intentional allusions, is but one example of such an approach.[16] This work, and others like it, may not claim that this approach to intertextuality exhausts its interpretive potential, but they certainly see it as one valid application of the term. As a result, biblical scholars need not apologize for using "intertextuality" in the methodological way it is now widely employed, both in biblical scholarship and beyond. However, Barton's warning is worth heeding, not only because biblical scholarship on intertextuality will likely be stronger to the degree

---

12   John Barton, "*Déjà lu*: Intertextuality, Method or Theory?," in *Reading Job Intertextually* (eds. Katharine Dell and Will Kynes; LHBOTS; New York: T&T Clark, forthcoming).

13   Stephen D. Moore and Yvonne Sherwood, *The Invention of the Biblical Scholar: A Critical Manifesto* (Minneapolis: Fortress Press, 2011), 35, 31; cf. 33.

14   Barton, "*Déjà lu*."

15   Will Kynes, "Intertextuality: Method and Theory in Job and Psalm 119," in *Biblical Interpretation and Method: Essays in Honour of Professor John Barton* (eds. K. J. Dell and P. M. Joyce; Oxford: Oxford University Press, forthcoming).

16   Scarlett Baron, "*Strandentwining Cable*": Joyce, Flaubert, and Intertextuality* (OEM; Oxford: Oxford University Press, 2012), 3.

it interacts with its theoretical background, but also because the theory and method of intertextuality need not be set at odds with one another, but may, in fact, be mutually enlightening, with methodological readings illustrating theoretical ideas and theoretical arguments informing the interpretation of texts.

Thus, though this study interacts with intertextual theory, it puts particular emphasis on method. The intertextual method developed in this chapter is applied systematically in the chapters that follow. I have done this primarily because this study is not merely an exploration of the connections between these two specific texts but also of how to identify and interpret connections between any two texts, especially those for which the relative dating of one before or after the other is unknown. My hope is that putting this method through its paces here will enable it to be used by others, perhaps with further refinement, to analyze other texts.

Given the disputes surrounding "intertextuality," it is not surprising that some biblical scholars choose to avoid the term altogether when studying biblical allusions.[17] However, the term is worth using, first, because "intertextuality" is now used so widely in biblical studies to describe any type of relationship between texts, acting as a sort of umbrella term,[18] that even a study of allusion that avoids the term cannot avoid the association. Some have argued that progressive intertextuality should exclusively claim the title "intertextuality," while the traditional approach should be called something else.[19] However, the broader use of the term is now so widespread that such a terminological correction is unlikely to be effective. In fact, this use has likely spread because, used that way, "intertextuality" fills an important void, since no word previously existed to encapsulate the many ways texts may be connected. Second, in my view, the development of intertextuality has provided some significant gains over traditional views of influence, and these deserve acknowledgment. At the same time, traditional insight may contribute to more progressive approaches, and this should not be excluded through strict terminological barriers.

The following presentation of my approach to intertextuality will involve three steps. First, focusing on the more methodological versions of intertextuality more prevalent in biblical studies, I will suggest that the polarization between

---

17   E.g., Sommer, *Prophet*, 6–10; Michael A. Lyons, *From Law to Prophecy: Ezekiel's Use of the Holiness Code* (LHBOTS 507; New York: T&T Clark, 2009), 50.

18   See, e.g., Peter D. Miscall, "Isaiah: New Heavens, New Earth, New Book," in *Reading Between Texts: Intertextuality and the Hebrew Bible* (ed. Danna Nolan Fewell; LCBI; Louisville, Ky.: Westminster John Knox, 1992), 44; Steve Moyise, "Intertextuality and Biblical Studies: A Review," *VeE* 23 (2002): 429–30.

19   E.g., Miller, "Intertextuality," 305; David M. Carr, "The Many Uses of Intertextuality in Biblical Studies: Actual and Potential," in *International Organization for the Study of the Old Testament Congress Volume: Helsinki 2010* (ed. Martti Nissinen; VTSup 148; Leiden: Brill, 2012), 531.

progressive and traditionalist types of intertextuality is a false dichotomy stemming primarily from the progressives' desire to differentiate themselves from their precursors. Second, I will describe how diachronic and synchronic approaches, the essence of the perceived polarization, may actually be mutually beneficial when practiced together. Finally, I will present my method for pursuing intertextual connections between Job and the Psalms, which, using the insight of studies on intertextuality from both progressives and traditionalists, works with the conviction that allusions are best addressed not only according to a text's historical enunciation (diachronic approaches) or its ever-present reception (synchronic approaches) but in the dialogue between them.

2.2. The False Dichotomy

Julia Kristeva coined the term "intertextuality" with the assertion that "any text is constructed as a mosaic of quotations; any text is the absorption and transformation of another. The notion of intertextuality replaces that of intersubjectivity, and poetic language is read as at least double."[20] As conceptions of intertextuality developed, poetic language began to be read not merely as double, but as infinite, as the sources that texts absorb and transform were seen to themselves absorb and transform others and thus create an expansive and unreconstructable intertextual web. Therefore, according to a progressive understanding, Kristeva's original intent for the term is "abused"[21] when it is applied to "a restricted conception"[22] of intertextuality that addresses questions of influence and sources. Kristeva herself later discarded the word for another, "transposition," to distinguish her conception of intertextuality from "the banal sense of 'study of sources.'"[23] However, this oft-repeated charge against traditional approaches is

---

20 Julia Kristeva, "Word, Dialogue, and Novel," in *Desire in Language: A Semiotic Approach to Literature and Art* (ed. Leon S. Roudiez; Oxford: Basil Blackwell, 1980), 66. This essay appeared as the fourth chapter of her *Semeiotikè: recherches pour une sémanalyse*, published in 1969. The essay is dated 1966 there. It was also published as "Bakhtine, le mot, le dialogue et le roman," *Critique* 23 (1967): 438–65.

21 Leon S. Roudiez, "Introduction," in *Desire in Language: A Semiotic Approach to Literature and Art* (ed. Leon S. Roudiez; Oxford: Basil Blackwell, 1980), 15.

22 Hans-Peter Mai, "Bypassing Intertextuality: Hermeneutics, Textual Practice, Hypertext," in *Intertextuality* (ed. Heinrich F. Plett; RTT 15; Berlin: de Gruyter, 1991), 30.

23 Julia Kristeva, *Revolution in Poetic Language* (trans. Margaret Waller; New York: Columbia University Press, 1984), 59–60.

both subjective[24] and exaggerated.[25] Furthermore, it is contradicted by the nature of progressive intertextuality, the practice of Kristeva herself, and the way words actually work.

First, there is the glaring irony of those who deny that meaning is fixed in the original author's intent attempting to fix the meaning of a word in its original author's intent. Second, Kristeva herself both practiced source-hunting, even claiming that the particular edition a scholar used was important,[26] and reinterpreted Mikhail Bakhtin's term "dialogic" to fit *her* new system just as later interpreters have used her term in ways she did not intend.[27] Third, despite the charge of inconsistency,[28] traditionalists who respect authorial intent and are sensitive to a word's original context need not affirm that Kristeva's use of the word is normative. Actually, words (as well as methods of interpreting texts) evolve with use. Should study of metaphor be restricted to Aristotle's initial understanding of it or the study of historical criticism to Spinoza's? The same could be said of the ideological baggage with which some claim intertextuality comes.[29] Though Kristeva and the *Tel Quel* group in Paris of which she was a part had Marxist leanings and

---

24   The subjective charge of banality could be thrown back at progressive intertextualists, as it has been on occasion, for their approach's "anticlimactic" and "idiosyncratic" conclusions (Culler, "Presupposition," 108, see also 110, where he uses the term "banal"; Irwin, "Intertextuality," 236).

25   Kristeva's characterization is "a metonymic 'mis-reading' … of the methodology of influence studies, which is surely more complex than 'the study of sources'" (Susan Stanford Friedman, "Weavings: Intertextuality and the (Re)Birth of the Author," in *Influence and Intertextuality in Literary History* [eds. Jay Clayton and Eric Rothstein; Madison: University of Wisconsin Press, 1991], 153).

26   Kristeva, *Revolution*, 341. Several scholars note this incongruous interpretive move. See Culler, "Presupposition," 106–7; Thaïs Morgan, "The Space of Intertextuality," in *Intertextuality and Contemporary American Fiction* (eds. P. O'Donnell and R.C. Davis; Baltimore, Md.: Johns Hopkins University Press, 1989), 261; Friedman, "Weavings," 154.

27   Clayton and Rothstein, "Figures," 18–20; Mai, "Intertextuality," 33; Orr, *Intertextuality*, 26–27. In fact, it is debatable whether Kristeva actually affirmed the belief in the death of the author common for later progressive intertextual scholars, such as Barthes. See Beth LaNeel Tanner, *The Book of Psalms Through the Lens of Intertextuality* (SBLit 26; New York: Lang, 2001), 20; Christopher B. Hays, "Echoes of the Ancient Near East? Intertextuality and the Comparative Study of the Old Testament," in *The Word Leaps the Gap: Essays on Scripture and Theology in Honor of Richard B. Hays* (eds. J. Ross Wagner et al.; Grand Rapids, Mich.: Eerdmans, 2008), 28–32. Mary Orr claims Barthes's ideas have been imported into Kristeva's work because, though his major work on intertextuality followed hers, it was translated into English before it (Orr, *Intertextuality*, 21–22).

28   Hatina, "Intertextuality," 32, 35.

29   Aichele and Philips, "Exegesis," 9–10. Similarly, Mai, "Intertextuality," 41; Hatina, "Intertextuality," 30. For more on the historical situation in which Kristeva's ideas developed, see Toril Moi, "Introduction," in *The Kristeva Reader* (ed. Toril Moi; Oxford: Basil Blackwell, 1986), 1–9; Graham Allen, *Intertextuality* (London: Routledge, 2000), 30–35.

she saw intertextuality as a means of actualizing that political philosophy in texts, this original intent need not be attached to the word forever.[30]

The weakness of these arguments suggests that progressive intertextualists' attempts to create an intertextual "orthodoxy"[31] through fixing the original radical meaning of the word have instead created a false dichotomy in order to define a separate space for their new interpretive system. They betray their own "anxiety of influence," to use Harold Bloom's conception of intertextuality in which later texts seek to deny their dependence on their literary ancestors,[32] with regard to their own methodological precursor, influence.[33] In fact, this anxiety is the result of the significant overlap between the two approaches demonstrated by several critics who have employed elements of both together.[34] Instead of defining inter-textual approaches in a binary way, a scale or spectrum is more appropriate for categorizing the range of approaches to intertextuality, or "intertextualities."[35] Instead of being mutually exclusive, diachronic and synchronic intertextualities may be mutually beneficial, even symbiotic. If intertextuality is defined only in its contrasting extremes, those extremes may "assume two different cultures of understanding"[36] with the two sides "separated by an unbridgeable chasm,"[37] but the progressives also risk being lost in an infinite text,[38] while the traditionalists are vulnerable to the accusation of merely using "trendy" terminology.[39] How-

---

30   Richard Hays responds to this criticism of his work: "I fail to see why my interest in intertextual echo should compel me to accept their ideological framework" (Richard B. Hays, "On the Rebound: A Response to Critiques of *Echoes of Scripture in the Letters of Paul*," in *Paul and the Scriptures of Israel* [eds. Craig A. Evans and James A. Sanders; JSNTSup 83; Sheffield: JSOT Press, 1993], 80–81). See also Richard B. Hays, *Echoes of Scripture in the Letters of Paul* (New Haven: Yale University Press, 1989), 227 n. 60.

31   Friedman, "Weavings," 153.

32   Harold Bloom, *The Anxiety of Influence: A Theory of Poetry* (2nd ed.; Oxford: Oxford University Press, 1997).

33   Friedman, "Weavings," 150–53.

34   E.g., Laurent Jenny, who claims, "Contrary to what Kristeva says, intertextuality in the strict sense is not unrelated to source criticism: it designates not a confused, mysterious accumulation of influences, but the work of transformation and assimilation of various texts that is accomplished by a focal text which keeps control over the meaning" (Laurent Jenny, "The Strategy of Form," in *French Literary Theory Today* [ed. T. Todorov; Cambridge: Cambridge University Press, 1982], 39–40). Also, see several of the contributors to Jay Clayton and Eric Rothstein, eds. *Influence and Intertextuality in Literary History* (Madison: University of Wisconsin Press, 1991).

35   Plett, "Intertextualities," 3–29; Orr, *Intertextuality*, 10.

36   Gerrie Snyman, "Who Is Speaking? Intertextuality and Textual Influence," *Neot* 30 (1996): 446.

37   Hatina, "Intertextuality," 41.

38   Timothy K. Beal, "Ideology and Intertextuality: Surplus of Meaning and Controlling the Means of Production," in *Reading Between Texts: Intertextuality and the Hebrew Bible* (ed. Danna Nolan Fewell; LCBI; Louisville, Ky.: Westminster John Knox, 1992), 28. See below.

39   Ellen van Wolde, "Trendy Intertextuality?" in *Intertextuality in Biblical Writings: Essays in Honour of Bas van Iersel* (ed. Sipke Draisma; Kampen: Kok, 1989), 43–49.

ever, an intertextual approach in the space between these poles would offer powerful hermeneutical insight not available through either individually.

2.3. Between Diachronic and Synchronic

Diachronic and synchronic intertextualities each have something to offer to the other. In fact, in Saussure's semiotics, one of the major influences on Kristeva,[40] though each approach provides its own insight, neither can exist alone. Thus, for example, in order to study a language synchronically, "all at one time," diachronic distinctions must be made between the language in the time being studied and what came before and after.[41] Therefore, though Saussure emphasized the synchronic aspect of language, he still claimed the two approaches were both autonomous *and* interdependent.[42]

In literary criticism, the mutually beneficial nature of the two approaches appears first in the way intertextuality has broadened traditional diachronic studies of "influence," which, as the term suggests, emphasized the effect earlier authors had on later ones as they "influenced" them. However, it is actually the later author who has agency in any reference to an earlier text, which is passive in the act.[43] Kristeva apparently recognized this deficiency in influence theory,[44] and her intertextual approach has opened the door for a new appreciation of allusions, which emphasizes the later author's use of the earlier text.[45] Though perhaps slightly exaggerating, Patricia Tull correctly perceives influence's negative influence on interpretation: "As long as the concept of 'influence' reigned, opportunities to examine the many ways in which later texts could and did interact with their predecessors were rendered invisible to the interpretive eye."[46] Udo Hebel claims, though, that allusion, and not influence, "may now serve as the over-arching category for an interpretation of verifiable relationships between texts."[47]

---

40   Allen, *Intertextuality*, 11.

41   James Barr, "The Synchronic, the Diachronic and the Historical: A Triangular Relationship?" in *Synchronic or Diachronic?: A Debate on Method in Old Testament Exegesis* (ed. Johannes C. de Moor; OtSt 34; Leiden: Brill, 1995), 2–3.

42   Saussure, *Course*, 87.

43   Michael Baxandall, *Patterns of Intention: On the Historical Explanation of Pictures* (New Haven, Conn.: Yale University Press, 1985), 58–59.

44   See the discussion in Clayton and Rothstein, "Figures," 21 and John Strazicich, *Joel's Use of Scripture and the Scripture's Use of Joel: Appropriation and Resignification in Second Temple Judaism and Early Christianity* (BIS 82; Leiden: Brill, 2007), 6–7.

45   Udo J. Hebel, "Towards a Descriptive Poetics of *Allusion*," in *Intertextuality* (ed. Heinrich F. Plett; RTT 15; Berlin: de Gruyter, 1991), 135.

46   Tull, "Intertextuality," 67.

47   Hebel, "Allusion," 135.

Though attention to the agency of the alluding author was not completely foreign to influence studies before the rise of intertextuality,[48] the study of allusion now emphasizes the evocative potential of these relationships instead of atomistically tracing covert allusions and listing them.[49] Thus, though traditional approaches to literary criticism and biblical scholarship have not embraced the progressive version of intertextuality, the development of that interpretive approach has moved the discussion from influence and source-hunting in the service of dating texts to allusions and their hermeneutical potential as interpreters attend to authors as readers of earlier texts.

However, traditional diachronic intertextuality may also benefit progressive intertextuality by providing a necessary limit for the infinite potential meanings the latter creates. Progressive intertextuality appeals to the mosaic nature of texts as a means of breaking the boundaries between one text and another, and even texts and the world. But, if texts become completely integrated into the broader communication process, they become indeterminable.[50] This view of intertextuality is an "invitation to chaos," in which the interpreter is asked to "read everything in light of everything, everywhere at once."[51] For texts to have any meaning, they must be pinned down somewhere.[52] Thus, though Kristeva claims intertextuality opens up a universe of discourse, the difficulty of interacting with this entire universe forces her to pursue identifiable discourses behind the text, such as her appeal to exact editions of the texts used by later authors.[53] Interpreters employ various "strategies of containment,"[54] and this "returns us to the reader who must decide what limits are to be placed on what is to be read and how it is to be read."[55]

---

48 Friedman, "Weavings," 155. See, e.g., T. S. Eliot, "Tradition and the Individual Talent," in *The Sacred Wood: Essays on Poetry and Criticism* (London: Methuen, 1920), 47–59.

49 Hebel, "Allusion," 136, 140.

50 Plett, "Intertextualities," 6.

51 Jacob Neusner, *Canon and Connection: Intertextuality in Judaism* (StJ; Lanham, Md.: University Press of America, 1987), xiii.

52 Plett, "Intertextualities," 6.

53 Culler, "Presupposition," 106–7.

54 Fredric Jameson, *The Political Unconscious: Narrative as a Socially Symbolic Act* (Ithaca, N.Y.: Cornell University Press, 1981), 52–53. See the discussion of various "strategies of containment" taken by prominent intertextual critics in Tanner, *Psalms*, 17–28.

55 Peter D. Miscall, "Texts, More Texts, a Textual Reader and a Textual Writer," *Semeia* 69/70 (1995): 252. Yvonne Sherwood observes that "all readers are always involved, in some sense, in textual management: we cannot let meaning ricochet in all directions, for that way interpretative vertigo and bad reviews lie" (Yvonne Sherwood, *A Biblical Text and its Afterlives: The Survival of Jonah in Western Culture* [Cambridge: Cambridge University Press, 2000], 215). She manages the intertextual potential of Jonah by claiming that it "participates in a specific network of texts" that is read "synchronically rather than diachronically" (214 n. 17).

Critics such as Culler and Michael Riffaterre have attempted to determine these limits while emphasizing the reader,[56] but a diachronic approach is another way this can be done. In a sense, the reader allows the author's own indications of intertextuality through intended allusions to limit the text's intertextual potential.[57] The concept of allusion itself suggests some degree of intention,[58] however circumscribed it may be in light of Wimsatt and Beardsley's famous "intentional fallacy."[59] Here allusion returns the favor to synchronic intertextuality by providing a means for channeling its infinite interpretive possibilities into a limited domain that is accessible trans-subjectively, beyond the personal responses of individual readers, due to its basis in the objective evidence of the text and history.[60] Though not the only way a text can be read, this does have the distinct advantage of historical plausibility, thus providing possible insight into what the text meant to the author(s) who composed it and the community that originally received it.

Thus, a diachronic approach can benefit intertextual interpretation by limiting the infinite number of possible intertexts to a more manageable number made

---

56   Clayton and Rothstein, "Figures," 24.

57   Thus, Stefan Alkier distinguishes between limited intertextuality, which only considers literary connections "that are written into the given text or can be postulated on the basis of the collection of signs in the text to be interpreted," and unlimited intertextuality, which may pursue intertexts in any text before or after (Stefan Alkier, "New Testament Studies on the Basis of Categorical Semiotics," in *Reading the Bible Intertextually* [eds. Richard B. Hays et al.; Waco, Tex.: Baylor University Press, 2009], 242).

58   Robert Alter, *The Pleasures of Reading in an Ideological Age* (New York: W. W. Norton, 1996), 115–16; William Irwin, "What is an Allusion?" *The Journal of Aesthetics and Art Criticism* 59 (2001): 291. Timothy Beal disagrees that intention is necessary (Timothy K. Beal, "Glossary," in *Reading Between Texts: Intertextuality and the Hebrew Bible* [ed. Danna Nolan Fewell; LCBI; Louisville, Ky.: Westminster John Knox, 1992], 21), as does Sommer, despite his emphasis on a diachronic approach (Sommer, *Prophet*, 208–9 n. 17). However, in his defense of attending to authorial intention in allusions and discussion of the "hidden intentions" of Romantic poets, James Chandler explains that without intention purported allusiveness would lose its force (James K. Chandler, "Romantic Allusiveness," *Critical Inquiry* 8 [1982]: 479, 464–65).

59   Appeals to the "intentional fallacy" could often themselves merit some moderation. Paul Ricoeur notes, "If the intentional fallacy overlooks the semantic autonomy of the text, the opposite fallacy forgets that a text remains a discourse told by somebody." Without some concept of the author, texts are reduced to "things which are not man-made, but which, like pebbles, are found in the sand" (Paul Ricoeur, *Interpretation Theory: Discourse and the Surplus of Meaning* [Fort Worth, Tex.: Texas Christian University Press, 1976], 30). Thus, just as van Wolde claims, "Without a reader a text is only a lifeless collection of words," the same could be said of a text without an author (van Wolde, "Intertextuality," 47). For further discussion, see John Barton, *Reading the Old Testament: Method in Biblical Study* (2nd ed.; London: Darton, Longman & Todd, 1996), 147–51, 167–70.

60   See Donald C. Polaski, *Authorizing an End: The Isaiah Apocalypse and Intertextuality* (BIS 50; Leiden: Brill, 2001), 36.

up only of those that could have been conceivably intended by the author. On the other hand, attention to the synchronic meaning of the text frees the traditional approach from merely being "source hunting." It puts the emphasis on the effect the text's interaction with those sources has on its meaning, and even on the reciprocal effect that interaction may have on our understanding of the source, as well as its reverberation through both. Gerrie Snyman depicts the conflict between traditional and progressive intertextualities with a question: "Is the critic's task to look into the *origins* of the voices in the text or to look at the *unlimited possibilities* of new arguments and texts opening up as a result of the interaction of these different voices?"[61] Thanks to the combined insights of both intertextualities, current approaches to allusion may stand between these two extremes.

2.4. Intertextuality and the Hebrew Bible

Recently, several scholars have explicitly integrated both diachronic and synchronic concerns into their studies of intertextuality in the HB. In his study of quotations in Isaiah, Richard Schultz, recognizing the impasse in historical analysis,[62] proposes intertextual connections be approached from both diachronic, author-centered and synchronic, reader-centered perspectives. He thus combines a focus on the text's origin with one on its effect.[63] He argues that one perspective without the other is lacking and the twofold analysis provides a check against both over-interpretation and under-interpretation. He admits, however, that he has not presented a method for exactly how the two are to be related, instead proposing "a new attitude" which recognizes the necessity and limitations of both.[64] Addressing the division between diachronic and synchronic approaches, he comments, "It is far too easy to advocate an exclusively diachronic or synchronic approach or to pay mere lip-service to one of the two without seriously considering how the one supplements, limits, corrects or gives guidance to the other."[65]

Pyeon, in this vein, attempts to read the intertextuality in Job both synchronically and diachronically. He pursues these two types of intertextuality as different "levels" of the text, with the synchronic referring to the literary connections

---

61 Snyman, "Intertextuality," 428. Emphasis original.

62 Richard L. Schultz, *The Search for Quotation: Verbal Parallels in the Prophets* (JSOTSup 180; Sheffield: Sheffield Academic Press, 1999), 332, cf. 252.

63 Schultz, *Quotation*, 232–33.

64 Schultz, *Quotation*, 237–39.

65 Schultz, *Quotation*, 332.

between the speeches of Job and the friends in the book as a whole and the diachronic referring to the book's allusions to earlier texts.[66] This insight into the dual nature of the dialogue in Job, both between the disputants and between the book of Job and earlier texts is vital for interpreting the book, and yet, in Pyeon's discussion of particular allusions, these levels tend to remain distinct. Though he proposes that Job and the friends "repeatedly use a variety of biblical texts as a means to respond to one another,"[67] he offers only a cursory treatment of the role references to biblical texts play in their argument, referring only to their differing uses of a general "past tradition" instead of their debate over the meaning of specific texts.[68] He does not explore the possibility that allusions to the same texts may be among the words and ideas that Job and the friends borrow from one another's speeches.[69]

More recently, Michael Stead has proposed a "contextual intertextuality," which is "attuned to both synchronic and diachronic issues."[70] He presents the "diversity of intertextualities" in three spectra, which address the identifiability of connections, the relationships they create between texts, and the reader's role in interpreting them.[71] He responds to those who see a dichotomy between intertextuality as a synchronic method and allusion or influence as a diachronic one by pointing out that "not all intertextualists are synchronic reader-response critics," including several biblical scholars who have defied such a normative categorization by explicitly including historical concerns in their definitions of intertextuality.[72] He then undertakes a synchronic account of how the text of Zechariah 1–8 operates limited by a diachronic awareness of the possible intertexts in circulation at its composition.[73] Stead, like Schultz and Pyeon, does not offer direction for how his integration of diachronic and synchronic perspectives should be carried out beyond limiting possible intertexts to those antedating the composition of Zechariah.

---

66   Pyeon, *Intertextuality*, 67.

67   Pyeon, *Intertextuality*, 2.

68   E.g., Pyeon, *Intertextuality*, 139.

69   He does note that Eliphaz refers to Ps 8:5–6 in 15:14–15 after Job had alluded to the same passage in 7:17–18, but only uses it as evidence for the initial allusion (Pyeon, *Intertextuality*, 136). Even when Job (10:8–12) and Zophar (11:7–9) both allude to Psalm 139 in the first cycle, which is the focus of Pyeon's study, he only mentions the latter allusion (186–88).

70   Michael R. Stead, *The Intertextuality of Zechariah 1–8* (LHBOTS 506; New York: T&T Clark International, 2009), 16, 18.

71   Stead, *Intertextuality*, 19–27.

72   Stead, *Intertextuality*, 22–23. For such a distinction, see Benjamin D. Sommer, "Exegesis, Allusion and Intertextuality in the Hebrew Bible: A Response to Lyle Eslinger," *VT* 46 (1996): 487.

73   Stead, *Intertextuality*, 28–29.

2.5. Intertextualities in Dialogue: Prolegomena

Building on the theoretical framework of these scholars, I have developed an approach for identifying inner-biblical allusions and interpreting them both historically and hermeneutically, labeling it "intertextualities in dialogue" to express my belief that the interpretation of allusions best lies in the interface between diachronic and synchronic approaches.[74] Each step alternates between primarily synchronic or diachronic concerns. This accords with Jay Clayton's suggestion that interpreters may address the same text from perspectives of both influence and intertextuality, but, in order for this compromise to work, at each point in the analysis, the interpreter would have to acknowledge "which assumptions were operative and which were being temporarily suspended."[75] Readers often alternate between these two approaches, and biblical criticism is made up of "a constant crisscrossing of synchronic and diachronic dimensions."[76] For example, the diachronic search for sources underlying biblical texts was motivated by inconsistencies perceived when it was read synchronically.[77] By combining both intertextualities, this approach is more than a sum of its parts, because the interaction between the two offers more insight than both do individually. In developing this approach, I am particularly indebted to the work of literary critic Ziva Ben-Porat on interpreting allusions and of New Testament scholar Richard Hays on identifying them,[78] though I have had to modify their approaches significantly to apply

---

74 I share this conviction with several of the contributors to Richard B. Hays et al., eds. *Reading the Bible Intertextually* (Waco, Tex.: Baylor University Press, 2009). In that collection, see Stefan Alkier, "Intertextuality and the Semiotics of Biblical Texts," 8; Marianne Grohmann, "Psalm 113 and the Song of Hannah (1 Samuel 2:1–10): A Paradigm for Intertextual Reading?" 122; Steve Moyise, "Intertextuality and Historical Approaches to the Use of Scripture in the New Testament," 32.

75 Jay Clayton, "The Alphabet of Suffering: Effie Deans, Tess Durbeyfield, Martha Ray, and Hetty Sorrel," in *Influence and Intertextuality in Literary History* (eds. Jay Clayton and Eric Rothstein; Madison, Wisc.: University of Wisconsin Press, 1991), 40.

76 Barton, *Biblical Criticism*, 188.

77 John Barton, "Intertextuality and the 'Final Form' of the Text," in *Congress Volume Oslo 1998* (eds. A. Lemaire and M. Sæbø; VTSup; Leiden: Brill, 2000), 36.

78 Ziva Ben-Porat, "The Poetics of Literary Allusion," *PTL* 1 (1976): 105–28; Hays, *Echoes*, 29–32. See also Richard B. Hays, *The Conversion of the Imagination: Paul as Interpreter of Israel's Scripture* (Grand Rapids, Mich.: Eerdmans, 2005), 34–45. The works of both have been used repeatedly in studies of intertextuality in the HB. For Ben-Porat, see Sommer, *Prophet*, 11–17; Tanner, *Psalms*, 72–73; Strazicich, *Joel*, 27; John S. Vassar, *Recalling a Story Once Told: An Intertextual Reading of the Psalter and the Pentateuch* (Macon, Ga.: Mercer University Press, 2007), 5–8. Michael Lyons builds on Ben-Porat's approach with several reservations (Lyons, *Law*, 51–53). Though he does not follow her method, Schultz calls Ben-Porat's article "one of the most helpful attempts to expound the semiotic workings of quotation" (Schultz, *Quotation*, 200). For Hays, see Patricia Tull Willey, *Remember the Former Things: The Recollection of Previous Texts in Second Isaiah* (SBLDS 161; Atlanta:

them to allusions within the HB, where the relative dates of texts are often unknown.

2.5.1. Terminology

This study is focused on allusions and not quotations or echoes because of qualitative differences I perceive between the three concepts, which all fit under the broader term intertextuality, which describes any connection between texts. The three terms are often used in an overlapping manner. Hays, for example, writes, "Quotation, allusion, and echo may be seen as points along a spectrum of intertextual references, moving from the explicit to the subliminal."[79] Similarly, Sommer notes, "The distinction between cases of allusion and echo is rarely clear-cut," but he distinguishes them by claiming echoes have little effect on the reading of the later text whereas allusions involve "the utilization of the marked material for some rhetorical or strategic end."[80] Sommer thus makes a qualitative distinction between the concepts (which is implied in Hays's comment) based on whether the author consciously intended the reference to an earlier text. Others, however, distinguish the concepts more quantitatively.[81] Stead, for example, claims quotation, allusion, and echo typically differ based on the number of shared vocabulary features they involve.[82]

I prefer a qualitative distinction because of the diverse manners in which each literary technique could be performed. If a quotation is introduced by an explicit citation formula, it could be one word (e.g., "As the raven said, 'Never-

---

Scholars Press, 1997), 82–83; Pyeon, *Intertextuality*, 63; Strazicich, *Joel*, 26; C. Hays, "Intertextuality," 35–43.

79   Hays, *Echoes*, 23. Following Hays, I focus on distinguishing these three types of intertextual connections. Another term occasionally debated is "citation." Yair Hoffman, for example, divides "quotation" into two categories: "*explicit quotation*," which uses a "quotation formula" and "citation," which does not use such a formula and is thus "in a sense, an *implicit quotation*" (Yair Hoffman, "The Technique of Quotation and Citation as an Interpretive Device," in *Creative Biblical Exegesis: Christian and Jewish Hermeneutics through the Centuries* [eds. Benjamin Uffenheimer and Henning Graf Reventlow; JSOTSup 59; Sheffield: JSOT Press, 1988], 72; emphasis original).

80   Sommer, *Prophet*, 15–17. Though he argues against limiting allusions to those intended by the author (208–9 n. 17), it is hard to imagine how an author could use an earlier text for a rhetorical or strategic end unintentionally.

81   In fact, elsewhere Hays speaks more quantitatively about the distinction between allusion and echo by claiming that in his work "*allusion* is used of obvious intertextual references, *echo* of subtler ones" (Hays, *Echoes*, 29; emphasis original).

82   Stead, *Intertextuality*, 22 n. 22. For him, quotations share four or more vocabulary features, allusion, two or three, and echo, one or two. Schultz states a preference for a quantitative distinction between the terms explicitly (Schultz, *Quotation*, 205).

more'"). In certain circumstances, an allusion could also be one word, particularly if that one word is a proper noun (e.g., "He was a real Romeo," or, "He was unnerved when all she said was, 'Nevermore'"). If an echo, however, is distinguished by lack of authorial intent, it could involve several words, though the more words were shared, the more likely it would seem that the repetition was intended. As the previous concession indicates, quantitative and qualitative distinctions often correspond, which may explain why the quantitative distinction is so widespread. However, when they do not correspond, as in the examples above, the qualitative distinction better represents the literary phenomena. As I understand that distinction, a quotation involves an explicit reference to an earlier expression, whether written or not, and is often indicated by a citation formula. Often a quotation represents its source verbatim, but it need not do so, as long as it involves an explicit reference (if it misrepresents its source, it is a "misquotation"). An allusion is an intentional implicit reference to an earlier expression.[83] It lacks a citation formula and often only loosely represents its source, though some verbatim repetition may occur. Echoes are unintentional implicit references to earlier expressions.[84]

Thus, quotation is distinguished from allusion and echo by its explicit reference to its source, and echo is distinguished from quotation and allusion by its lack of authorial intent. Implicit and yet intended, allusion stands in between the two, as the following diagram illustrates:

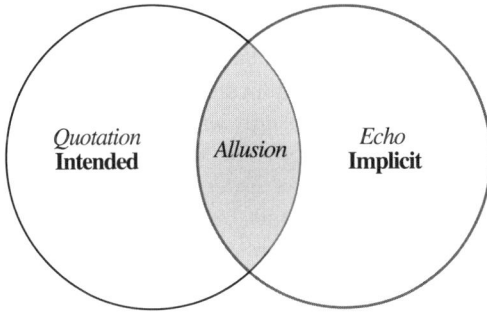

Admittedly, both the distinctions between explicit and implicit references and intended and unintended ones have their difficulties. Theoretically, the lines between them are clear, as in the chart, but in practice they become blurred.

---

83   For more on the definition of allusion, see Carmela Perri, "On Alluding," *Poetics* 7 (1978): 289–307; Earl Miner, "Allusion," in *The Princeton Handbook of Poetic Terms* (ed. A. Preminger; Princeton, N.J.: Princeton University Press, 1986), 10–11; Irwin, "Allusion," 287–97.

84   "Echo is a metaphor of, and for, alluding, and does not depend on conscious intention" (John Hollander, *The Figure of Echo: A Mode of Allusion in Milton and After* [Berkeley, Calif.: University of California Press, 1981], 64).

When distinguishing the explicit from the implicit, the general lack of source attribution in the HB means this category would rarely apply if it were to rely on citation formulas. Yet, should a nearly verbatim citation of several verses from an earlier source (e.g., 1 Chr 13:6–14 // 2 Sam 6:2–11) be called an "allusion"? This difficulty drives scholars to introduce a quantitative distinction between quotation and allusion instead of a qualitative one, but this is once again a confusion based on the correspondence of the two criteria. Actually, a certain amount of verbatim repetition has changed the reference qualitatively from implicit to explicit.[85] Where exactly this line is crossed would be a matter worthy of further discussion, but it is superfluous to this study because none of Job's intertextual connections to the Psalms involve more than a half-verse of verbatim repetition, which I believe is still on the implicit side of that line.

The distinction between intended and unintended connections to earlier texts is more challenging. David Carr argues that the scribes who composed the HB would memorize large portions of texts and, with their minds so thoroughly saturated in those traditions, would draw fluidly on texts both consciously and probably unconsciously, as well.[86] That some repetition of earlier influential texts was unconscious is hard to dispute, and determining which repeated words and phrases were intended and which were not is even more difficult. This is why, again, interpreters often revert to quantitative distinctions between allusions and echoes, since the more words that are repeated, the more likely it is that the reference was intended. But once again, this quantitative distinction is actually just a method for attempting to determine the qualitative one. The attraction of this approach is understandable, since the minds of ancient authors are inaccessible to us. Indeed, I employ quantitative arguments in this study. However, if quantitative measures are used not just to identify allusions, as I use them, but to define them, setting the question of intention aside, then the term "echo" does not serve a distinctive function and it would be clearer to refer simply to "weak allusions." If, however, the repetition of elements from an earlier text seems to serve a "rhetorical or strategic end," as Sommer says, authorial intention is likely.[87] Thus, like quantitative observations, rhetorical ones may help identify allusions, but they

---

85 Instead of depending on the external indication from a citation formula, the degree of verbal reproduction itself makes the reference explicit. For this reason, though I appreciate the distinction he is aiming for, I hesitate to embrace Hoffman's definition of citation as "implicit quotation," since it would either make a citation an implicit explicit reference to an earlier text or make it indistinguishable from an allusion. See p. 30 n. 79.

86 Carr, "Intertextuality," 524. Sommer makes a similar point to argue that allusions may be unintentional (Sommer, *Prophet*, 208–9 n. 17).

87 Similarly, Nogalski claims an allusion must refer to an earlier text "for a specific purpose" (J. D. Nogalski, "Intertextuality and the Twelve," in *Forming Prophetic Literature* [eds. James W. Watts and P. R. House; Sheffield: Sheffield Academic Press, 1996], 109).

do not define them. If this argument is built not from assumptions about the author's psychology based on criteria external to the text, but from the text itself, it avoids running aground on the intentional fallacy. If, on the other hand, echoes, as unintended traces of other texts, do not serve a rhetorical or strategic end, then their interpretive relevance is limited. If we can identify the sources of these echoes, they may indicate what texts the author knew and which texts were influential at the time, but they give little insight into the meaning of the author's composition. Therefore, because quotations of the Psalms are absent in Job and psalmic echoes have minimal interpretive value, this study will address the allusions in the book.

2.5.2. The Text

When pursuing these allusions, I will focus on those passages in which they are the strongest, most concentrated, and seem to have the greatest interpretive significance. For the book of Job, this is the dialogue between Job and his three friends in chs. 3–27, in which allusions appear in the speeches of both Job and his friends, acting as a subtext to their debate. Though the contribution these psalms offer to the debate makes the dialogue the most significant section of the book for psalmic allusions, this is likely not the only section in which they occur. For example, a strong case could be made for allusions to Psalm 104 in ch. 38 of the divine speeches.[88] Also, parallels between the Elihu speeches and Psalm 107 have led some to argue the psalm is alluding to Elihu's words,[89] but given that, as I will argue, the psalm is repeatedly alluded to in the dialogue, these allusions, if they exist, would most likely go in the other direction. If these are indeed psalmic allusions, it could suggest that the same poet composed all these sections in which this literary technique is employed. However, it could also suggest that later authors picked up on the use of psalmic allusions in the dialogue and imitated it.

  Despite the quests to excise purported later additions and recover the original form of Job, which have been both extensive, and, ultimately, inconclusive,[90] a recent movement toward reading Job as a unity has developed.[91] Beyond the

---

88 Köhlmoos, *Textstrategie*, 339–40, 361.

89 See p. 82 n. 16.

90 Several studies addressed this question around the turn of the twentieth century, such as Julius Grill, *Zur Kritik der Komposition des Buchs Hiob* (Tübingen: Fuesi, 1890) and Baumgärtel, *Hiobdialog*. A renewed interest in the issue has recently arisen, particularly in German scholarship. For an overview, see Jürgen van Oorschot, "Die Entstehung des Hiobbuches," in *Das Buch Hiob und seine Interpretationen: Beiträge zum Hiob-Symposium auf dem Monte Verità vom 14.–19. August 2005* (eds. Thomas Krüger et al.; ATANT 88; Zürich: Theologischer Verlag, 2007), 166–71.

91 Ellen F. Davis, "Job and Jacob: The Integrity of Faith," in *Reading Between Texts: Intertextuality and the Hebrew Bible* (ed. Danna Nolan Fewell; LCBI; Louisville, Ky.: Westminster/John Knox, 1992).

debates over which sections of the book are original, which this study avoids by focusing on the dialogue section, these quests for the original form involve investigation into possible later, smaller interpolations into the text. Though I recognize that these may exist, because of the unavoidable subjectivity of attempting to identify them and the inability of more than a century of critical study to do so, I would prefer to study the text in its final form,[92] reconciling this with my interest in authorial intent by assuming this form of the text is as reliable a reproduction of the work as the author intended it as any scholarly reconstruction.

Though my study only addresses allusions in the dialogue, it invites further investigation into how this literary technique not only affects our understanding of this section, but also of the book in its entirety. Whereas the framing of the Job dialogue with prose invites the reader to interpret one section in light of the other, the formal distinction between the poetry of the dialogue and the prose narrative that surrounds it demands the reader approach the two sections differently. This interplay between unity and diversity legitimates interpreting the dialogue independently of the prose narrative, but then makes this only a step toward the final interpretation of the book, since both parts are "dialogically engaged."[93]

2.5.3. The Intertext

As with my focus on the dialogue between Job and his friends, I have limited my study of its psalmic intertexts to psalms where the allusions are the strongest and most concentrated. Because the allusion to Ps 8:5 in Job 7:17–18 has become a scholarly commonplace, I have used it as a standard and only addressed psalms that have received at least one allusion of at least that "volume," to use Hays's term, and that then prove their importance to the dialogue by appearing in several more allusions of nearly the same volume. Using this criteria, I have identified six psalms, 1, 8, 39, 73, 107, and 139, which act as subtexts to the dialogue between Job and his friends. This list is not exhaustive, and the author of Job likely alludes

---

For earlier intimations of this move, see James Barr, "The Book of Job and its Modern Interpreters," *BJRL* 54 (1971–1972): 29. Examples of this approach include Norman C. Habel, *The Book of Job: A Commentary* (OTL; Philadelphia: Westminster Press, 1985) and Newsom, *Contest*. The contrast between Habel's narrative analysis of the "plot" of the book and Newsom's emphasis on the dialogical relationship between its disparate parts demonstrates the diversity among these holistic readings.

92   For a cogent argument against searching for later interpolations in the text, see Robert Gordis, *The Book of God and Man: A Study of Job* (Chicago: University of Chicago Press, 1978), 169–72.

93   Newsom, *Contest*, 24.

to other psalms as well, but, in my view, these six appear to play the most pronounced role in the dialogue.[94]

As with Job, a tendency has developed in Psalms scholarship to read individual psalms and even the Psalter itself in their final form.[95] I do not argue that the author of Job is alluding to the Psalter in its final form, so when and how individual psalms were gathered into the five-book collection in the HB does not affect this study. The actual original form of the psalms in question also is of limited relevance because only the form of the psalm to which the author of Job had access is important, whether that form is the result of a lengthy textual development or not. As Edward Greenstein observes, when a text in Job parallels one found elsewhere in the HB, whether the allusion is to that text in its present context or in an earlier source is unclear.[96] Thus, since we can only know which sections of any given psalm were available to the author of Job by his allusions to them, I build my argument more on what Job and his friends mention than what they omit. However, this does not exclude consideration of the broader context of texts to which the author alludes. If several different parts of the same psalm appear in the book, such as Job's references to both Ps 8:5 (Job 7:17–18) and 8:6 (Job 19:9) along with the friends' allusions to Ps 8:4–6 in Job 15:14–16 and 25:5–6,[97] then we may assume at least that much of the psalm existed together when he wrote. Further, if the nature of the section of a psalm suggests strongly that it was unified, such as if it naturally coheres thematically, like the alternation between affliction and deliverance in Psalm 107, then the Job poet's omission of a notable aspect of a psalm, such as his exclusion of the deliverance in Psalm 107 in Job 12:13–25, may be considered significant. When the Job poet's apparent allusions to different aspects of the same psalms are all grouped together, and the consistent interpretive use he has given them becomes evident, it seems unduly cautious and the less probable explanation of the evidence to argue that he is referring to isolated traditions rather than alluding to the psalms where this language is gathered.[98]

---

94   Other psalms, such as Psalm 126, have a single marked parallel with the Job dialogue (Ps 126:2 // Job 8:21) but lack recurrence (see p. 39), while others, such as Psalm 37, have several possible allusions but none which are especially marked (see p. 42 n. 119).

95   See J. Kenneth Kuntz, "Continuing the Engagement: Psalms Research Since the Early 1990s," *CBR* 10 (2012): 321–78, esp. 364.

96   Edward L. Greenstein, review of Yohan Pyeon, *You Have Not Spoken What is Right About Me: Intertextuality and the Book of Job*, *RBL* 11 [http://www.bookreviews.org] (2003). This does not prevent him from claiming Job is dependent on the text of Jeremiah at several points, however. See Edward L. Greenstein, "Jeremiah as an Inspiration to the Poet of Job," in *Inspired Speech: Prophecy in the Ancient Near East: Essays in Honor of Herbert B. Huffmon* (eds. John Kaltner and Louis Stulman; JSOTSup 378; London: T&T Clark International, 2004), 98–110.

97   See ch. 3.

98   Greenstein acknowledges the possibility that the author of Job may allude to a large section of

Though Westermann has emphasized Job's use of the lament genre, the psalms to which the Job poet alludes are not restricted to that form. In fact, the six psalms which act as subtexts to the dialogue could be generally classified as praise (8, 107), supplication (39, 139), and instruction[99] (1, 73), and I will address them in three sections according to those broad categories.[100] Though grouping the psalms this way has heuristic value, as it highlights similar themes that appear in each pair of psalms and enables comparison of how they are treated in the dialogue, these formal classifications should not be strictly applied. In fact, the individual features of several of the psalms I will be discussing push the boundaries of form to such a degree that their classification is a matter of continuing debate.[101] As a result, I will not attempt to classify these psalms more specifically than these categories, which reflect the general tenor of the composition, whether as praise, they primarily intend to inspire worship or thanksgiving, or as supplication, they try to move God to act on the psalmist's behalf, or as instruction, they attempt to convey some message to others. These categories are not mutually exclusive, and these three intentions often overlap in the same text. For example, Psalm 139 praises God for the first eighteen verses before turning to supplication in the last six. When the information the psalmist conveys to his readers inspires worship of God, as it does in Psalm 73 (see v. 25), the line between praise and instruction is exceedingly thin. The author of Job himself seems to relish flouting genre expectations, which should further encourage the categories to be held lightly, but it does not necessitate rejecting them altogether.

---

an earlier text when he says "a very good argument could be made" that Job 12 parodies Isa 41–45 (Greenstein, review of Pyeon).

99   I prefer "instruction" to "wisdom" or "didactic" because it is a noun describing the intent of the psalms like the other two labels. For instructional use as the unifying feature of wisdom literature both in the HB and at Qumran, see John J. Collins, "Wisdom Reconsidered, in Light of the Dead Sea Scrolls," *DSD* 4 (1997): 265–81.

100 This accords with Kugel's suggestion that Fishbane could make his discussion of inner-biblical exegesis more useful and objective by categorizing it according to the genre of the material being interpreted (James L. Kugel, "The Bible's Earliest Interpreters," *Proof* 7 [1987]: 277).

101 For succinct overviews of the debates surrounding the form of each of these psalms, see the relevant passages in Erhard S. Gerstenberger, *Psalms and Lamentations* (2 vols.; FOTL 14–15; Grand Rapids, Mich.: Eerdmans, 1988, 2001).

2.6. Intertextualities in Dialogue: Eight Steps

2.6.1. Identification

My identification and interpretation of the allusions to these six psalms in the Job dialogue is based on an eight-step process. The first is synchronic and involves identifying marked parallels which may be allusions while leaving the question of relative chronology open. Because this step is the basis for all which follow, it merits a more extended discussion. Scholars vary widely on what literary features actually constitute an allusion. Ben-Porat defines the indicator of an allusion quite broadly as "an element or pattern belonging to another independent text."[102] Hays calls the correspondence between the text and its precursor its "volume," which is determined primarily by the degree of lexical and syntactical repetition.[103] Thematic similarity is also a necessary, though rarely sufficient, indicator of allusions, since allusions are difficult to identify without the lexical similarity of at least two repeated words. Syntactical similarity may or may not be present, but greatly strengthens an allusion when combined with lexical and thematic affinities. Allusions may be signaled through situational or thematic similarities instead of direct verbal borrowing,[104] but because Job and the Psalms already share much situational and thematic resonance, and so that my findings will be as compelling as possible, I concentrate on intertextual connections that either share at least three significant words, excluding conjunctions and prepositions, or two words with close syntactical similarity, when identifying initial allusions linking Job and a psalm.[105] The more rare the shared words as a group, the less verbal repetition is necessary to claim an allusion, particularly when the texts are related thematically.[106] Repeated stylistic techniques, such as sound and word play, repeated or reversed word order, and parody, may also strengthen the case for an allusion.[107] Once an allusion has been established, thereby forming a bond between the texts, further connections between them need not be held to as high a standard, and I

---

102 Ben-Porat, "Allusion," 108.

103 Hays, *Echoes*, 30.

104 See Alter, *Pleasures*, 122; Stead, *Intertextuality*, 29–30, 37.

105 For principles for using shared language to determine allusions, see Nogalski, "Intertextuality," 109–10; Jeffery M. Leonard, "Identifying Inner-Biblical Allusions: Psalm 78 as a Test Case," *JBL* 127 (2008): 246.

106 For rarity as a vital criterion for determining allusions, see Sommer, "Exegesis," 484–85. However, Stead rightly questions the assumption that biblical authors limited their allusions to "rare" expressions (Stead, *Intertextuality*, 30). The rarity of the expression does, however, make the argument that the author had a particular text in mind, and not merely a common phrase, more convincing.

107 See Jenny, "The Strategy of Form," 54–58; Sommer, *Prophet*, 68–70; Lyons, *Law*, 88–99.

will argue that two shared words, and even occasionally one, may indicate an allusion.[108]

2.6.1.1. Formula or Text?

In every case, the possibility that a third shared source or a common formula explains the parallel should be considered.[109] In addition to intertextual allusions, reference to common formulas could also be a widespread technique in Job.[110] Occasionally, the recurrence of a common formula is clearly a preferable explanation, such as with formulaic language that recurs several times across the HB,[111] common word-pairs (sometimes called "fixed" or "standing" pairs), such as עלה ("to ascend") and ירד ("to descend") in Ps 107:26 and elsewhere,[112] and words that naturally belong together such as "clap" and "hands," even if the combination is rare.[113] However, four other factors may militate against allusion even in parallels between Job and the Psalms where the verbal similarity is both extensive and rare.

First, though some thematic similarity is necessary for an allusion, too much similarity can actually count against arguing for direct dependence. If the shared words and imagery perform the same function in both texts with no evidence of reworking on the part of one author, then not only is the direction of dependence nearly impossible to determine without additional evidence, but dependence itself must be questioned. For example:

---

108 Similarly, Greenstein claims that in view of the extensive impact of Jeremiah on Job, weaker parallels, which could be due to the common use of stock vocabulary, may also be attributed to direct influence (Greenstein, "Jeremiah," 99). See p. 55 n. 191 below for the cumulative nature of arguments for allusion.

109 See Avi Hurvitz, *A Linguistic Study of the Relationship between the Priestly Source and the Book of Ezekiel* (CahRB 20; Paris: J. Gabalda, 1982), 13–14; Sommer, *Prophet*, 219–20 n. 12.

110 For the suggestion that the author of Job interacts with both formulaic language and specific texts, see Köhlmoos, *Textstrategie*, 2; Greenstein, "Jeremiah," 98. For Job's sustained and sophisticated interaction with common forms, see Fohrer, "Form," 60–77; Dell, *Sceptical*.

111 For a study of formulaic language in the Psalms, see Robert C. Culley, *Oral Formulaic Language in the Biblical Psalms* (Toronto: University of Toronto Press, 1967). However, Culley at times overstates the case for a formula when either the rarity of an image or the distinctive use to which it is put suggest a phrase is anything but "formulaic." See p. 168 n. 35 below.

112 See the discussion in Wilfred G. E. Watson, *Classical Hebrew Poetry* (JSOTSup 26; Sheffield: JSOT Press, 1984), 128–42.

113 The verb מחא ("to clap") is combined with a word for "hands" all three times it appears, so the combination does little to strengthen the possibility of allusion. For a similar list of indications against allusion, see Sommer, *Prophet*, 32.

Job 27:15[114]

שְׂרִידוֹ [שְׂרִידָיו] בַּמָּוֶת יִקָּבֵרוּ וְאַלְמְנֹתָיו לֹא
תִבְכֶּינָה

Those who survive them the pestilence buries,

and their widows make no lamentation.

Ps 78:64

כֹּהֲנָיו בַּחֶרֶב נָפָלוּ וְאַלְמְנֹתָיו לֹא תִבְכֶּינָה

Their priests fell by the sword,

and their widows made no lamentation.

The exact repetition of an entire half verse that appears nowhere else in the HB would be a compelling indication of an allusion if it were not for the thematic similarity, which fails to provide evidence of intentional use. As part of a description of God's wrath against rebellious Israel, this image is appropriate for Job's depiction of the fate of the wicked, so appropriate, in fact, that dependence cannot be affirmed without other evidence. This could be merely a common phrase used to describe the demise of the guilty.

Second, even where the thematic interplay between two parallel passages might suggest some reworking on the part of one of the authors, there still may not be adequate evidence to indicate that an allusion and not the repetition of a common formula has caused the parallel, such as when the purported allusion lacks recurrence (for this criterion, see below). For example, to encourage Job to plead to God for mercy, Bildad uses imagery that appears in one of the Psalms of Ascent to describe the joy experienced by those in the restored Zion:

Job 8:21

עַד־יְמַלֵּה שְׂחוֹק פִּיךָ וּשְׂפָתֶיךָ תְרוּעָה

He will yet fill your mouth with laughter,

and your lips with shouts of joy.

Ps 126:2

אָז יִמָּלֵא שְׂחוֹק פִּינוּ וּלְשׁוֹנֵנוּ רִנָּה אָז יֹאמְרוּ
בַגּוֹיִם הִגְדִּיל יְהוָה לַעֲשׂוֹת עִם־אֵלֶּה

Then our mouth was filled with laughter,

and our tongue with shouts of joy;

then it was said among the nations,

"The LORD has done great things for them."

Bildad's transformation of the community's declaration into an individual promise for Job should he repent fits with the friends' parenetic reworking of other psalms.[115] Combined with the nearly exact repetition in the first half of the verse (though changed to the second person) and the synonymous imagery with similar syntax in the second half, this thematic reworking would suggest a direct allusion if it were not for the lack of other connections between Job and this

---

114 Here and throughout the *qere* is in brackets.

115 See, e.g., the discussion of Eliphaz's use of Psalm 107 in 5:9–16 on pp. 87–89.

psalm.[116] Only one other fairly weak possibility exists in the dialogue section of the book (4:8 // Ps 126:5). Without recurring connections between the texts and thus the benefit of a cumulative argument, it is difficult to argue that the author of Job was familiar with the psalm and alluding to it directly instead of simply using a common formula for expressing joy, though this does not rule out the possibility of this being a lone allusion to the psalm.

A third factor which may indicate that formulaic language and not a direct allusion explains a textual parallel is a stronger connection in another passage. Consider the following parallel:

Job 5:18

כִּי הוּא יַכְאִיב וְיֶחְבָּשׁ יִמְחַץ וְיָדוֹ [וְיָדָיו] תִּרְפֶּינָה
    For he wounds, but he binds up;
    he strikes, but his hands heal.

Ps 147:3

הָרֹפֵא לִשְׁבוּרֵי לֵב וּמְחַבֵּשׁ לְעַצְּבוֹתָם
    He heals the brokenhearted,
    and binds up their wounds.

Isa 30:26b

בְּיוֹם חֲבֹשׁ יְהוָה אֶת־שֶׁבֶר עַמּוֹ וּמַחַץ מַכָּתוֹ יִרְפָּא
    ... on the day when the Lord binds up the
    injuries of his people, and heals the wounds
    inflicted by his blow.

חבשׁ ("to bind") and רפא ("to heal") only appear together in five verses in the HB. However, of the three other passages where the two verbs are used (Isa 30:26; Ezek 34:4; Hos 6:1), the first and last also refer to God healing wounds he has caused and, in Isaiah, the noun form of the verb מחץ ("to shatter") in Job also appears, and the shared words appear in the same order, making a stronger connection. When a stronger lexical connection is discovered in another passage, it moves the likelihood either to the use of a common formula or to direct dependence with the passage with the greater affinity. However, there may be cases where other factors, such as the relative frequency with which the author refers to the two passages or other connections in the near context, may still indicate an allusion to the passage with the weaker lexical affinity.[117]

A fourth factor that militates against direct dependence is equal connection in multiple passages. For example, Eliphaz's concluding statement on the wicked in his second speech (15:35) is strikingly similar to both Ps 7:15 and Isa 59:4:

---

116 Friedländer mentions this parallel as evidence of the friends' use of psalmic language (Friedländer, *Griechische Philosophie*, 103).

117 Both of these factors contribute to my conclusion that Job 21:18 is an allusion to Ps 1:4, though the verse in Job shares closer verbal similarities with other passages. See pp. 145–148.

Job 15:35

הָרֹה עָמָל וְיָלֹד אָוֶן וּבִטְנָם תָּכִין מִרְמָה They conceive mischief and bring forth
evil
and their heart prepares deceit.

Ps 7:15

הִנֵּה יְחַבֶּל־אָוֶן וְהָרָה עָמָל וְיָלַד שָׁקֶר See how they conceive evil,
and are pregnant with mischief,
and bring forth lies.

Isa 59:4

אֵין־קֹרֵא בְצֶדֶק וְאֵין נִשְׁפָּט בֶּאֱמוּנָה בָּטוֹחַ No one brings suit justly,
עַל־תֹּהוּ וְדַבֶּר־שָׁוְא הָרוֹ עָמָל וְהוֹלֵיד אָוֶן no one goes to law honestly;
they rely on empty pleas, they speak lies,
conceiving mischief and begetting
iniquity.

The triple repetition of natal imagery, as wicked action develops from conception
to birth, involving nearly exact wording, would suggest dependency if only two
passages were involved.[118] The nearly identical context of the passages does little
to help, so dependence between the three texts in either direction is possible, as is
the shared phraseology being merely formulaic. For Job and Psalm 7, the possibility of an allusion here is also hindered by a lack of recurrence since this is the
only notable lexical connection between Job and the psalm.

This phenomenon may also occur within Job's parallels to the Psalms. For
example:

Job 16:9

אַפּוֹ טָרַף וַיִּשְׂטְמֵנִי חָרַק עָלַי בְּשִׁנָּיו צָרִי יִלְטוֹשׁ He has torn me in his wrath, and hated me;
עֵינָיו לִי he has gnashed his teeth at me;
my adversary sharpens his eyes against me.

Ps 35:16

בְּחַנְפֵי לַעֲגֵי מָעוֹג חָרֹק עָלַי שִׁנֵּימוֹ They impiously mocked more and more,
gnashing at me with their teeth.

Ps 37:12

זֹמֵם רָשָׁע לַצַּדִּיק וְחֹרֵק עָלָיו שִׁנָּיו The wicked plot against the righteous,
and gnash their teeth at him …

The similarity of these passages is striking, especially when the rarity of the verb
חרק ("to gnash"), which only appears five times in the HB, is taken into account.
Job's use of this imagery, which is elsewhere used of "profane mockers" (Ps

---

118 Hitzig claims Job is dependent on the psalm (Hitzig, *Hiob*, xl–xli). Olympiodorus and Grotius
also note the connection (Grotius, *Annotata*, 408; Olympiodorus, Deacon of Alexandria, *Kommentar zu Hiob* [ed. U. Hagedorn and C. Hagedorn; PTS 24; Berlin: de Gruyter, 1984], 143).

35:16) and "the wicked" (Ps 37:12), for God (cf. 16:7) is also stunning, and demonstrates a significant thematic reworking. Ps 37:12 may be a stronger possibility for the allusion because it has parallels throughout the dialogue,[119] but the equal connection in Psalm 35 draws that allusion into question. Wright considers this passage in Job to be a quotation of both psalms,[120] but because of this equal connection in the three passages, it could be recurring formulaic language, as well.

Finally, when it comes to larger psalmic forms, such as the hymn or the lament, the author of Job demonstrates a greater propensity for employing general forms than specific texts.[121] Though his use of larger forms, such as the hymn in 5:9–16 and the parody of that form in 12:13–25, or the lament in ch. 7, is widespread,[122] he rarely interacts extensively with one psalm in a single passage, though, for example, 12:13–25 incorporates several images from Psalm 107 and, in the divine speeches, ch. 38 repeats a series of images from Psalm 104 in the same order.[123]

2.6.1.2. Job and Ancient Near Eastern Texts

Job also shares broad connections with several texts from the ancient Near East [ANE]. The texts most similar to Job are the Sumerian poem Man and His God and two Babylonian texts, The Babylonian Theodicy and *Ludlul bel nemeqi*, sometimes referred to as "The Babylonian Job."[124] All three share an interest in the suffering of righteous individuals, though none of the sufferers proclaim their innocence with Job's vehemence. At times, the thematic and narratival similarities between the texts are expressed with considerable verbal affinity. For example,

---

119 Parallels between Psalm 37 and Job include: v. 1 // 5:2; v. 2 // 14:2; v. 4 // 22:26 and 27:10; v. 5 // 21:31; v. 6 // 11:17; v. 10 // 8:22 and 24:24; v. 12 // 16:9; v. 19 // 5:19–20; v. 23 // 21:14; vv. 25, 28 // 4:7; v. 31 // 12:5 and 23:11; vv. 35–36 // 5:3. See Wright, *Job*, 239. Though the extent of these allusions might have warranted further discussion of the psalm in the current study, it lacks any single strongly marked parallel.

120 Wright, *Job*, 240.

121 I have followed Hugh Williamson in distinguishing the smaller common phrases discussed above from "forms" in the form-critical sense by calling the former "formulas" instead (H. G. M. Williamson, review of Marvin A. Sweeney and Ehud Ben Zvi, *The Changing Face of Form Criticism*, *JJS* 56 [2005]: 139). However, in previous discussion of this issue in Job, these shorter phrases have also occasionally been called "forms" (see, e.g., Fohrer, *Hiob*; Dell, *Sceptical*).

122 See Fohrer, *Hiob*, 50–53.

123 Jamieson-Drake, "Job 38," 225. He denies that this indicates direct dependence.

124 See R. G. Albertson, "Job and Ancient Near Eastern Wisdom Literature," in *Scripture in Context II: More Essays on the Comparative Method* (eds. William W. Hallo et al.; Winona Lake, Ind.: Eisenbrauns, 1983); Moshe Weinfeld, "Job and its Mesopotamian Parallels–A Typological Analysis," in *Text and Context: Old Testament and Semitic Studies for F. C. Fensham* (ed. W. Claasen; JSOTSup 48; Sheffield: Sheffield Academic Press, 1988).

Man and His God lines 35–42, *Ludlul* I.82–92, and Job 19:13–18 all describe the experience of social ostracism with common references to friends turning to foes, and youths or slaves (in Job it is both) rising up against the sufferer.[125] Whether or not the shared language in these texts indicates that the author of Job is referring to them particularly, it certainly suggests that the depiction of Job's experience accords with a widespread convention in the ANE, which should therefore be considered in any study of intertextuality in Job.[126]

In fact, when attempting to identify allusions in any HB text, ANE witnesses to the broader culture surrounding the authors must always be taken into account because they may also testify to common forms and formulas or even be the specific texts the author has in mind.[127] However, the results of this comparison are often overstated. Robert Gordis remarks that in an attempt to rectify the isolation of the Bible, scholars often go to the opposite extreme and see Hebrew borrowing in every similarity with ANE sources. But, he argues, similarity does not prove dependency without "an unusual sequence of thought or some striking and exceptional feature common to the two documents being compared," and the basic human concerns dealt with in Hebrew wisdom would naturally produce "similarities in outlook, mood, and form of expression."[128]

Even when an interpreter does not intend to affirm dependence on an ANE source but merely to use the similarity of the ANE text to indicate the widespread existence of a form or formula in the culture, therefore drawing a possible allusion into question, a closer examination of the evidence may actually have the opposite effect, further strengthening the case for the allusion instead. For example, in Job 11:7–8, Zophar asks Job, "Can you find out the deep things of God? Can you find out the limit of the Almighty? It is higher than heaven—what can you do? Deeper than Sheol—what can you know?" Both Ps 139:7–12 and Amos 9:1–6 also contain contrasts between heaven and Sheol, and Pyeon suggests these are the sources behind Zophar's speech.[129] Greenstein, however, criticizes Pyeon for not considering possible ANE parallels to Job 11:7–8, which he claims come even closer to the passage.[130] Based on the parallels in the Babylonian Dialogue

---

125 Weinfeld, "Parallels," 219–20. Weinfeld mentions that similar descriptions may be found in several other biblical texts. He also discusses further similar passages in Job and "The Babylonian Theodicy" (222–24).

126 Greenstein, review of Pyeon.

127 See Sommer, *Prophet*, 33–35, 219–20 n. 12. He claims certain cumulative arguments, such as a sustained pattern of reformulating marked vocabulary or repeated reference to certain texts may indicate an allusion even where ANE similarities are evident.

128 Gordis, *Book*, 55, 59–60.

129 Pyeon, *Intertextuality*, 186.

130 Greenstein, review of Pyeon. He refers to the following works on this purported common proverb: Frederick E. Greenspahn, "A Mesopotamian Proverb and Its Biblical Reverberations," *JAOS* 114 (1994): 33–38; Raymond C. Van Leeuwen, "The Background of Proverbs 30:4aα," in

between a Master and His Servant and the Sippar recension of the Sumerian poem of the early rulers, he argues Zophar is adapting a widespread proverbial saying. Greenstein's characterization of the relative vicinity of these phrases to Job 11:7–8 is questionable, however, because he does not consider 11:9, where Zophar creates a horizontal totality through the merism "earth" (ארץ) and "sea" (ים), which is similar to the psalmist's horizontal merism of the "wings of the morning" (כנפי־שחר), which likely meant the east, and "sea" (ים), which was west for the Israelites.[131] Thus, Zophar and the psalmist both use four locations to communicate the entirety of the cosmos, and three of the same locations in the same order to do so, while the other instances of this proposed proverbial saying only use two, even if we add two more examples to those identified by Greenstein:

Dialogue between a Master and His Servant[132]

Who is so tall as to ascend to the heavens?
Who is so broad as to compass the underworld?

Sippar recension of the Sumerian poem of the early rulers[133]

Like [the remote heavens], can my hand reach them?
Like the deep netherworld, no one knows them!

Fragmentary Sumerian composition[134]

(Even) the highest one cannot reach heaven,
(Even) the broadest one cannot cover the mountains.

Amarna letter 264[135]

If we go up to the heavens or down to the earth,
our heads are still in your hands.

Wisdom, You Are My Sister: Studies in Honor of Roland E. Murphy, O. Carm., on the Occasion of His Eightieth Birthday (ed. Michael L. Barré; CBQMS 29; Washington, D.C.: Catholic Biblical Association of America, 1997), 102–21. See pp. 112–115 below for further discussion of this possible allusion.

131   Unlike these two passages, Amos uses ים to create a second vertical totality by contrasting it with ראש הכרמל ("top of Carmel"), and he has heaven and Sheol in the opposite order (vv. 2–3).

132   W. G. Lambert, *Babylonian Wisdom Literature* (Oxford: Clarendon Press, 1960), 148–49: lines 83–84.

133   J. Klein, "'The Ballad about Early Rulers' in Eastern and Western Traditions," in *Languages and Cultures in Contact: At the Crossroads of Civilizations in the Syro-Mesopotamian Realm* (eds. Karel van Lerberghe and Gabriella Voet; OLA 96; Leuven: Uitgeverij Peeters, 2000), 210: lines 16–17.

134   Bendt Alster, *Studies in Sumerian Proverbs* (CSA 3; Copenhagen: Akademisk Forlag, 1975), 88: lines 17–18.

135   J. A. Knudtzon, *Die El-Amarna-Tafeln* (2 vols.; Aalen: Otto Zeller, 1964), 1:826–27: lines 15–19. Van Leeuwen notes the similar hypothetical conditional structure this passage shares with Psalm 139 (Van Leeuwen, "Background," 119).

Thus, though this evidence does testify to a common use of merisms, particularly those including heaven, to express the totality of the cosmos, it also demonstrates the diversity of this purported formula that actually makes the similarity between Job 11 and Psalm 139 even more striking.

In addition, this type of argument, in which the apparent existence of a common formula is used against the affirmation of an allusion, rests on a false dichotomy in which the interpreter is forced to choose between the two explanations of the textual parallel. In fact, there is no reason why Zophar could not be doing both by referring to the particular use of this formula in Psalm 139. This, of course, depends on identifying further similarities between the passages beyond the mere formulaic language, but in light of Job's allusions to Psalm 139 in the previous chapter (10:8–12), and further allusions to the psalm later in the book, including to this fourfold representation of totality (23:8–9), this seems to be the more probable explanation.[136] Greenstein himself apparently recognizes this, because even though he acknowledges the attestation of a motif of cursing or seeking to abolish a certain day in order to express grief or despair in Mesopotamian literature, he does not let this prevent him from claiming the use of this motif in Job 3:1–12 is an allusion to Jer 20:14–18 because only these two texts apply that more general form to the day of one's birth.[137]

Because the allusions between Job and the Psalms that I will discuss have marked lexical similarities and are each part of a sustained dialogue between the book and certain psalms, closer parallels in ANE texts are doubtful. Though the book of Job shows knowledge of the broader thought-world in which it arose and even of interacting consciously with its popular beliefs and genres,[138] the HB, as mentioned earlier, is its main contextual and intertextual background.[139] That being said, it must be acknowledged that the texts preserved in the HB are likely only a small percentage of the compositions, both oral and literary, that were known in ancient Israel and upon which the author could have drawn. Similarly, the inscriptions discovered from the ANE cultures that surrounded Israel are also a limited sample of a far more extensive corpus, which also could have influenced the author of Job. As Carr argues, our restricted knowledge of these broader potential intertexts should chasten biblical scholars against overconfident assertions about identifying specific intertexts.[140] To make his point, Carr refers to the

---

136 See ch. 5.

137 Greenstein, "Jeremiah," 102.

138 For example, Bruce Zuckerman claims that the Job poet parodies the general dialogue/appeal model found in ANE wisdom literature, such as The Babylonian Theodicy (Zuckerman, *Job*, 93–103). Zuckerman argues for Job's interaction with the broader ANE context throughout his work.

139 Köhlmoos, *Textstrategie*, 14–15. Similarly, Fohrer, *Hiob*, 48.

140 Carr, "Intertextuality," 505–35.

poststructuralist version of intertextuality, with its appeal to the infinite intertextual web of literary, oral, and even visual cultural artifacts surrounding any text to draw into question the tendency in biblical scholarship to restrict the group of potential intertexts to some sort of "proto-canon." Even so, though Carr and the poststructuralist intertextualists on whom he relies are right that the potential influences on a given text encompass far more than some circumscribed literary canon, this does not mean that identifying specific intertexts is impossible (as one could locate Carr's work itself as an influence on this paragraph). Works that have made it into the canon have done so precisely because of their importance in the culture, and thus they could be expected to be prominent among the literary intertexts for later works. Without assuming that the HB contains the sum-total of its intertexts (something Carr warns against), one can still argue that in certain cases, where the evidence is strong enough, the author of a later canonical work is referring to the work of an earlier one.[141] That there may be influences on a text that we can no longer discover should not invalidate the significance of the ones we can find.

2.6.1.3. Allusions within Job

Authors' intratextual allusions to their own work are cases where references to specific texts are difficult to deny. According to Gordis, prominent in the Job poet's widespread use of quotation is Job's repeated quotation of his opponents before refuting them.[142] Gordis gives examples from 21:19–34, ch. 12, and 42:2–6, and claims that the three-fold repetition of this technique, appearing at crucial junctures of the book, demonstrates that the poet favored this rhetorical device.[143] This technique is also part of the book's thoroughly allusory character, a feature it shares with all poetry, which involves a penchant for leaving implications to be felt and understood by readers, engaging them through connotations, allusions, analogies, and symbols.[144]

---

141 Carr acknowledges the possibility of determining specific intertexts when he claims that "blind motifs," which suggest a motif fits more naturally in one text than another where its presence is elsewhere unexplained, may indicate unassimilated borrowing from extra-biblical sources (Carr, "Intertextuality," 528).

142 Gordis, *Book*, 185.

143 Gordis, *Book*, 185–88.

144 Gordis, *Book*, 196, 198. Gordis suggests that this approach, which makes great demands on the reader, would have been embraced in the ancient Semitic world, where an appreciation for the difficulty of reading (the texts lacked vowel letters, word and paragraph divisions, and punctuation) was combined with a love for riddles (191–93, 201). This may help explain why the allusions to the Psalms in Job have been largely overlooked throughout history; the author did not intend them to be easy to find.

A closer look at this technique will further illuminate the poet's use of quotation, or, since Gordis includes "oblique restatement," allusion. First, in ch. 21, immediately before the passage Gordis addresses, Job alludes to a point made by Bildad in order to refute it by transforming it into a question:[145]

Job 18:5–6

גַּם אוֹר רְשָׁעִים יִדְעָךְ וְלֹא־יִגַּהּ שְׁבִיב אִשּׁוֹ 5 Surely the light of the wicked is put out,
and the flame of their fire does not shine.

אוֹר חָשַׁךְ בְּאָהֳלוֹ וְנֵרוֹ עָלָיו יִדְעָךְ 6 The light is dark in their tent,
and the lamp above them is put out.

Job 21:17

כַּמָּה נֵר־רְשָׁעִים יִדְעָךְ וְיָבֹא עָלֵימוֹ אֵידָם חֲבָלִים יְחַלֵּק בְּאַפּוֹ How often is the lamp of the wicked put out?
How often does calamity come upon them?
How often does God distribute pains in his anger?

The thematic, lexical, and syntactical similarity between the passages combine to make a compelling case for allusion. Given the setting of Job's question in a dispute with his friends, even if Job is using a common formula, he likely has Bildad's specific use of the imagery in mind.[146] However, that being the case, the Job poet tellingly refrains from quoting the earlier text verbatim. He repeats just enough of the passage to indicate the allusion but makes several changes, such as replacing the word אוֹר ("light") with נר ("lamp") from the next verse, changing the parallel phrase, and making the verse into a question.[147] This example of intratextual allusion sets a precedent for intertextual allusions between Job and the Psalms, in which allusions will involve changes and only enough similarity to make them evident. It also demonstrates that the argument in the dialogues does not proceed in a directly linear fashion. Words and ideas from previous speeches may be taken up several chapters later with speeches by other characters intervening, as I will argue is often the case in the disputes over particular psalms.

Michael Cheney suggests that the intratextual precedent for intertextual allusions to the Psalms is evident in another allusion Job makes to Bildad's speech:[148]

---

145 See, e.g., Dhorme, *Job*, 315; Clines, *Job*, 2:528–29.
146 The extinguishing lamp of the wicked also appears in Prov 13:9; 24:20 with exactly the same wording as Job 21:17. The author of Job apparently has the characters debate the meaning of this proverb similar to the way I will argue they contest the interpretation of several psalms.
147 The free adaptation of sources seems to be a widespread allusive technique. See, e.g., Sommer, *Prophet*, 21–22; Stead, *Intertextuality*, 37.
148 Michael Cheney, *Dust, Wind and Agony: Character, Speech and Genre in Job* (ConBOT 36; Stockholm: Almqvist & Wiksell International, 1994), 120–21.

Job 18:2

עַד־אָנָה ׀ תְּשִׂימוּן קִנְצֵי לְמִלִּין תָּבִינוּ וְאַחַר נְדַבֵּר   How long will you hunt for words?
                                                                        Consider, and then we shall speak.

Job 19:2

עַד־אָנָה תּוֹגְיוּן נַפְשִׁי וּתְדַכְּאוּנַנִי בְמִלִּים   How long will you torment me,
                                                              and break me in pieces with words?

He observes that the similarities that indicate the allusion between these texts are comparable to those in Job's parody of Psalm 8 in 7:17, where he also repeats the leading phrase and preserves the basic poetic dynamics of the first bicolon, though changing the verb to invert its meaning while retaining the formal resemblance and paragogic *nun*.[149] If Job 7:18 is also considered, then this allusion also shares the repetition and negative intonation of a word in the second bicolon of the source text.

Another intratextual allusion appears in 25:4, as Bildad conflates Job's question in 9:2 with Eliphaz's in 15:14:

Job 9:2

אָמְנָם יָדַעְתִּי כִי־כֵן וּמַה־יִּצְדַּק אֱנוֹשׁ עִם־אֵל   Indeed I know that this is so;
                                                               but how can a mortal be just before God?

Job 15:14

מָה־אֱנוֹשׁ כִּי־יִזְכֶּה וְכִי־יִצְדַּק יְלוּד אִשָּׁה   What are mortals, that they can be clean?
                                                            Or those born of woman, that they can
                                                            be righteous?

Job 25:4

וּמַה־יִּצְדַּק אֱנוֹשׁ עִם־אֵל וּמַה־יִּזְכֶּה יְלוּד אִשָּׁה   How then can a mortal be righteous before
                                                                   God?
                                                                   How can one born of woman be pure?

By combining it with Eliphaz's question, Bildad puts Job's query to a different purpose. Job had used it to attempt to demonstrate the impossibility of proving one's righteousness before God's divine strength (9:3–4), while Bildad uses it to declare that the obstacle is the innate unrighteousness of every human, including Job, as Eliphaz's question had suggested. As he has done here with two different speeches, the author of Job may conflate allusions to two different psalms, or a psalm and another text, and thereby draw the two texts into dialogue with both his work and one another.[150]

---

149 For a comparison of these texts, see p. 63.

150 For the author's conflation of passages from elsewhere in the HB, see Wilson, *Judaism*, 5 n. 4. This technique is also evident in the Qumran *Hodayot* (Svend Holm-Nielsen, *Hodayot: Psalms from Qumran* [ATDan 2; Aarhus: Universitetsforlaget, 1960], 315).

The divergences between the wording of the Psalms and the allusions in Job, including their conflation with other texts, may possibly result from memory error, since the effort of unrolling a scroll would likely make the author rely on memory whenever he could.[151] Greenstein sees evidence for memory errors of this type at Qumran.[152] However, the fact that these same types of verbal differences appear within the book of Job itself indicates that, at least in some cases, they are intentional. These subtle allusions would then accord with the book's thoroughly allusory character, though this subtlety means interpreters must be careful to distinguish direct allusions from repeated common formulas. However, in many cases, the lexical, thematic, and syntactical links are strong enough to suggest a direct allusion. The following steps provide a means for determining the direction of that allusion and drawing out its hermeneutical significance for both texts.

2.6.2. Date

The second, diachronic step investigates the two texts' likely dates of composition to determine which direction of dependence is possible, or at least most probable.[153] Though discovering exact dates is difficult in the HB, plausible date ranges, broader for some books than for others, are identifiable. To this end, the possible development of the texts,[154] and the relative date of the Hebrew they use should be examined.[155]

Because neither Job nor any of the six psalms in this study refer explicitly to historical events, their dates elude definitive determination. Arguments attempting to suggest a plausible period for their composition are based primarily on inner-biblical parallels, linguistic evidence, and the development of Israel's religion. However, conclusions based on evidence in each of these categories are tenuous. Inner-biblical parallels can often be interpreted in either direction, and thus

---

151 Carr suggests Israelite scribes often relied on their memory (David M. Carr, *Writing on the Tablet of the Heart: Origins of Scripture and Literature* [Oxford: Oxford University Press, 2005], 159–62).

152 Edward L. Greenstein, "Misquotation of Scripture in the Dead Sea Scrolls," in vol. 1 of *The Frank Talmage Memorial Volume* (ed. Barry Walfish; 2 vols.; Haifa: Haifa University Press, 1993), 71–83.

153 This is similar to Hays's "availability" criterion (Hays, *Echoes*, 29–30).

154 See Hurvitz, *Linguistic Study*, 16–17. As mentioned above, attempts to determine the textual development of Job have thus far been inconclusive.

155 These comparisons are also often inconclusive. See David M. Carr, "Method in Determination of Direction of Dependence: An Empirical Test of Criteria Applied to Exodus 34,11–26 and Its Parallels," in *Gottes Volk am Sinai. Untersuchungen zu Ex 32–34 und Dtn 9–10* (eds. Matthias Köckert and Erhard Blum; Gütersloh: Chr. Kaiser, Gütersloher Verlaghaus, 2001), 125.

regularly serve only to confirm unstated presuppositions.[156] Arguments built on linguistic evidence and the development of Israel's religion both rely on the assumption that Israel's language and theology developed in a linear chronological fashion, but distinctions between texts can also be explained sociologically, geographically, or even stylistically.[157] For Job and many of these psalms, contradictory conclusions have been drawn from the evidence in each of these categories, leaving the dates of all the texts disputed, and, according to some, unknowable.[158] For example, unusual linguistic features in Job have been interpreted as either later incursions of Aramaic,[159] archaic elements,[160] archaisms that imitate an earlier style,[161] or even imitations of foreign dialects.[162] Thus, J. J. M. Roberts declares, "The chronological significance of the so-called Aramaisms is a moot point."[163] Or, similarly, Gordis and Marvin Pope disagree over the chrono-

---

156 For example, both Michael Goulder and Walter Beyerlin claim Psalm 107 is dependent on Job. However, Goulder dates the psalm in the late sixth century, which means he must dismiss the general consensus that Job was written between the fifth and third centuries as so many "speculations" to reconcile his date for the psalm with its dependence on Job (Michael D. Goulder, *The Psalms of the Return: Book 5, Psalms 107–150* [JSOTSup 258; Sheffield: Sheffield Academic Press, 1998], 127). Beyerlin, on the other hand, following the consensus on the dating of Job, pushes his date for the psalm into the late third century, against the consensus on the psalm, to account for this (Walter Beyerlin, *Werden und Wesen des 107. Psalms* [BZAW 151; Berlin: Walter de Gruyter, 1979], 84). No scholarly consensus is inviolable, but these two examples demonstrate how malleable they can be when driven by assumptions about dependence.

157 For language, see Ian Young, *Diversity in Pre-Exilic Hebrew* (FAT 5; Tübingen: Mohr, 1993). For theology, see James L. Crenshaw, *A Whirlpool of Torment: Israelite Traditions of God as an Oppressive Presence* (OBT 12; Philadelphia: Fortress Press, 1984), 95. He observes that "pockets of a culture invariably preserve older values." Dell suggests general scholarly commitment to these types of reconstructions is in need of review (Katharine J. Dell, "On the Development of Wisdom in Israel," in *Congress Volume: Cambridge 1995* [ed. J. A. Emerton; VTSup 66; Leiden: Brill, 1997], 135–51).

158 Clines, for example, states, "Of [Job's] author or date of composition I frankly know nothing, and my speculations are not likely to be worth more than the many guesses that already exist" (Clines, *Job*, 1:xxix). For the difficulty of dating the psalms in this study, see the respective chapters.

159 Driver and Gray, *Job*, xlvi–xlvii; Harold Henry Rowley, *Job* (NCB; Grand Rapids, Mich.: Eerdmans, 1980), 22.

160 David A. Robertson, *Linguistic Evidence in Dating Early Hebrew poetry* (Missoula, Mont.: Society of Biblical Literature, 1972), 155.

161 Avi Hurvitz, "The Date of the Prose-Tale of Job Linguistically Reconsidered," *HTR* 67 (1974): 17–34.

162 Edward L. Greenstein, "The Language of Job and its Poetic Function," *JBL* 122 (2003): 651–66.

163 J. J. M. Roberts, "Job and the Israelite Religious Tradition," *ZAW* 89 (1977): 109. This is all the more the case if Young is right that though the so-called Aramaisms are, in fact, indications of Archaic Biblical Hebrew, this type of Hebrew is distinguished stylistically through its free use of forms and not chronologically from Standard Biblical Hebrew. See Young, *Diversity*, 123, 130–37; Ian Young, "Is the Prose Tale of Job in Late Biblical Hebrew?" *VT* 59 (2009): 606–29.

logical relationship between Job and Isaiah 40–55, each appealing to inner-biblical parallels and the development of Israel's religion in their arguments.[164]

Thus, discussions of the inconclusive nature of the evidence for Job's date have become standard fare in commentaries.[165] Throughout history, suggestions have ranged from the Mosaic age to the Maccabean period,[166] but, in recent scholarship, the book's date is generally placed between the fifth and third centuries B.C.E. based on cumulative evidence, particularly the book's language, mention of a Satan figure, and challenge of a developed view of retribution,[167] though the occasional argument for a seventh-century date may be found.[168]

The psalms in this study are also often dated in the postexilic period.[169] Similarities to Job, either through the parallels pursued in this study, the thematic resonance that likely occasioned those parallels, or the evidence of "wisdom influence" deduced from those lexical and thematic affinities, widely contribute to these conclusions, which gives them an air of circularity. Therefore, the overlapping date range should be neither surprising nor a hindrance to attributing dependence to Job. The vital point is that no definitive evidence exists to preclude the possibility of Job's diachronic dependence on these psalms (nor, it should be said, the psalms' dependence on Job). Recognizing the tenuous nature of diachronic arguments built on inner-biblical parallels, I do not intend to prove definitively that Job is later than the psalms in question. Given that this relationship is entirely possible, I do, however, believe a strong case can be made that it is also the probable explanation of the lexical and thematic connections between the texts.

---

164 Gordis believes Job came after Isaiah 40–55; Pope thinks Job is more likely earlier (Marvin H. Pope, *Job* [3rd ed.; AB 15; Garden City, N.Y.: Doubleday, 1973], xxxix–xl; Gordis, *Book*, 216).

165 E.g., Habel, *Job*, 40–42.

166 Brevard S. Childs, *Introduction to the Old Testament as Scripture* (Philadelphia: Fortress Press, 1979), 530. For a succinct overview of the various positions on the date of the book in critical scholarship up to the mid-twentieth century, see Harold Henry Rowley, "The Book of Job and its Meaning," in *From Moses to Qumran: Studies in the Old Testament* (London: Lutterworth Press, 1963), 173–74.

167 E.g., Fohrer, *Hiob*, 42; Gordis, *Book*, 216; Dell, *Sceptical*, 162; John Gray, *The Book of Job* (ed. David J. A. Clines; THB 1; Sheffield: Sheffield Phoenix Press, 2010), 35.

168 E.g., Pope, *Job*, xl; Hartley, *Job*, 20.

169 Though she declares the specific dating of any of the Psalms "impossible," Susan Gillingham offers a broad outline, in which she puts Psalms 1, 8, 39, 73, and 107 in the postexilic period but does not mention Psalm 139 (Susan E. Gillingham, *The Poems and Psalms of the Hebrew Bible* [OBS; Oxford: Oxford University Press, 1994], 251–54).

2.6.3. Coherence

If, as in the connections between Job and many of the psalms, diachronic study is unable to determine which text is referring to the other, the decision is pushed into this third, synchronic step, in which the possibility of an allusion is evaluated in both texts simultaneously in the hope that a simultaneous comparison will shed light on the sequence of the texts. Though the result hoped for from this comparison is diachronic, the method of comparing the possible meaning of the allusion in both directions involves imagining at least one relationship between the texts that could not have historically existed, since both texts cannot be dependent on each other in a single parallel, so this step is best considered synchronic.

The coherence of the parallel texts is evaluated, first, internally, in their immediate context, and then externally, in relation to the context of the parallel text.[170] When comparing internal coherence, the text in which the possible allusion fits more awkwardly is more likely the later text, based on the assumption that words and images fit better in their original settings than in new contexts to which they are later adapted.[171] This can involve either thematic or linguistic inconsistency. Thus, for example, Hare claims that Psalm 107 is dependent on Job because the participle שֹׁפֵךְ that begins the shared phrase in Ps 107:40 and Job 12:21 is part of a series of participles in Job but diverges in tense from the surrounding verbs in the psalm. Hare's argument, however, turns out to be inconclusive,[172] as do many arguments based on internal coherence when the authors show literary skill and a willingness to adapt earlier material to new surroundings.

The comparison of external coherence builds on the assumption that allusions carry with them their surrounding contexts, since authors allude to texts and not merely words. In other words: "The work alluded to reflects upon the present context even as the present context absorbs and changes the allusion."[173] Therefore, as Schultz, who uses the word "quotation" where many would use "allusion," says, "One should seek in quotation such a use of the borrowed phrase that a knowledge of the *quoted* context is essential in order to properly understand the *quoting* context."[174] Greenstein makes this sort of argument when he reasons that the Job poet's more radical version of the imagery he shares with

---

170 Hays addresses similar issues in his criterion of "thematic coherence" (Hays, *Echoes*, 30).

171 For this criterion for determining direction of dependence, see Risto Nurmela, *The Mouth of the Lord Has Spoken: Inner-Biblical Allusions in Second and Third Isaiah* (StJ; Lanham, Md.: University Press of America, 2006), viii; Lyons, *Law*, 62–64.

172 See p. 83.

173 H. Davidson, *T. S. Eliot and Hermeneutics: Absence and Interpretation in the Waste Land* (Baton Rouge: Louisiana State University Press, 1985), 117.

174 Schultz, *Quotation*, 227. Emphasis original.

Jeremiah more likely results from his use of Jeremiah than from Jeremiah's domestication of Job.[175]

This attention to external coherence is similar to Lyle Eslinger's suggestion that when literary evidence is insufficient to suggest a particular direction of dependence, the interpreter should address the intertextual connections "from both ends,"[176] but its intent is to use that synchronic comparison to come to a diachronic conclusion with more optimism that such a comparison can be persuasive, though admittedly not definitive. So, for example, Eslinger challenges Fishbane's interpretation of Job's parody of Ps 8:5 in Job 7:17–18 because, he claims, given the lack of evidence for the relative chronology of the two texts, "we could as easily read the Psalm as an allusive corrective of Job's excessive cynicism, a pious riposte to Job's exaggerated sense of personal right and freedom."[177] Though it is true that we *could* read the relationship between the passages in this way, it is doubtful that we could do so *as easily*.[178] Whereas parody contributes naturally to Job's accusations against God, an allusion to Job's lament would mar the positive tone of the psalmist's hymn.[179]

Admittedly, in some cases this comparison of the internal and external coherence of the parallel passages is going to be inconclusive, particularly when the two texts share the same tone, as in the parallels between Job and some lament psalms. As S. R. Driver says, "Nothing is more difficult (except under specially favourable circumstances) than from a *mere* comparison of parallel passages to determine on which side the priority lies."[180] To address this difficulty, several scholars have proposed various possible criteria, but comparing the internal and external coherence of the passages basically encompasses them all.[181] If dependence cannot be determined, the interpretation of the two possible directions of allusion may simply have to be left side by side,[182] though the probability for

---

175 Greenstein, "Jeremiah," 99.

176 Lyle Eslinger, "Inner-Biblical Exegesis and Inner-Biblical Allusion: The Question of Category," *VT* 42 (1992): 56.

177 Eslinger, "Inner-Biblical," 55.

178 See Michael Fishbane, "The Book of Job and Inner-Biblical Discourse," in *The Voice From the Whirlwind* (eds. Leo G. Perdue and W. Clark Gilpin; Nashville: Abingdon, 1992), 89–90.

179 See p. 69. Similarly, referring to the allusions to the plague narrative of Exodus 9 in Psalms 78 and 105, Jeffery Leonard points to the difficulty of imagining how either example could have functioned in the opposite direction as an important factor in determining the direction of dependence (Leonard, "Identifying," 264).

180 S. R. Driver, *An Introduction to the Literature of the Old Testament* (9th ed.; ITL; Edinburgh: T&T Clark, 1929), 312. Emphasis original.

181 Risto Nurmela, *Prophets in Dialogue: Inner-Biblical Allusions in Zechariah 9–14* (Åbo: Åbo Akademi University Press, 1996), 29–33; Carr, "Method," 107–40; Leonard, "Identifying," 241–65; Lyons, *Law*, 60–67.

182 E.g., Thomas Dozeman, "Inner-Biblical Interpretation of Yahweh's Gracious and Compassion-

dependence should lean in the direction of the text that shows a more widespread proclivity for allusion.[183]

2.6.4. Use

After establishing the direction of dependence, the interpreter can pursue the meaning of the allusion diachronically by asking how the later author is using this earlier text in its new context. The possible uses of an allusion are manifold.[184] In each case, certain questions must be addressed, such as: How has the author changed the precursor?[185] Are the similarities or the differences between the passages emphasized? What attitude is the author taking toward the precursor? And, to how much of the precursor's context is the allusion referring?[186]

Sommer argues that Deutero-Isaiah's allusions relate to their sources, like the two versets in biblical parallelism, by employing structures of specification, antithesis, and intensification.[187] This analogy elucidates the use of the Psalms in Job, as well. Sometimes Job and his friends specify general psalmic statements by applying them directly to Job and his situation (e.g., Job 23:10–11 // Ps 1:1, 6; Job 22:13 // Ps 73:11).[188] Job's repeated parodies of the Psalms put his words in an antithetical relationship with theirs (e.g., Job 7:17–18 // Ps 8:5), though the friends' use of the Psalms may also reverse their meaning (e.g., Job 25:5–6 // Ps 8:4–5). Also, Job often elaborates on passages from the Psalms, thereby intensifying their imagery (e.g., Job 12:21–24 // Ps 107:40; Job 10:20–22 // Ps 39:14).

---

ate Character," *JBL* 108 (1989): 207–23. He reads the "mutual relationship" between Jonah and Joel in both directions.

183 Leonard mentions this among his criteria for determining the direction of dependence (Leonard, "Identifying," 258).

184 See the lists in Anthony Johnson, "Allusion in Poetry," *PTL* 1 (1976): 581–82; Thomas M. Greene, *The Light in Troy: Imitation and Discovery in Renaissance Poetry* (New Haven: Yale University Press, 1982), 38–46; Sommer, *Prophet*, 29–30. For similar lists of purposes for quotation, see Stefan Morawski, "The Basic Functions of Quotation," in *Sign, Language, Culture* (ed. A. J. Greimas; The Hague: Mouton, 1970), 692–95; Schultz, *Quotation*, 195–99.

185 For an extensive taxonomy of types of intertextual relationships between texts, see Gérard Genette, *Palimpsests: Literature in the Second Degree* (trans. C. Newman and C. Doubinsky; Stages 8; Lincoln: University of Nebraska Press, 1997).

186 See Alter's distinction between whole-to-part, part-to-part, part-to-whole, and whole-to-whole allusions (Alter, *Pleasures*, 129–33).

187 Sommer, *Prophet*, 160–61.

188 See the relevant chapters for discussion of these and the following allusions.

2.6.5. Recurrence

As Robert Alter observes, "allusions often radiate out to contiguous allusions."[189] This step pursues further recurring allusions to the same text, as, like a stone dropped into water, the original allusion sends ripples through the entire work. The search should also extend throughout the precursor text, because, having drawn an earlier text into the work once, the author is likely to do so again, and may even appeal to other aspects of that text.[190] In fact, further recurrence of allusions to the same text may strengthen the evidence for the allusion in the first place.[191] The search here is, like the first step, mainly a synchronic comparison of the two texts searching for similarities that may be allusions. However, because the texts have already been linked and the direction of dependence already established, additional allusions need not be quite as strong as the initial connection, and the direction may be assumed.[192] However, in each case, steps one to four could be repeated, particularly if there is doubt as to the seams of the texts in question, leaving the possibility that some parts could be later than others.

2.6.6. Holistic Interpretation

The significance of these recurring allusions is addressed in the sixth step, which is like the fourth except that it now approaches the author's diachronic use of the earlier text holistically instead of focusing on one particularly marked allusion. The goal is to examine the text's "deep structure,"[193] which stretches out through the alluding text and its precursor at once, as "a current of sense" flows between the texts through the allusions that solder them together.[194] Thus, Ben-Porat defines allusion as "a device for the simultaneous activation of two texts."[195] The

---

189 Alter, *Pleasures*, 118.

190 For example, Stead notices "sustained allusion" to particular texts in Zechariah 1–8 (Stead, *Intertextuality*, 253).

191 Sommer observes the cumulative nature of the argument for allusion (Sommer, *Prophet*, 35), and Hays makes "recurrence" one of his criteria for echoes (Hays, *Echoes*, 30). Similarly, Leonard, "Identifying," 253, 262. Schultz warns, however, that cumulative arguments are not compelling in themselves since ten subjective arguments are not necessarily stronger than one convincing one (Schultz, *Quotation*, 70–71). Also, if the case for each individual allusion is dependent on the recognition of them all, the argument is circular, thus this criterion cannot stand on its own.

192 Thus, Sommer claims, "When a text in Deutero-Isaiah shares vocabulary with one of Deutero-Isaiah's favorite sources, one can argue more confidently that the Deutero-Isaianic text in question depends on that source" (Sommer, *Prophet*, 71–72).

193 See Plett, "Intertextualities," 9–10.

194 Johnson, "Allusion," 586. He calls this "metaliterary allusion."

195 Ben-Porat, "Allusion," 107.

allusion may act as a synecdoche, standing in *pars pro toto* for the precursor text,[196] while that earlier text becomes a "recurrent thread" in the design of the later one.[197]

A pattern emerges in the Job poet's holistic interpretation of many of the psalms. With the exception of Psalm 39, each of the psalms is alluded to by both Job and the friends, but the characters interpret them in different ways to further their arguments against one another. By embodying contrasting positions in different characters, the author of Job presents them *dialogically*. This concept derives from the work of Mikhail Bakhtin. In his work on the nineteenth-century novelist Fyodor Dostoevsky, Bakhtin praised his dialogical style of presenting truth, in which each character represented a different idea, and did so with such authenticity that the author's voice receded into the background. There is a "profound personalism" in his work; "For Dostoevsky there are no ideas, no thoughts, no positions which belong to no one, which exist 'in themselves.'"[198] Bakhtin contrasted this with the monological form of most writing, in which a single authoritarian voice declares a unitary truth.[199] Bakhtin's ideas were popularized by Kristeva in the 1970s and have recently made their way into biblical scholarship.[200]

The clashing voices in Job have offered rich opportunities to apply Bakhtin's insight. Several scholars have argued that Job is a dialogical work in which the author uses the dialogue to create a space where the consciousnesses of his characters can interact, thereby presenting his message in a multivalent polyphony, and even that the structure of the book as a whole draws further views into that debate.[201] Though the present study does not attempt to be dialogical in the sense of embracing Bakhtin's broader approach to interpreting texts, this basic understanding of the way truth may be refracted into various voices is a helpful concept for explaining how the Job poet is using the Psalms. Therefore, I will build on previous dialogical research on Job by tracing the way that the "profound personalism" of the work is expressed not merely through the characters debating

---

196 See Mettinger, "Intertextuality," 264.

197 Alter, *Pleasures*, 127. Thus, Stead argues that the "sustained allusions" in Zechariah 1–8 give the book a "meta-intertextuality" that warrants "reading Zechariah against the wider context of the specific passages being alluded to" (Stead, *Intertextuality*, 254).

198 Mikhail M. Bakhtin, *Problems of Dostoevsky's Poetics* (trans. Caryl Emerson; THL 8; Manchester: Manchester University Press, 1984), 31.

199 See, e.g., Bakhtin, *Dostoevsky's Poetics*, 97.

200 Kristeva, "Word," 64–91. In biblical studies, see, e.g., Walter L. Reed, *Dialogues of the Word: The Bible as Literature According to Bakhtin* (Oxford: Oxford University Press, 1993); Carol A. Newsom, "Bakhtin, the Bible, and Dialogic Truth," *JR* 76 (1996): 290–306; Barbara Green, *Mikhail Bakhtin and Biblical Scholarship: An Introduction* (Atlanta: Society of Biblical Literature, 2000).

201 Reed, *Dialogues*, 114–38; Carol A. Newsom, "The Book of Job as Polyphonic Text," *JSOT* 97 (2002): 87–108; Newsom, *Contest*; Mandolfo, "Renegade," 45–63.

theological ideas, but also scriptural texts, and, in so doing, embodying not only different concepts but contrasting interpretive approaches.

These interpretations of the Psalms reflect another Bakhtinian conception of the dialogical nature of speech, "double-voicedness." By this Bakhtin refers to a type of speech in which the original semantic intention of another earlier speaker is discernible along with that of the present speaker. Parodies, like those Job repeatedly makes of the Psalms, are prime examples of this. Thus Bakhtin observes that "in parody two languages are crossed with each other, as well as two styles, two linguistic points of view, and in the final analysis two speaking subjects."[202] As Newsom puts it, "[Job] uses the worlds [*sic*] of psalmic discourse, yet overlays them with his own intentions, so that assumptions and ideological commitments which were obscure when those words were voiced monologically suddenly become evident."[203] However, Newsom argues that the friends also employ double-voiced discourse, but do so differently than Job. Whereas Job's parodies create a contrast between his voice and earlier speech, the friends use what Bakhtin calls "stylization" to present their speech as in harmony with earlier discourse. In so doing, they attempt to add weight to the authority of their words and encourage Job to acquiesce to their interpretation of traditional speech.[204] By investigating in more detail how Job and the friends interpret the same texts, this study will support Newsom's conclusion that Job and the friends interact with earlier voices in different ways, while nuancing the way she presents that interaction, as Job's parodies are actually seen to be more faithful to the meaning of the psalms.

---

202 Mikhail M. Bakhtin, "From the Prehistory of Novelistic Discourse," in *The Dialogic Imagination: Four Essays* (ed. Michael Holquist; trans. Caryl Emerson and Michael Holquist; Austin: University of Texas Press, 1981), 76. For more on Bakhtin's understanding of parody, see Gary S. Morson, "Parody, History and Metaparody," in *Rethinking Bakhtin: Extensions and Challenges* (eds. Gary S. Morson and C. Emmerson; Evanston: Northwestern University Press, 1989). Though Bakhtin argues that in parody discourse "becomes an arena of battle between two voices" (Bakhtin, *Dostoevsky's Poetics*, 93), I have argued elsewhere that a parodied text may be employed as a weapon instead of a target, and thus the relationship between the two texts need not be hostile. See Will Kynes, "Beat Your Parodies into Swords, and Your Parodied Books into Spears: A New Paradigm for Parody in the Hebrew Bible," *BibInt* 19 (2011): 276–310.

203 Newsom, "Bakhtin," 297–98.

204 Newsom, "Polyphonic," 100.

2.6.7. Reciprocation

Since allusions involve interpretation, they serve as "commentary" on earlier texts.[205] As a "bilaterally operative signal," allusion can go against the historical grain.[206] Steve Moyise, who calls this "dialogical intertextuality," speaks of the "two-way" influence between texts, in which "the new affects the old while the old affects the new."[207] Thus, this synchronic step treats the alluding text as an early stage in the history of interpretation of its precursor and examines how the allusions enrich our understanding of it. Though there is a diachronic contribution to this step, the sequential aspect here, in which the later text is considered to interpret the earlier one, is approached from a more synchronic perspective, which emphasizes the reader's ability to compare the texts and see new features of the earlier text through the connections with the later one. This accords with Fishbane's description of aggadic exegesis, which he claims, is "not content to supplement gaps in the *traditum*, but characteristically draws forth latent and unsuspected meanings from it."[208]

As an example of this reciprocal effect, often the repeated allusions to the psalms in Job highlight tensions or ambiguities within them. Their double-voiced use uncovers features of the texts that were obscure in their monological expression. Since ambiguity is "any verbal nuance, however slight, which gives room for alternative reactions to the same piece of language,"[209] the contrasting interpretations given the psalms by Job and the friends expose its presence in those psalms. Further, while arguing for "deliberate ambiguity" in the Psalms, Paul Raabe suggests that much of it involves issues of weighty theological significance.[210] Allusions to these psalms in Job demonstrate this to be the case, as this ambiguity often concerns the theological tensions at their heart.

2.6.8. Historical Implications

Finally, the eighth step seeks to answer historical questions about what these allusions say about the earlier text's standing when the later author alluded to it and about the interpretive techniques employed at that time. This can extend to a

---

205 Hebel, "Allusion," 139. Thus, Sommer claims help in understanding the earlier text is a secondary feature of some allusions (Sommer, *Prophet*, 18).

206 Hebel, "Allusion," 140.

207 Moyise, "Intertextuality," 424–25. Similarly, Ben-Porat, "Allusion," 114 n. 9.

208 Fishbane, *Interpretation*, 283. This does not change the meaning of the earlier text, but it may enable readers to see aspects of its meaning they had not seen before. See Barton, *Biblical Criticism*, 86.

209 William Empson, *Seven Types of Ambiguity* (3rd ed.; Harmondsworth: Penguin, 1960), 1.

210 Paul R. Raabe, "Deliberate Ambiguity in the Psalter," *JBL* 110 (1991): 227.

broader consideration of the historical setting and culture of the alluding text, including questions of scribal training and habits. Intertextuality in the HB not only suggests that "the religion of the ancient Israelites was already a text-based religion,"[211] it indicates which texts had authority in the community and how much flexibility was allowed in their interpretation.[212] Because our knowledge of the historical settings of both Job and these psalms is so limited, this discussion can offer little more than suggestions. Though a synchronic reading of the relationship between the texts may occasionally contribute insight here, because this step is primarily concerned with the texts' place in history, it is best considered diachronic.

In summary, the eight steps of intertextualities in dialogue are as follows. They are best followed in this order, though they inevitably overlap with one another.

1.   Identification (synchronic): Where does this text point to another and to which text(s) does it point?
2.   Date (diachronic): Which order of texts is historically plausible?
3.   Coherence (synchronic): Which order makes better sense of the internal and external context?
4.   Use (diachronic): How is the author using the allusion?
5.   Recurrence (synchronic): What other allusions connect the two texts?
6.   Holistic interpretation (diachronic): How do allusions to the precursor contribute to the meaning of the alluding text as a whole?
7.   Reciprocation (synchronic): How does the use of the precursor affect our understanding of it?
8.   Historical implications (diachronic): What do these allusions say about the standing of the earlier text at this time and the interpretive techniques at play?

2.7. Conclusion

The astute reader may have noticed that the concept of dialogue appeared four times in this chapter with slightly different nuances each time. In his work, the author of Job has capitalized on the potential of dialogue to communicate meaning in a rich and engaging way, and, following his lead, this study draws on a number of dialogical features, which have been developed throughout this chapter. First, it takes a dialogical approach to the question of intertextuality, in which diachronic and synchronic concerns are put into a conversation where they com-

---

211 Sommer, *Prophet*, 2.
212 See James A. Sanders, "Intertextuality and Canon," in *On the Way to Nineveh: Studies in Honor of George M. Landes* (eds. Stephen L. Cook and S. C. Winter; Atlanta: Scholars Press, 1999), 316.

plement one another. Second, it focuses on the dialogue section of the book of Job, in which the author's narratival control recedes into the background as he creates a space for his characters to represent and explore different ideas and even varying interpretive approaches. Third, in this way, my reading draws on Bakhtin's dialogical insight. Fourth, it points to the "dialogical intertextuality" created between the book of Job and the Psalms by the allusions that solder the texts together and create a reciprocal hermeneutical relationship between them. It is to that dialogue, in all its facets, that I now turn.

Part I

Praise

3. Hubris and Humility: Psalm 8 in Job

What a chimera, then, is man! what a novelty, what a monster, what a chaos, what a subject of contradiction, what a prodigy! A judge of all things, feeble worm of the earth, depository of the truth, cloaca of uncertainty and error, the glory and the shame of the universe![1]

If the sheer volume of scholarly work is any indication, Köhlmoos is certainly right to assert, "Der wichtigste Intertext für die Hiob-Dichtung ist der mehrfach rezipierte Ps 8."[2] Despite the widespread attention this intertextual connection has received, the breadth and depth of the book's interaction with the psalm has yet to be fully explored. This study is essential because the extensive and sophisticated use of Psalm 8 in Job both invites the search for allusions to other psalms in Job and creates a framework for how those other allusions may be understood.

3.1. Identification

The marked parallel drawing Job and this hymn together is Job's "bitter parody" of Ps 8:5 in his first response to Eliphaz:

Job 7:17–18

מָה־אֱנוֹשׁ כִּי תְגַדְּלֶנּוּ וְכִי־תָשִׁית אֵלָיו לִבֶּךָ 17   What are human beings, that you make
         so much of them,
         that you set your mind on them,

וַתִּפְקְדֶנּוּ לִבְקָרִים לִרְגָעִים תִּבְחָנֶנּוּ 18   visit them every morning,
         test them every moment?

Ps 8:5

מָה־אֱנוֹשׁ כִּי־תִזְכְּרֶנּוּ וּבֶן־אָדָם כִּי תִפְקְדֶנּוּ   What are human beings that you are
         mindful of them,
         mortals that you care for them?

---

1   Blaise Pascal, *The Thoughts, Letters and Opuscules of Blaise Pascal* (trans. O. W. Wight; New York: Derby & Jackson, 1859), 244.

2   Köhlmoos, *Textstrategie*, 362.

The lexical similarities between these two passages are too numerous to be a coincidence.[3] First, the question "What are human beings?" (מה־אנוש) is repeated.[4] Second, the extended forms of both questions have a similar structure ([verb] + כי + ו + [verb] + כי), with the addition of בן־אדם (literally, "son of man") in the psalm.[5] Third, Job's use of the verb גדל ("to make great") recalls the exalted status of humanity in Ps 8:6–9,[6] though in its context it has a negative connotation,[7] ironically contrasting with the verb חסר ("to make less"), which is used positively in Ps 8:6.[8] Fourth, תשית אליו לבך ("you set your mind/heart") in Job recalls זכר ("to be mindful of") in the psalm.[9] Fifth, the same verb פקד is set in a context which reverses its meaning from condescending care in the psalm to overbearing observation in Job.[10] Sixth, both verbs in the psalm and three of the four verbs in Job have suffixes with an energic *nun*, and these are the only two passages in the HB where the verb פקד has an energic *nun*. The extent of these lexical and semantic ligatures strongly suggest an allusion, which has led to the widespread affirmation that Job is here parodying the psalm. As Clines remarks, "In every respect the language of [Psalm 8] is reapplied ironically by Job."[11]

This view has not, however, gained universal approval. Gunkel claims the parallel between the texts is insufficient to determine their relative dates, and Yair Hoffman declares that the linguistic relation between the two passages falls short of providing sufficient proof of an ironic dialogue between them.[12] Eslinger, how-

3   Francis I. Andersen, *Job* (London: Inter-Varsity Press, 1976), 138.

4   This exact phrase only appears in three places in the HB: these two verses and Job 15:14, which is likely another reference to the psalm.

5   Fishbane, "Job," 87.

6   Habel, *Job*, 164; Clines, *Job*, 1:192; Carol A. Newsom, "The Book of Job," in *1 & 2 Maccabees, Introduction to Hebrew Poetry, Job, Psalms* (NIB 4; Nashville: Abingdon Press, 1996), 396.

7   E.-J. Waschke, "'Was ist der Mensch, daß du seiner gedenkst?' (Ps 8,5): Theologische und anthropologische Koordinaten für die Frage nach dem Menschen im Kontext alttestamentlicher Aussagen," *TLZ* 116 (1991): 807. Michaela Bauks observes that by replacing זכר ("to be mindful of") in the psalm with גדל, Job is exchanging the psalmist's admiration at God's allotment of creaturely greatness to humans for a mocking allusion to their purely physical growth. See Michaela Bauks, "Was ist der Mensch, dass du ihn großziehst? (Hiob 7,17)," in *Was ist der Mensch, dass du seiner gedenkst? (Psalm 8,5): Aspekte einer theologischen Anthropologie* (ed. Michaela Bauks; Neukirchen-Vluyn: Neukirchener Verlag, 2008), 2.

8   Fishbane, "Job," 87.

9   Clines, *Job*, 1:192. שית in Job also contrasts with Ps 8:7, where it communicates God's gracious bestowal of earthly dominion to humans (Hans Klein, "Zur Wirkungsgeschichte von Psalm 8," in *Konsequente Traditionsgeschichte* [eds. Rüdiger Bartelmus et al.; OBO; Göttingen: Vandenhoeck & Ruprecht, 1993], 187). Fishbane also observes the common use of the verb (Fishbane, "Job," 87).

10 See HALOT and comments in Clines, *Job*, 1:192.

11 Clines, *Job*, 1:192.

12 Hermann Gunkel, *Die Psalmen* (Göttingen: Vandenhoeck & Ruprecht, 1926), 29; Yair Hoffman,

ever, finds the literary connection clear, but argues dependence could just as easily be in the other direction.[13] Raymond Van Leeuwen devotes an entire article to
challenging this "scholarly commonplace."[14] He argues that the lexical links
between the texts are better explained as variations on a shared "living, oral formula" that was used in the ANE to communicate the insignificance of humans
and the unworthiness of servants before their masters. In support of this interpretation, he points to several more general uses of the formulaic structure used
in the two passages ("Who/What is X // that X/Y has/should ... ?"), including
three further appearances of the formula in Job (15:14; 21:14–15; 25:4–6), and
one in Lachish Letter 2:3–5 ("who is your servant, a dog, that my lord remembers
his servant?"), which employs the same Hebrew verb זכר ("to remember") as Ps
8:5. He concludes that Psalm 8, and not Job 7, "subverts" the ancient formula by
indirectly asserting human splendor.[15]

Van Leeuwen's argument has had little effect on the scholarly consensus, and
that may be because it rests on a false disjunction. He attempts to prove that a
common formula and not Ps 8:5 is the subtext for Job 7:17. However, both could
be true.[16] Even if the similar structure between the passages is evidence of a common formula, the Job poet could be using the formula to parody its earlier usage
by the psalmist. Further lexical and thematic connections between the two passages like those noted above, which Van Leeuwen either ignores or attempts to
explain away as "lexemes appropriate to the rhetoric of the formula,"[17] suggest a
closer connection between the two passages than the mere repetition of a common formula. In fact, by reducing the similarity between the texts to merely its
shared structure Van Leeuwen has created a straw man. Additionally, because of
the anthological character of Psalm 144 and the Job poet's proclivity to refer to
the same psalm at several points in the dialogue, the biblical passages which Van
Leeuwen claims as evidence of this formula that share more than the same bare
structure could all actually be allusions to Psalm 8. As I shall demonstrate below,
that these other allusions to Psalm 8 in Job incorporate other aspects of the
psalm beyond Van Leeuwen's purported formula in v. 5 further indicates that the
psalm itself and not a common formula is repeated in 15:14–16 and 25:4–6.[18]

A Blemished Perfection: The Book of Job in Context (JSOTSup 213; Sheffield: Sheffield Academic
Press, 1996), 212 n. 45.

13   Eslinger, "Inner-Biblical," 55. See p. 53 above.

14   Van Leeuwen, "Psalm 8.5," 205–15, 206.

15   Van Leeuwen, "Psalm 8.5," 213–14.

16   See p. 45.

17   Van Leeuwen, "Psalm 8.5," 210.

18   These further similarities distinguish these passages from Job 21:14–15, which only repeats the
     structure (כי + [noun] + מה).

Helmut Schnieringer makes a slightly different argument against the literary dependence of Job 7:17–18 on Ps 8:5.[19] He claims that the differences between the passages make dependence uncertain. He appeals to the variance in both syntax and the number of verbs used (with the repeated verb פקד only in the extra synonymous parallel in Job), as well as to Job's use of the verb גדל, which, as he understands it, does not refer to the exalted view of humanity in Ps 8:6–7. He claims these differences negate all the commonly suggested connections between the texts, leaving the evidentiary burden solely on the repetition of the verb פקד, which, with its apparently reversed sense in Job, often serves as the prime evidence of Job's parody of the psalm. However, Schnieringer argues that the negative sense of פקד in Job is actually more common than the positive sense in Ps 8:5, which, he claims, indicates that the use in Job does not result from a parody of the psalm. Therefore, he maintains that the similarities between the two texts are too vague to be the result of direct dependence, and thus, shared dependence on a common element of tradition is a completely adequate explanation.

Though the possibility that both Job and Psalm 8 are referring to a common tradition cannot be definitively disproven, Schnieringer overstates his case against dependence. First, his argument that the differences between the texts negate their similarities reflects a simplistic view of how a later author may interact with an earlier text that overlooks the possibility that the Job poet may have interpreted the psalm as he alluded to it. Even when the author has characters allude to earlier speeches within the dialogue, he exercises considerable freedom in his representation of those passages (e.g., Job 21:17; cf. 18:5–6).[20] The elaboration of the psalmist's phrase in Job's version corresponds to other psalmic allusions in Job, where the author shows a propensity to embellish his source (e.g., Job 12:21–24; cf. Ps 107:40; Job 10:20–22; cf. Ps 39:14). Second, though Schnieringer claims to have explained away all the similarities between the texts except the common use of פקד, he never actually counters the striking repetition of the phrase מה־אנוש כי, which only appears three times in the HB (Ps 8:5; Job 7:17; 15:14). Third, the predominance of the negative meaning of פקד in the HB does not mean that Job's use of it in that sense cannot be a parody. In fact, the usage of that verb across the HB indicates that it was a *vox media*, its meaning varying according to its context.[21] This polyvalence allows for Job's word play.[22] A parody need not employ the rarer meaning of a word, and even if פקד appears more often with a negative connotation, the positive meaning is not uncommon (e.g.,

---

19   Helmut Schnieringer, *Psalm 8: Text – Gestalt – Bedeutung* (ÄAT 59; Wiesbaden: Harrassowitz, 2004), 432–33, 503.

20   See p. 47.

21   HALOT gives three possibilities: 1. to miss, worry about; 2. to see something remarkable, or alternatively examinable, in someone or something; 3. to seek, seek out, visit.

22   Habel, *Job*, 164; Newsom, "Job," 396.

Gen 21:1; 50:24; 1 Sam 2:21; Pss 80:14; 106:4). Thus, ultimately, Schnieringer's arguments against Job's parody of Psalm 8 are unconvincing.

A final objection to reading Job 7:17–18 as Job's parody of Ps 8:5 is the possibility that Job is alluding to Psalm 144 instead. Van Leeuwen suggests that Job 7 and Psalm 144 may actually be closer to one another in terms of common vocabulary than to Psalm 8 because they both refer to life as הבל ("vanity"; Job 7:7, 16; Ps 144:4).[23] He denies that the repetition of the phrase מה־אנוש כי in Job 7:17 and Ps 8:5 is significant because מה and כי are formulaic and Ps 144:3 simply switches אנוש with its synonym אדם in the second clause. However, without taking a position on possible dependence, Edouard Dhorme observes that though Psalm 144 and Job 7 both use הבל, because Psalm 144 lacks כי, Psalm 8 and Job 7 actually have a more similar structure.[24] Van Leeuwen asserts, "Indeed, in these three texts the formula displays a number of small variants that suggest not literary allusion but free literary use of a common oral formula."[25] However, he fails to account for the use of פקד in Job 7 and Psalm 8, and it is unclear why a writer may freely use an oral formula but not an earlier text. He, like Schnieringer, has based his argument on an unduly high of allusive imitation that disregards the interpretive changes a later author may make to an earlier text. Addressing the relation of the three texts, Leo Perdue states that Job "parodies Ps. 8.5–6 in the fashion of the lament in Ps. 144.3–4."[26] Perdue is not explicit about whether Job is aware of the use of Psalm 8 in Psalm 144 and responding to it, but in light of the common use of the word הבל in the latter psalm and Job 7:16, and the Job poet's conflation of sources in his intratextual allusions (e.g., 25:4; cf. 9:2; 15:14), this is certainly a possibility. Therefore, the similarity between Job 8 and Psalm 144 need not invalidate the many connections between Job and Psalm 8, which strongly suggest dependence.

3.2. Date

The first factor to consider in order to determine the direction of this likely dependence is the evidence for the relative date of the two texts. Four features of the psalm have contributed to a general view that it comes from the early postexilic period. First, Psalm 8 has parallels with Gen 1:26–28; Job 7:17–18; and Ps 144:3–4, and the psalm appears to be dependent on the first text while acting as a

---

23 Van Leeuwen, "Psalm 8.5," 210–11.

24 Dhorme, *Job*, 108.

25 Van Leeuwen, "Psalm 8.5," 211.

26 Leo G. Perdue, *Wisdom and Cult: A Critical Analysis of the Views of Cult in the Wisdom Literatures of Israel and the Ancient Near East* (SBLDS 30; Missoula, Mont.: Scholars Press, 1976), 130.

subtext for the latter two.[27] Based on current views on the dating of each of these texts, this would date the psalm soon after the exile. Second, some scholars appeal to words in the psalm that they claim only appear in postexilic texts, particularly the appellation "our Lord" (אֲדֹנֵינוּ; vv. 2, 10).[28] Third, the mix of forms in the psalm would indicate, according to the tenets of form criticism, that the psalm is late.[29] Fourth, scholars note indications of later religious thought, such as conscious monotheism,[30] universalism,[31] postexilic wisdom,[32] and the aftershocks of a theological crisis, such as the exile.[33] All this evidence is open to dispute, however, leading many to conclude that the date of Psalm 8 cannot be established with certainty.[34] Even if an early postexilic date for the psalm were accepted, however, this would not rule out dependence in either direction for its parallel with Job 7 because Job was also likely written in the postexilic period. This evidence is particularly inconclusive because the strongest argument offered for dating the psalm is Job's allusion to it, which would make for a circular argument if it contributed to determining which text came first.

27 For the psalm's dependence on Genesis 1, see, e.g., Hans-Joachim Kraus, *Psalms: A Continental Commentary* (trans. Hilton C. Oswald; 2 vols.; Minneapolis: Fortress Press, 1993), 1:180; Frank-Lothar Hossfeld and Erich Zenger, *Die Psalmen* (2 vols.; NEchtB 29, 40; Würzburg: Echter, 1993, 2002), 1:77; James Luther Mays, *Psalms* (Interpretation; Louisville, Ky.: Westminster John Knox, 1994), 67. For Job's dependence on Psalm 8 as a *terminus ante quem* for the psalm's date, see Erich Zenger, "'Was ist das Menschlein, daß du seiner gedenkst.?' (Ps 8,5). Die Sorge für den Menschen in Theologie und Verkündigung," in *Der Dienst für den Menschen in Theologie und Verkündigung* (eds. Reinhard M. Hübner et al.; Regensburg: Friedrich Pustet, 1981), 130; Hubert Irsigler, *Vom Adamssohn zum Immanuel* (ATAT 58; St. Ottilien: EOS, 1997), 37. For the dependence of Psalm 144 on Psalm 8, see Gunkel, *Psalmen*, 29; Alfons Deissler, "Zur Datierung und Studierung der 'Kosmischen Hymnen' Pss 8, 19, 29," in *Lex tua veritas* (eds. Heinrich Groß and Franz Mußner; Trier: Paulinus-Verlag, 1961), 48; Hermann Spieckermann, *Heilsgegenwart: Eine Theologie der Psalmen* (FRLANT 148; Göttingen: Vandenhoeck & Ruprecht, 1989), 237.
28 Deissler, "Datierung," 48–49; Kraus, *Psalms*, 1:180.
29 W. H. Schmidt, "Gott und Mensch in Ps. 8: Form- und überlieferungsgeschichtliche Erwägungen," *TZ* 25 (1969): 14. Also, Kraus, *Psalms*, 1:180.
30 Bernhard Duhm, *Die Psalmen* (KHC 14; Leipzig: Mohr, 1899), 29.
31 Gerstenberger, *Psalms*, 1:68.
32 Deissler, "Datierung," 48, 50; Walter Beyerlin, "Psalm 8: Chancen der Überlieferungskritik," *ZTK* 73 (1976): 17–19, 20.
33 Irsigler, *Adamssohn*, 37; Ute Neumann-Gorsolke, "'Mit Ehre und Hoheit hast Du ihn gekrönt' (Ps 8,6b): Alttestamentliche Aspekte zum Thema Menschenwürde," *JBTh* 15 (2000): 61–62; Samuel L. Terrien, *The Psalms: Strophic Structure and Theological Commentary* (ECC; Grand Rapids, Mich.: Eerdmans, 2003), 132.
34 E.g., A. A. Anderson, *The Book of Psalms* (2 vols.; NCB; Grand Rapids, Mich.: Eerdmans, 1981), 1:100; Gert T. Prinsloo, "Polarity as Dominant Textual Strategy in Psalm 8," *OTE* 8 (1995): 377; Peter C. Craigie, *Psalms 1–50* (WBC 19; Nashville: Thomas Nelson, 2004), 106.

3.3. Coherence

Given the inconclusiveness of the evidence for the dates of the two texts, a synchronic comparison of the coherence of the allusion in its respective contexts is the best indicator of the direction of dependence. Without any strong signals of either text lacking internal coherence, a comparison of external coherence is the best evidence available, and this strongly suggests that Job is the later text. Bernhard Duhm, one of the few to argue that the psalm was written after Job, tellingly explains the psalmist's allusion to Job as "eine wohl unbewusste Reminiscenz."[35] As Duhm apparently realizes, because the psalmist would be integrating words from Job's accusation against God into his worship, a conscious allusion would be unlikely. As one early twentieth-century commentator put it, "If the words were first used in Job's sense, would it be possible ever to take the acid out of them?"[36] In other words, though a positive text may be parodied, its praise twisted into complaint, it is much more difficult to imagine complaint transformed into praise without the negative aspect of the former text lingering and tainting the attempted worship. Thus, in light of the striking lexical parallels and thematic reversals between the two texts, most commentators agree with Fishbane, who claims, "Indeed, it seems far more likely than not that the fixed form of the psalmist's praise preceded and inspired Job's rhetoric."[37]

3.4. Use

The strong likelihood that Job is alluding to Ps 8:5 invites consideration of the role it plays in Job's argument with his friends and God. Fishbane argues that in this allusion to Psalm 8, Job exploits the "latent ambiguity" in the psalmist's question, transforming marvel at human exaltation into "a sarcastic, contentious sneer."[38] Given the "bitterness" of Job's words, many interpreters agree.[39] Hermann Spieckermann even proclaims this parody "das Ende der Theologie der Heilsgegenwart."[40] Following Dell, Mettinger sees the parody as evidence that the book "emanates from a sceptical tradition."[41] In this skepticism, he claims, "The

35 Duhm, *Psalmen*, 28.
36 James Strahan, *The Book of Job Interpreted* (Edinburgh: T&T Clark, 1913), 85.
37 Fishbane, "Job," 89–90.
38 Fishbane, *Interpretation*, 285.
39 See, e.g., Clines, *Job*, 1:193; Klein, "Wirkungsgeschichte," 188; Irsigler, *Adamssohn*, 43.
40 Spieckermann, *Heilsgegenwart*, 237.
41 Mettinger, "Intertextuality," 267. See Dell, *Sceptical*, 126.

proud proclamation of the glory of humanity that is the very point of Ps. 8.5–6 is left out," and thus, "Ps. 8.6 has no counterpart in the Job passage."[42]

But the ambiguity of the psalmist's question has two sides, and Frevel denies this negative assessment because he claims that the positive sense of Psalm 8, including Ps 8:6, stands in the background of the allusion, as Job uses the parody to demand the glory and honor that it attributes to humankind for himself.[43] He sees this type of argumentation as consistent with Köhlmoos's description of Job as a book that shares the characteristic exilic dialogue with established normative texts.[44] For Frevel, the normative nature of Psalm 8, and the Psalms in general, enables Job's parody to act not as an expression of sapiential skepticism, but as an argumentative device against God.[45] He claims, "Das Menschenbild von Ps 8 bleibt auch für Ijob Paradigma des Menschenbild."[46]

Comparing the message of the psalm with his own suffering, Job encounters another tension between his life and the tradition of the privileged place of humanity in creation.[47] However, instead of coming to believe, as Brevard Childs suggests, that "man is dead and lacks utterly any value,"[48] which would negate both the foundation and motivation for his appeal to God, by relying on Psalm 8 as a paradigm, Job can appeal to the God it presents against the God who has afflicted him. Thus Gerhard von Rad, suggesting that Job's link "with the old Yahwistic traditions" may actually be stronger than that of his friends, describes his general argument as an appeal "against the terrible God of his experience to the God who, from of old, had offered himself as savior of the poor and the sick and as the defending counsel of those who had been deprived of justice."[49] As Psalm 8 proclaims, this benevolent God has bestowed royal dignity on humankind, and so Job uses the psalm to demand this for himself.[50] Fishbane

---

42　Mettinger, "Intertextuality," 267.

43　Frevel, "Menschenwürde," 261. See the discussion of Job's allusion to Ps 8:6 in 19:9 below (p. 73).

44　Köhlmoos, *Textstrategie*, 1–2.

45　Frevel, "Menschenwürde," 262. A lingering eighteenth-century understanding of parody, which assumes that it must ridicule its literary precursor, may have misled commentators into believing Job is mocking Psalm 8. However, Job's antithetical allusion to the psalm need not necessarily indicate that he is subverting its authority. See Kynes, "Parody," 283, 306.

46　Frevel, "Menschenwürde," 262.

47　Brevard S. Childs, "Psalm 8 in the Context of the Christian Canon," *Int* 23 (1969): 29.

48　Childs, "Psalm 8," 29.

49　Gerhard von Rad, *Wisdom in Israel* (trans. James D. Martin; Harrisburg, Pa.: Trinity Press International, 1993), 222.

50　"The bitterness Job expresses through his savage parody of the language of psalms arises from his sense of contradiction between the image of God as it has been traditionally rendered in psalms and the image of God that seems necessary to account for Job's recent experiences" (Newsom, "Job," 397).

himself observes this type of appeal to earlier texts to remind God of the deity's own nature and motivate God to intervene when the divine attribute formulary (Exod 34:6–7a) is cited in Mic 7:18–20 and Psalms 103 and 109.[51] As Westermann notes, Job's complaint is consistent with complaints against God throughout the HB. These sufferers consistently cling to the God who causes their suffering because this God is the only one who can end it. Their accusations are neither condemnations nor objective theological declarations but appeals intended to cause change.[52] Therefore, Job's words can stand in tension with his beliefs, and, in my view, Job's parody of Psalm 8 and his other parodies throughout the dialogue, are intended for rhetorical effect, not to reject the psalms or the God they describe, but to break through God's apparent injustice to the just God that Job believes resides behind it.

3.5. Recurrence

3.5.1. Eliphaz: 15:14–16

Eliphaz seems to recognize that Job is not rejecting the psalmist's high view of humanity but actually using his parody of Psalm 8 to accuse God of not bestowing on him the royal place it describes, because he responds with a parody of his own, in which he denies Job this possibility:

Job 15:14

מָה־אֱנוֹשׁ כִּי־יִזְכֶּה וְכִי־יִצְדַּק יְלוּד אִשָּׁה   What are mortals, that they can be clean?
Or those born of woman, that they can
be righteous?

Ps 8:5

מָה־אֱנוֹשׁ כִּי־תִזְכְּרֶנּוּ וּבֶן־אָדָם כִּי תִפְקְדֶנּוּ   What are human beings that you are
mindful of them,
mortals that you care for them?

As in Job 7:17–18, the introductory כי מה־אנוש and similar structure connect Eliphaz's question with that of Ps 8:5. Eliphaz may also use the assonant verb זכה ("to be pure") to match זכר in the psalm.[53] Recalling his earlier revelation from a nocturnal spirit (4:17–19), he continues, "God puts no trust even in his holy ones [קְדֹשָׁיו][54], and the heavens [שָׁמַיִם] are not clean in his sight; how much less one

---

51 Fishbane, *Interpretation*, 439.
52 Claus Westermann, "The Complaint Against God," in *God in the Fray: A Tribute to Walter Brueggemann* (eds. Tod Linafelt and Timothy K. Beal; Minneapolis: Fortress Press, 1998), 237–39.
53 Cheney, *Dust*, 130.
54 This is the *qere*, the *kethib* is קדשׁו.

who is abominable and corrupt, one who drinks iniquity like water!" (vv. 15–16). Fishbane considers this a "caustic rejoinder" to Job's earlier allusion to Ps 8:5, in which Eliphaz has "ironically re-established the original *traditum*" by answering the question of Ps 8:5 himself.[55] However, since the original *traditum* in Psalm 8 expresses an exalted view of humanity, Eliphaz is not reestablishing it, but twisting it into its opposite in order to support his argument. Samuel Balentine, who recognizes that these two passages represent a "debate about the theology of Psalm 8," similarly argues that the whole of 15:7–16 is intended to respond to "Job's misplaced hubris."[56] However, if Job's parody of the psalm sarcastically rejects its presentation of the human being as "royal steward," instead depicting a "powerless victim," as Balentine suggests, where is Job's hubris? He does indeed challenge God, but if his parody dismisses the psalm, it does so through denying his exalted place in creation. If, however, as I have suggested, Job appeals to Psalm 8 as a paradigm from which he accuses God of departing through his parody, then Balentine rightly notes the latent ambiguity that would result, and to which Eliphaz is reacting, when he asks, "Is it *misguided hubris* or *radical faith* to believe that human beings are created in the image of God and are thereby specially prepared for delightful communion and shared partnership with the deity?"[57] Job's faith is expressed in his tenacious commitment to the belief that the psalmist is right.[58]

Frevel, however, argues that Eliphaz is not referring to Psalm 8 because his low view of humans conflicts with the exalted place given them in Psalm 8.[59] This overlooks the possibility, though, that Eliphaz may be interpreting the psalm's message in his own way as he alludes to it.[60] In fact, Psalm 8 reverberates even more widely in Eliphaz's answer. The psalmist wonders at God's concern for humans as he considers their lowliness in comparison with the "heavens" (שמים) (vv. 4–5) and the apparent inappropriateness of their place a little lower than the

---

55 Fishbane, "Job," 93.

56 Samuel E. Balentine, "'What are Human Beings, That You Make So Much of Them?': Divine Disclosure from the Whirlwind: 'Look at the Behemoth,'" in *God in the Fray: A Tribute to Walter Brueggemann* (eds. Tod Linafelt and Timothy K. Beal; Minneapolis: Fortress Press, 1998), 262–64.

57 Balentine, "Divine Disclosure," 264.

58 Elsewhere Balentine acknowledges this possibility (Samuel E. Balentine, *Job* [Macon, Ga.: Smyth & Helwys, 2006], 385).

59 Frevel, "Menschenwürde," 268. Irsigler similarly denies that the question of Job 15:14 goes back to Psalm 8 (Irsigler, *Adamssohn*, 43).

60 Markus Witte suggests that 15:11–16, along with ch. 25 (see below) and several other passages, is part of a redaction of the book that represents a low view of humanity (a *Niedrigkeitsredaktion*). See Markus Witte, "Die dritte Rede Bildads (Hiob 25) und die Redaktionsgeschichte des Hiobbuches," in *The Book of Job* (ed. W. A. M. Beuken; BETL 114; Leuven: Leuven University Press, 1994), 349–55. However, this tension between divergent views of humanity could be intended by the author as a reflection of the tension already evident in the psalm.

"heavenly beings" (אלהים)[61] (v. 6). Eliphaz, who also contrasts humanity with the "heavens"[62] and God's "holy ones,"[63] regards these comparisons as declarations of the lowly place of humankind instead of their exaltation, and even as indications of moral impurity. While speaking of humanity generally, Eliphaz implicitly rebukes Job for using Psalm 8 to suggest that he deserves better.

3.5.2. Job: 19:9

When Job returns to Psalm 8 several chapters later, he seems to have Eliphaz's low view of humanity in mind:

Job 19:9

כְּבוֹדִי מֵעָלַי הִפְשִׁיט וַיָּסַר עֲטֶרֶת רֹאשִׁי He has stripped my glory from me,
and taken the crown from my head.

Ps 8:6

וַתְּחַסְּרֵהוּ מְּעַט מֵאֱלֹהִים וְכָבוֹד וְהָדָר תְּעַטְּרֵהוּ Yet you have made them a little lower than God,
and crowned them with glory and honor.

Frevel claims this is a clear allusion to Psalm 8 that has received much less attention than the parody in ch. 7.[64] According to Frevel, the words "glory" (כבוד) and "crown" (עטרה) in Job's lament allude to Ps 8:6, where God is praised because he has "crowned" (root: עטר) humanity with "glory" (כבוד) and honor.[65] This con-

---

61 The NRSV translates אלהים in Ps 8:6 as "God." However, A. A. Anderson and Hans-Joachim Kraus, following the LXX, the Targum, the Syriac Version, and the Vulgate, argue that "angels" or "heavenly beings" is a better translation (Anderson, *Psalms*, 1:103; Kraus, *Psalms*, 1:183). For the "holy ones" in Job 15:16 as angels, see, e.g., Fohrer, *Hiob*, 271; Pope, *Job*, 116. This corresponds to the similar statement in Eliphaz's first speech where he compares humans to God's "angels" (מלאכים) (4:18). Considering that Eliphaz there claimed that God charges his angels with error, in his view, being a little lower than the angels is not a commanding moral position.

62 When Eliphaz mentions the "heavens" he may mean the place or its inhabitants. Either way, this comparison resonates with Psalm 8. Following the Targum, Clines even suggests that Eliphaz is referring to the heavenly bodies (cf. Job 25:5), which would parallel with the psalmist's mention of the moon and stars (v. 4) (Clines, *Job*, 1:353).

63 Janzen notes the parallel between Eliphaz's words and Ps 8:4 (J. Gerald Janzen, *Job* [Interpretation; Atlanta: John Knox Press, 1985], 117). See also Johannes Hempel, "Mensch und König: Studie zu Psalm 8 und Hiob," *FF* 35 (1961): 123.

64 Frevel, "Menschenwürde," 262. Several scholars note that Job's words here "recall" or "echo" Ps 8:6, e.g., Perdue, *Wisdom and Cult*, 174; Luis Alonso Schökel and José Luis Sicre Díaz, *Job: Comentario teológico y literario* (NBE; Madrid: Ediciones Cristiandad, 1983), 287; Habel, *Job*, 300.

65 Lam 5:16 also refers to the loss of a communal "crown" (עטרה) as an indication of disgrace. It does not repeat any other words from the psalm, but it does share the word "head" (ראש) with Job 19:9. Because Job 19:7–11 is reminiscent of other passages in Lamentations (e.g., 3:7–9), Job may have both texts in mind, or his allusion to Ps 8:6 may take into account an earlier allusion in

tinues Job's contrast of his experience with positive statements from the psalm.[66] For Job to accuse God of tearing the crown from his head, he must assume that this is where it intrinsically belongs, and thus, though he parodies the psalm, a conviction of the worth of humankind, which Psalm 8 declares,[67] motivates his lament and accusation of God.[68]

3.5.3. Bildad: 25:5–6

Following Eliphaz's lead, and even repeating his words, Bildad also denies Job's appeal to royal human dignity in a final allusion to Psalm 8. First, mimicking Eliphaz's earlier allusion to the psalm (15:14), he asks, "How then can a mortal be righteous before God? How can one born of woman be pure?" (25:4). Then, he continues:

Job 25:5–6

הֵן עַד־יָרֵחַ וְלֹא יַאֲהִיל וְכוֹכָבִים לֹא־זַכּוּ בְעֵינָיו <u>5</u> If even the moon is not bright
and the stars are not pure in his sight,

אַף כִּי־אֱנוֹשׁ רִמָּה וּבֶן־אָדָם תּוֹלֵעָה <u>6</u> how much less a mortal, who is a maggot,
and a human being, who is a worm!

Ps 8:4–5

כִּי־אֶרְאֶה שָׁמֶיךָ מַעֲשֵׂי אֶצְבְּעֹתֶיךָ יָרֵחַ וְכוֹכָבִים <u>4</u> When I look at your heavens, the work of
אֲשֶׁר כּוֹנָנְתָּה   your fingers,
the moon and the stars that you have
established;

מָה־אֱנוֹשׁ כִּי־תִזְכְּרֶנּוּ וּבֶן־אָדָם כִּי תִפְקְדֶנּוּ <u>5</u> what are human beings that you are
mindful of them,
mortals that you care for them?

Lam 5:16 as may have occurred with Ps 8:5 and Ps 144:3. For the reminiscences between Job 19:7–11 and Lam 3:7–9 see, e.g., Alonso Schökel and Sicre Díaz, *Job*, 287; Mettinger, "Intertextuality," 272–74.

66   Frevel, "Menschenwürde," 264.

67   Because this imagery is used metaphorically of humanity in general in Psalm 8, it need not be taken literally to indicate Job's previous royal status as Samuel Terrien, following Andre Caquot, asserts (Samuel L. Terrien, *Job* [2nd ed.; CAT 13; Geneva: Labor et Fides, 2005], 193; cf. Andre Caquot, "Traits royaux dans le personnage de Job," in *Maqqel shaqedh: La branche d'amandier: Hommage à Wilhelm Vischer* [ed. Daniel Lys; Montpelier: Cause Graille Castelnau, 1960], 32–45).

68   Frevel, "Menschenwürde," 266. Similarly, Ute Neumann-Gorsolke claims that in Job 19:9 "geradezu in Umkehrung der Begrifflichkeit von Ps 8,6b, formuliert Hiob seinen Vorwurf gegen Gott" (Neumann-Gorsolke, "Menschenwürde," 55).

Beyerlin considers the comparison between humankind and the moon and stars an indicator of an allusion to Psalm 8.[69] Notably, in both cases, the sun is lacking.[70] The parallel terms אנוש and בן־אדם, though common, provide a further connection,[71] as well as the repetition of the key word "dominion" (משל) in Job 25:2 from Ps 8:7.[72] Thus, Psalm 8 stands behind Job 25, though Bildad highlights the pitiable state of humans and not their exaltation.[73]

Because of this adverse anthropology, Frevel also denies that Bildad is alluding to Psalm 8.[74] However, Bildad actually appears to be repeating Eliphaz's allusion to the psalm's comparison between humans and the inhabitants of the heavens, as he contrasts the worm-like existence of humanity with the heavenly bodies. Yet, as Gerald Janzen, who affirms that this passage is an allusion to the psalm, observes, "Bildad has missed the point of the comparison in Psalm 8."[75] He only refers to the negative side of the ambiguous tension surrounding the psalmist's question and omits the positive message which follows. Thus, by appealing to only one pole of the psalm's tensive anthropology and making moral fallibility a correlate of physical frailty,[76] he distorts the psalm's message to attack Job by declaring that humans "are not a little less than the angels of God (Ps. 8:6 [5E]), but little more than maggots."[77]

3.6. Holistic Interpretation

Psalm 8 expresses a "mixture of humility at man's insignificance and pride at man's exalted place within the creation."[78] Job uses the exalted place of humanity in the psalm as the grounds of his appeal to God for restoration, while, in response, the friends highlight humanity's insignificance to teach Job humility.[79]

---

69   Beyerlin, "Psalm 8," 18.

70   Schmidt, "Gott," 7.

71   Perdue, *Wisdom and Cult*, 178.

72   Janzen, *Job*, 174; David Wolfers, *Deep Things out of Darkness: The Book of Job* (Kampen: Kok Pharos, 1995), 257. The word only appears in the *hiphil* in these two passages and Dan 11:39 (Deissler, "Datierung," 48).

73   Klein, "Wirkungsgeschichte," 188.

74   Frevel, "Menschenwürde," 268.

75   Janzen, *Job*, 174, 176.

76   Irsigler, *Adamssohn*, 22 n. 48.

77   Habel, *Job*, 370.

78   Reed, *Dialogues*, 136.

79   Referring to many of the passages in this dispute, Habel argues that Job appeals to traditions about "the potential of humanness" to counter the friends' low anthropology (Norman C. Habel, "'Naked I Came …': Humanness in the Book of Job," in *Die Botschaft und die Boten* [eds. Jörg Jeremias and Lothar Perlitt; Neukirchen-Vluyn: Neukirchener Verlag, 1981], 373–92).

Thus, though Frevel does not consider Job 15:14–16 and 25:4–6 to be allusions to Psalm 8, seen in this light, they actually support his contention that the psalm acts as a normative paradigm in Job. He argues that Job uses his allusions to Psalm 8 to strengthen his claim against God, and thus, that Job's lament aims and hopes for restitution.[80] But it also appears that the friends use their allusions to the psalm to support their argument against Job. Thus, in their contrasting uses of the same text, the characters represent conflicting interpretive models.[81] The author of Job has picked up on a tension in this text and exploited it to develop the characters of Job and his friends and provide a textual locus for their conflict.[82] Fishbane argues that the "skein of argument and counter-argument that binds Ps. 8:5–7, Job 7:17–18 and 15:14–15" makes it "appear quite contrived to presume that these three texts are not exegetically correlated, and that they are simply independent versions of a rhetorical topos."[83] When the contributions that the allusions in Job 19:9 and 25:5–6 make to that dialogue are considered as well, the author of Job's use of Psalm 8 becomes even more difficult to dispute.[84]

3.7. Reciprocation

In this use of the psalm, the Job poet has produced a sophisticated dialogic interpretation in which his reading incorporates the contrasting interpretations of Job and his friends. To do so, he exploits the tension and ambiguity in the psalm itself. Commentators have often noticed this feature of the psalm, and the Job poet's reading reinforces their insight. Gert Prinsloo claims polarity "becomes the

---

80 Frevel, "Menschenwürde," 266.

81 Köhlmoos, *Textstrategie*, 364.

82 Though he only briefly touches on Eliphaz's allusion to Psalm 8 in ch. 15 and overlooks the allusion in ch. 19, Janzen similarly notes that both Job and Bildad "are shown as offering variations on Psalm 8," in which Bildad attempts "to denude humankind of the royal honor and vocation bestowed on it by God," while Job "sustains a sense of that special attention and vocation" given to humans in the psalm (Janzen, *Job*, 176). However, Janzen claims that, instead of appealing to the psalm against God in ch. 7, Job "sees things differently" than the psalmist because his experience "disillusions the fond dream of Psalm 8" (83). Only at the end of the dialogue (31:35–37) does Janzen claim that Job gains "a transformed royal consciousness" which "has in effect reestablished the vision of Psalm 8, though on new bases" (83).

83 Fishbane, *Interpretation*, 286.

84 There may be a further allusion to Ps 8:8–9 in Job 12:7–8, where Job lists a similar sequence of "beasts," "birds of the heavens" (with a different word for "bird"), and "fish of the sea." However three other passages mention the same animals in similar lists (Gen 1:26; Deut 4:17–18; Zeph 1:3), and in the latter two, they are also in the same order. This repeated use of the common elements combined with the limited thematic interplay between Job's use of the imagery and Psalm 8 make it difficult to argue that this is not simply the repetition of common formulaic language.

dominant textual strategy in Psalm 8," existing "in every single line," and expressing the message, "Man is at the same time insignificant and important, humble and dignified."[85] This tension is focused in the ambiguous question, "What is humanity?" at the center of the psalm, and the repeated allusions in Job indicate how its meaning is open to dispute. As the contending interpretations of Job and the friends demonstrate, the description of God's creation of the vast heavens with his mere fingers (v. 4) preceding this question at first suggests the answer, "Nothing!"[86] However, the question is followed by an affirmation of the exalted place of these lowly humans in the created order (v. 6–9), which reverses the reader's expectation. Thus, between these two poles, the question "What is humanity?" means two things at once, depending on whether one reads it with what precedes or what follows. In fact, the humble depiction of humanity may have been intended to create a sense of despair in order to make the human exaltation in vv. 6–9 all the more powerful.[87]

That both Job and the friends find resources for their diametrically opposed anthropologies in the same psalm highlights the tension between hubris and humility at its heart. In the dialogue this tension is unresolved, but the final form of the book offers a resolution. In the end, when God restores Job and rejects the friends (42:7–8), God vindicates Job, his lament, and his high view of humanity against the friends and their low anthropology and thereby endorses his interpretation of Psalm 8 over theirs,[88] just as the psalmist, by describing human dominion over creation (vv. 7–9), transforms the tension at the psalm's heart into an affirmation of human exaltation.

3.8. Historical Implications

The repeated appeals to Psalm 8 suggest it had an authoritative status in the community which could be employed to support an argument, even one against God. However, though the text was considered authoritative, Job's interpretive dispute with his friends indicates that its meaning was open to debate. This might at first seem contradictory, but it actually accords with the text's normative status. As is still the case with authoritative texts, because Psalm 8 was considered authoritative, its meaning was considered worth dispute; it could not simply be dismissed.

---

85 Prinsloo, "Polarity," 383, 382. This summary of the psalm's message is common. See, e.g., Walther Zimmerli, "Was ist der Mensch?" in *Studien zur alttestamentlichen Theologie und Prophetie: Gesammelte Aufsätze Band II* (ed. Walther Zimmerli; TBü 51; Munich: Chr. Kaiser Verlag, 1974), 314; Klein, "Wirkungsgeschichte," 185; Irsigler, *Adamssohn*, 25.

86 Craigie, *Psalms*, 108.

87 Craigie, *Psalms*, 108.

88 See Frevel, "Menschenwürde," 269.

In fact, the more authoritative a text is considered, the more debate its meaning is likely to receive, as continuing modern disputes over the meaning of the Bible demonstrate.

Another example of the disputes normative texts can engender is midrash. Daniel Boyarin attempts to explain the "scandal" of the contradictory interpretations filling "the authoritative commentaries on the holiest text of Judaism" by identifying an implicit intertextual theory of reading in the midrash.[89] Looking specifically at the Mekilta on Exodus, he argues that it "is aware of true ambiguities in the biblical narrative, and that while each of the readers it presents work in their readings toward reduction of the ambiguity, the cumulative effect of the midrash as compiled is to focus on the ambiguity and the possibilities for making meaning out of it."[90] He gives the example of two rabbis (Yehoshua and El'azar of Modi'in), who interpret ambiguities in the narratives of the bitter water at Mara and giving of manna (Exod 15:22–26; 16:2–36) differently to substantiate their contrasting positive and negative views of Israel in the wilderness.[91] Instead of smoothing out these ambiguities, the midrash indicates its awareness of textual ambiguity by setting these opposed views side by side.[92] Even though each of the rabbis only hears one of the two conflicting voices embedded in this ambiguity, the midrash hears them both, dialectically revealing the text's ambiguity through both rabbis' attempts to eradicate it.

Though the differences between the Job dialogue and the midrash are manifold, this hermeneutical phenomenon is remarkably resonant, as Job and the friends, like those two rabbis, each represent opposite sides of the psalm's ambiguity. The dialogue holds these two readings in tension, highlighting that ambiguity for the reader. This dispute not only demonstrates the authoritative status of the psalm at the time Job was written, but suggests a possible precursor for rabbinic interpretation, which, as Fishbane has argued, carried on the intertextual approach to reading practiced in the HB itself.[93]

3.9. Conclusion

By clinging to Psalm 8, Job displays not misguided hubris but radical faith. As the suffering outcast cries to God, even accuses the Almighty, while clinging to the deity, he, like the babes and infants in Psalm 8, paradoxically proves the power of

---

89   Boyarin, *Intertextuality*, 58.
90   Boyarin, *Intertextuality*, 58.
91   Boyarin, *Intertextuality*, 57–79.
92   Boyarin, *Intertextuality*, 77.
93   Fishbane, *Interpretation*, 527.

God's name on earth.[94] His appeal to the God who is treating him as his enemy (Job 13:24), is, as Roland de Pury puts it, "la démarche suprême de la foi."[95] The friends, who recognize Job's appeal to Psalm 8 as undergirding his audacious accusations, attempt to silence him by appealing to the other side of the psalm's tensive presentation of humans before God. This dialectic demonstrates both the ambiguity at the heart of Psalm 8 and its authority when the Job dialogue was composed.

---

94   Zenger, "Sorge," 140.
95   Roland de Pury, *Job ou l'homme révolté* (Cahiers du renouveau 12; Geneva: Éditions labor et fides, 1958), 29.

4. Doxology in Disputation: Psalm 107 in Job

I would even exult in unrelenting pain;
for I have not denied the words of the Holy One (Job 6:10).

"Without a doubt," claims Hartley, the author of Job "knew Pss. 8 and 107."[1] Though the parody of Ps 8:5 in Job 7:17–18 has received significant scholarly attention, the closest textual parallel with the Psalms in the book of Job is actually between Job 12:21, 24 and Ps 107:40. This connection was the locus of early debate over which of the two books has historical priority,[2] but the meaning of this possible allusion has generally been overlooked.[3] However, the striking lexical affinity between the two passages, the indications of further resonances between the two texts (e.g., Ps 107:42; cf. Job 5:16; 22:19), and the exegetical significance already widely recognized in the parody of Psalm 8 in Job 7:17–18, all suggest that the intersection of these two texts in Job 12 is no coincidence, and that, in fact, the Job poet's use of Psalm 107 may be part of a larger rhetorical and theological purpose. Thus, Clines claims, "The connections with Ps 107 are so close and numerous that it seems right to term it a 'source' of the present hymn, in the way that Ps 8 was the 'source' of Job 7:17–18."[4] Currently, though, scholars are not even agreed on whether the author of Job is referring to the psalm or vice versa, with a few arguing that both are simply using a common source. Thus, the probability that the Job poet is alluding to Psalm 107 must first be established before the contributions these allusions have in the dialogue between Job, his friends, and God may be examined.

4.1. Identification

The marked parallel signaling the interface between the two texts appears in Job 12:21, 24 and Ps 107:40:

---

1   Hartley, *Job*, 13.
2   See p. 7.
3   Clines provides the most thorough discussion I have found (Clines, *Job*, 1:287, 297–304).
4   Clines, *Job*, 1:297. Elsewhere he claims, "There is obvious dependence upon Ps 107" (287). Similarly, Janzen, *Job*, 103.

Job 12:21, 24

שֹׁפֵךְ בּוּז עַל־נְדִיבִים וּמְזִיחַ אֲפִיקִים רִפָּה 21 He pours contempt on princes
and looses the belt of the strong …

מֵסִיר לֵב רָאשֵׁי עַם־הָאָרֶץ וַיַּתְעֵם בְּתֹהוּ 24 He strips understanding from the leaders
לֹא־דָרֶךְ   of the earth
and makes them wander in a pathless
waste.

Ps 107:40

שֹׁפֵךְ בּוּז עַל־נְדִיבִים וַיַּתְעֵם בְּתֹהוּ לֹא־דָרֶךְ   He pours contempt on princes
and makes them wander in trackless
wastes.

Besides the division of the two halves of the verse in the psalm, the only difference between the two texts is a slightly different spelling of the first word in Ps 107:40a (שֹׁפֵךְ) and Job 12:21a (שֹׁפֵךְ). The addition of the *waw* as a *mater lectionis* in Job to indicate the historically long vowel is an orthographic feature that appears with more frequency in later books. However, active *qal* participles like this one are often written defectively without the *waw*, and this one may have been a later scribal addition, so, for determining the relative date of the texts, this slight difference is suggestive but inconclusive.[5]

This extensive and exact correspondence cannot be a coincidence. Though some have suggested that it results from common dependence on a stock phrase, the manner[6] and multiplicity of parallels between the two texts, which extend beyond this one allusion, militate against seeing these shared phrases merely as "standard formulas for expressing humiliation and aimlessness"[7] or the result of common dependence on a source that no longer exists, such as N. H. Tur-Sinai's proposal of a description of travelers caught in a storm at sea, which involves a strained reading of Job 12:21–25 to make it fit a nautical context.[8]

---

5   See Paul Joüon and T. Muraoka, *A Grammar of Biblical Hebrew* (2 vols.; SubBi 14/1–2; Rome: Editrice Pontificio Istituto Biblico, 2005), 1:49.

6   Beyerlin, *Werden*, 14 n. 6.

7   Habel, *Job*, 214.

8   N. H. Tur-Sinai (H. Torczyner), *The Book of Job: A New Commentary* (Revised ed.; Jerusalem: Kiryath Sepher, 1967), 217–19. Similarly, though without such specificity, Friedrich Horst, *Hiob 1–19* (BKAT 16/1; Neukirchen-Vluyn: Neukirchener Verlag, 1968), 195.

4.2. Date

A comparison of the dates of the texts unfortunately does little to determine in which direction this likely dependence lies. Though evidence is lacking to assign a definitive date to Psalm 107, three primary factors have created a widespread consensus that the psalm in its final form is postexilic, though it may incorporate a preexilic hymn (vv. 1, 4–32).[9] First, there may be several implicit references to the exile and return in the mention of "the redeemed of the Lord"[10] who are "gathered in from the lands"[11] (vv. 2–3), the four descriptions of affliction and deliverance which follow (vv. 4–32),[12] and the underlying narrative of the reversals in vv. 33–41.[13] Second, the message of the psalm, in its encouragement to give thanks for God's deliverance from distress fits well with this period in Israel's history.[14] Third, the psalm appears to be drawing on Isaiah 40–55 in vv. 2–3, 33–43, which has contributed to the general acceptance of a postexilic date for those portions of the psalm, though Deutero-Isaianic influence may be evident throughout.[15] Possible dependence on Job has also figured into discussions of the date of the psalm, in Beyerlin's case pushing it back into the late third century to account for the allusions he sees to the Elihu speeches,[16] but, as I will argue, dependence more likely lies in the other direction. If this rather tenuous evidence does suggest a postexilic date for Psalm 107, then, because both texts likely come from the postexilic period, either could be alluding to the other, and their relative dates must be based on a synchronic comparison of the coherence of the allusions.

---

9   E.g., J. Mejía, "Some Observations on Psalm 107," *BTB* 5 (1975): 56; Kraus, *Psalms*, 2:327.

10   This phrase only appears elsewhere in Isa 62:12 (J. W. Roffey, "Beyond Reality: Poetic Discourse and Psalm 107," in *A Biblical Itinerary: In Search of Method, Form and Content: Essays in Honor of George W. Coats* [JSOTSup 240; Sheffield: Sheffield Academic Press, 1997], 73).

11   Some take this as a reference to the Diaspora, but it may simply refer to return from exile. See Goulder, *Return*, 119.

12   Goulder claims these depictions of desert wandering (vv. 4–9), imprisonment (vv. 10–16), sickness (vv. 17–22), and storm at sea (vv. 23–32) are "four traditional images of Israel in exile" (Goulder, *Return*, 126).

13   Frank-Lothar Hossfeld and Erich Zenger, *Psalmen 101–150* (HTKAT; Freiburg: Herder, 2008), 142, 156.

14   See Ernst Wilhelm Hengstenberg, *Commentary on the Psalms* (trans. Patrick Fairbairn and John Thomson; 3 vols.; CFThL 1–2, 12; Edinburgh: T&T Clark, 1845–1848), 3:286; Goulder, *Return*, 126–27.

15   See the chart in Roffey, "Beyond Reality," 72. Similarly, Goulder, *Return*, 117.

16   Beyerlin, *Werden*, 84. Both have similar descriptions of deliverance from sickness (Job 33:19–28; Ps 107:17–22) and prison (Job 36:8–12; Ps 107:10–16). Goulder also argues Psalm 107 is alluding to Job here, but then pushes the date of the final form of Job back into the sixth century instead (Goulder, *Return*, 127).

4.3. Coherence

Regarding the internal coherence of the parallel passages in their respective contexts, the participle with which Ps 107:40 begins diverges from the surrounding verses, where the imperfect tense predominates, while it corresponds with the other participles in the Job passage. In the mid-eighteenth century Hare concluded on this basis that the psalmist had alluded to Job.[17] However, referring to this verse in the psalm as an example, Gunkel identifies the use of participles as a common indicator of hymnic form, so the syntactical divergence is not unprecedented,[18] and Erich Zenger claims the participle begins a new section of the psalm in vv. 40–41, which reflects Israel's exilic situation.[19] Additionally, the verse in the Job passage has its own stylistic divergence. The *shin* with which it begins breaks up a long alliterative series of verses each beginning with *mem*.[20] Thus, this comparison is inconclusive.

Hermeneutically, commentators have also struggled to understand vv. 39–40 of the psalm in their present context because the transition from blessing in v. 38 to oppression in v. 39 is abrupt, and the relation of the princes in v. 40 to the hungry who have been the subject of vv. 36–38 and possibly v. 39 is unclear. This leads some to suggest that one or both verses should be removed,[21] some that the verses should be transposed,[22] and others that the awkwardness results from the

---

17   Hare, *Psalmorum Liber*, 1418. Similarly, though without reference to Job, Christian Friedrich Schnurrer, *Disputatio philologica ad Psalmum centesimum septimum* (Tübingen: Litteris Sigmundianis, 1789), 28–29.

18   Hermann Gunkel and Joachim Begrich, *Introduction to Psalms: The Genres of the Religious Lyric of Israel* (MLBS; Macon, Ga.: Mercer University Press, 1998), 30–31.

19   Hossfeld and Zenger, *Psalmen 101–150*, 142, 156. Carbajosa points out that the second and fourth strophes also begin with participles (vv. 10, 23). He argues that in all three cases, the participles introduce a *casus pendens*, which is resolved in the following verse (I. Carbajosa, "Salmo 107: Unidad, Organización y Teología," *EstBib* 59 [2001]: 471).

20   The four verses that precede the parallel passage and the three that follow it all begin with a *mem*. The verses that immediately precede and follow this alliterative series (vv. 16 and 25) also start with a *mem* sound. Six of these *mems* are used to form *hiphil* or *piel* participles and may merely result from the sequence of participles, but in v. 18 the author reverses the repeated verse order, putting the object (מוסר) at the beginning instead of the verb (פתח) as in every other verse, which suggests the alliteration is intentional and the divergence in v. 21 may be the result of the citation of an external source. Alternatively, in v. 18, the author could have put the verb in participial form, which would have then begun with a *mem* like the others because it is in the *piel*, but he may have chosen not to do this because the other two words in the hemistich both start with a *mem*.

21   Gunkel, *Psalmen*, 473.

22   E.g., Kraus, *Psalms*, 2:325. Though the meaning of the inverted *nun* in the margin of the MT is unknown, some have suggested it is an indicator that the verse has been moved from its original context. See Franz Delitzsch, *Biblical Commentary on the Psalms* (trans. David Eaton; 3 vols.;

psalmist inserting words from Job in v. 40 without alteration.[23] Those who follow the MT suggest either that v. 39 serves as the protasis to v. 40[24] or that the sudden oppression of the restored hungry is consistent with the message of reversal of fortunes in the psalm.[25] However, Job commentators have questioned the authenticity, not only of a single verse, as in the psalm, but the entire section 12:13–25, because of its apparent stylistic and thematic discontinuity with Job's speeches, and the similarities between this passage and Psalm 107 contribute to these arguments.[26]

These inconclusive arguments from the contexts of the possible allusions are reflected among the commentators, who are split in their attribution of priority, with Psalms commentators tending to claim the psalm is later while Job commentators often give this position to Job. Few, though, have considered the external coherence of the parallel passages in relation to the context of the purportedly cited text by asking the question, Why did the author choose to allude to these phrases from this particular text? John Goldingay is one of the few who addresses the relationship between the contexts of the two texts. He claims that the psalmist "combines" the two phrases from the passage in Job, which is "part of a long declaration that has rather cynical implications on Job's lips but quite positive ones here."[27] Yet, this observation only presses the question further. Why would the psalmist choose cynical lines to convey his positive message? While interpreting the final verses of the psalm as an attempt to encourage the returning exiles, Goulder suggests that "comfort was to be taken from the book of Job."[28] But, even if these words from Job are employed to describe the downfall of oppressive leaders, understood in their cynical context, as they praise the wisdom of a God who destroys arbitrarily, they are far from comforting and seem to con-

---

CFThL 29–31; Edinburgh: T&T Clark, 1887–1889), 3:145 n. 1. However, the symbol also appears next to vv. 21–26, where its intent is even less clear. See the discussion in Kraus, *Psalms*, 2:326.

23   A. F. Kirkpatrick, *The Book of Psalms* (3 vols.; Cambridge: Cambridge University Press, 1892–1901), 3:645; Goulder, *Return*, 125.

24   Anderson, *Psalms*, 2:757.

25   Craig C. Broyles, *Psalms* (NIBCOT 11; Peabody, Mass.: Hendrickson, 1999), 410; John Goldingay, *Psalms* (3 vols.; BCOTWP; Grand Rapids, Mich.: Baker Academic, 2006–2008), 3:258 n. 33. The Targum inserts the words "when they sinned" in v. 39 to bring the meaning of the text closer to that found in vv. 11 and 17, where affliction is the result of iniquity (David M. Stec, *The Targum of Psalms* [ArBib 16; Collegeville, Minn.: Liturgical Press, 2004], 199).

26   Baumgärtel, *Hiobdialog*, 19; Fohrer, *Hiob*, 245.

27   Goldingay, *Psalms*, 3:259. It appears that Goldingay considers the psalm to be dependent on Job (see 260), but he does not address the issue explicitly.

28   Goulder, *Return*, 125. Similarly, Leslie C. Allen, *Psalms 101–150* (WBC 21; Nashville: Thomas Nelson, 2002), 65.

tradict the message of the psalm.[29] If, however, the Job poet is alluding to the psalm, he has extracted two negative phrases from the psalm that integrate well into Job's bitter hymn parody.

Clearly, the external coherence of this possible allusion deserves more attention. Further connections between the texts aid this evaluation. Goulder mentions three other texts from Job that he suggests the psalmist cited to encourage the returned exiles: Job 5:16, 21:11, and 22:19. The first and last of those texts are often mentioned as possible allusions because they include phrases that are almost exactly the same as the two halves of Ps 107:42:

Job 22:19

יִרְאוּ צַדִּיקִים וְיִשְׂמָחוּ וְנָקִי יִלְעַג־לָמוֹ The righteous see it and are glad;
the innocent laugh them to scorn …

Job 5:16

וַתְּהִי לַדַּל תִּקְוָה וְעֹלָתָה קָפְצָה פִּיהָ So the poor have hope,
and injustice shuts its mouth.

Ps 107:42

יִרְאוּ יְשָׁרִים וְיִשְׂמָחוּ וְכָל־עַוְלָה קָפְצָה פִּיהָ The upright see it and are glad;
and all wickedness stops its mouth.

In the first shared phrase (Ps 107:42a; Job 22:19a) the only difference is a change of the adjective that stands in for the subject: יׁשרים ("upright [ones]") versus צדיקים ("righteous [ones]"). In the second shared phrase (Ps 107:42b; Job 5:16b), כל ("all") appears in the psalm but not in Job, and עולה ("iniquity") is spelled slightly differently in Job.[30] In contrast to the affinities between Ps 107:40 and Job 12:21, 24, these general platitudes have a greater chance of being mere instances of formulaic phraseology. Their proximity to Ps 107:40, however, makes this less likely.[31] Even if these were widely used formulas, their use in a text that is alluded

29 Even Beyerlin, who speaks of the importance of the context of the passages to which he understands the psalmist to be alluding (Job 12:12–25), fails to recognize this (Beyerlin, *Werden*, 62–63).

30 In Job, the word has what has been called a "double feminine ending" (Bernhard Duhm, *Das Buch Hiob* [Freiburg: Mohr, 1897], 33), though the exact nature of this ending is disputed. Hurvitz claims it is an archaic feature of the language (Avi Hurvitz, "Originals and Imitations in Biblical Poetry: A Comparative Examination of 1 Sam 2:1–10 and Ps 113:5–9," in *Biblical and Related Studies Presented to Samuel Iwry* [eds. Ann Kort and Scott Morschauser; Winona Lake, Ind.: Eisenbrauns, 1985], 116–19). The combination of *patah* and *waw* with a silent *schewa* in the first syllable of the word has also apparently turned into a *holem*, though Beyerlin suggests this indicates the psalm is providing an easier reading (Beyerlin, *Werden*, 13). Given the possibility that the author of Job employs archaisms, these linguistic features are insufficient to draw a conclusion on relative dating.

31 Also, the shared word קפץ ("to shut") only appears seven times in the HB, and only here with an abstract subject. Only here and Isa 52:15 does it have "mouth" as its object.

to elsewhere by one of these authors suggests that the particular literary use of this formula is what is being cited here.[32]

Considered together, these textual parallels offer more insight into the direction of influence between the two works. Both Job 5:16 and 22:19 appear in Eliphaz's speeches. Goldingay, who noted the cynical sense of Job's words in their original context, remarks that when the psalm uses words that correspond with Eliphaz's, it "means them in the same sense as Eliphaz does."[33] Thus, if the psalmist is quoting the book of Job, he has placed Eliphaz's words a verse away from Job's without distinguishing their conflicting original contexts.[34]

If, however, the Job poet is quoting from the psalm, because of his work's dialogical form, he is able to give the phrases to different characters who use them in contrasting ways. Job receives two negative phrases from the psalm that integrate well into his hymn parody in 12:13–25. Eliphaz, however, repeats didactic maxims that carry a subtle hint of accusation. Thus, both disputants use lines commensurate with the character they demonstrate throughout the dialogue. This more plausible explanation of the allusions' external coherence further substantiates Job's dependence on the psalm.

4.4. Use

The comparison of the external coherence of the parallel texts also provides insight into the purpose of Job's allusion. His selective use of negative imagery from Psalm 107 uses the psalm's words against itself. Not only does Job quote v. 40 while omitting its context, in which the princes' affliction is a judgment for

---

32 Gordis claims that 5:16b is "clearly based" on Ps 107:42, and that the two verses which follow it also draw on earlier texts (17a // Ps 94:12; 17b // Prov 3:11; 18a // Hos 6:1; 18b // Deut 32:34 [he probably means Deut 32:39]). He then claims, "Obviously, it is Job who has borrowed from older writers" (Robert Gordis, *The Book of Job: Commentary, New Translation, and Special Studies* [Moreshet 2; New York: Jewish Theological Seminary of America, 1978], 57).

33 Goldingay, *Psalms*, 3:259–60. C. Rosenmüller similarly claims that Job 5:16 has "eadem verba et sententia" as Ps 107:42 (C. Rosenmüller, *Psalmi* [3 vols.; SVT 4; Leipzig: Ioh. Ambros. Barthii, 1821–1823], 3:1643).

34 Beyerlin argues that Psalm 107 is dependent on Job because he finds it hard to believe that passages from what he considers the original Job composition (5:11a, 16b; 22:19a) and a later addition (12:12–25) would refer to the same three verses in the psalm (Beyerlin, *Werden*, 14). However, this argument could work the other way, since Beyerlin argues that Ps 107:33–43 is a later addition to the psalm, which was originally made up of just the first three strophes (vv. 4–22) (82), and yet parallels to the same passage in Job (12:13–25) appear in both (see below). Significantly, Beyerlin mentions the common word pair חשׁך and צלמות in Ps 107:10, 14 and Job 3:5; 10:21 as evidence of the first three strophes' dependence on Job, but does not mention Job 12:22, where those terms also appear (17, 84).

oppressing the people,[35] in Job's version the generalized "leaders of the earth" receive the punishment with no moral distinction indicated.[36] He also omits the positive contrast in the psalm that immediately follows: "but he raises up the needy out of distress, and makes their families like flocks." This omission is not due to his ignorance of this verse, because he alludes to the imagery of families like flocks later in 21:11, though he again parodies it, applying it to the wicked (see below). Thus, as with Psalm 8, in his allusion to Psalm 107, Job parodies the psalm.[37]

4.5. Recurrence

4.5.1. Eliphaz: Ch. 5

Job's parodic interpretation of the hymn becomes clearer when further allusions to Psalm 107 are considered, particularly when his use is compared with that of Eliphaz. In ch. 5, Eliphaz begins to apply subtly to Job the message he had received from a spirit that all mortals are sinful and thus liable to God's judgment. In 5:2–5 he describes the "fool" in a way that only indirectly hints that Job might be in mind.[38] The word used here for "fool" (אֱוִיל) is common in Proverbs but appears only here in Job and only in Ps 107:17 in the Psalms.[39] If Eliphaz is here alluding to Psalm 107, he has chosen the one strophe from the psalm (vv. 17–22) that most clearly supports his point that human sinfulness leads to affliction and that best applies to Job's case, as the emphasis sickness receives in the dialogue demonstrates (e.g., Job 19:1–22).[40] Eliphaz may be directing Job to this strophe because it ends happily with the afflicted crying to the Lord in their distress and being healed (vv. 19–20), just as Eliphaz advises Job to do in vv. 8–9,

---

35   Clines, *Job*, 1:301. Similarly, Edward J. Kissane, *The Book of Psalms* (2 vols.; Dublin: Browne and Nolan Ltd., the Richview Press, 1953–1954), 2:180. This interpretation is based on reading v. 40 connected with v. 39, but even Zenger, who claims the participle in v. 40 indicates a new subsection, argues the text presents the "princes" as answerable for the exile, which he considers to be the affliction there described (Hossfeld and Zenger, *Psalmen 101–150*, 142, 156).

36   Klaus Seybold notes this as a contrast between Job's hymn and Psalm 107, especially vv. 34, 39 (Klaus Seybold, *Die Psalmen* [Tübingen: Mohr, 1996], 430). Similarly, Clines, *Job*, 303.

37   Clines, *Job*, 1:287.

38   Clines, *Job*, 1:138–39.

39   Noting the similarity between Ps 107:17 and Job 5:2–3 and Prov 5:21–23, Beyerlin argues that the psalmist is here dependent on the Israelite wisdom tradition (Beyerlin, *Werden*, 18, 29).

40   For the significance of sickness in Job, see R. E. Clements, *Wisdom in Theology* (The Didsbury Lectures; Carlisle: Paternoster, 1992), 84–89.

using the word נפלאות ("wondrous deeds") that describes God's miraculous intervention in the second part of the psalm's repeated refrain (vv. 8, 15, 21, 31).[41]

With v. 9, Eliphaz sets into a hymn praising this wonder-working God that parallels Psalm 107, especially its concluding section (vv. 33–42).[42] In fact, Baumgärtel finds the parallels between this section and the psalm so clear that he suggests the author of the psalm has adapted this passage from Job.[43] Both passages focus on divine reversals. Both mention the provision of water to the land (Job 5:10; Ps 107:33, 35), the exaltation of the lowly (Job 5:11; Ps 107:41a),[44] and the overturning of the powerful (Job 5:12–13; Ps 107:40a) leaving them lost (Job 5:14; Ps 107:40b); both have the same hymnic-parenetic tone,[45] and both end with the same words (Job 5:16b; Ps 107:42b).[46] Newsom claims that Eliphaz cites doxology in 5:9–16 to add weight to his words,[47] but his allusions to a specific doxological psalm gives them even greater authority.[48]

Eliphaz begins a new section in vv. 17–27, where he promises that God will "deliver" from various "troubles" (v. 19), now summoning words from the first part of the psalm's refrain (vv. 6, 13, 19, 28), which declares the deliverance of those who cried to the Lord.[49] Like the psalmist, Eliphaz lists distresses from which Job may expect deliverance, though the situations are different and less detailed. He concludes with blessings, including numerous offspring (v. 25; cf. Ps 107:38, 41), and an admonition for Job to consider what he has said (v. 27; cf. Ps 107:42–43).

---

41   Habel claims Eliphaz has "extracted this expression from its cultic context and employed it as a proof text to justify his argument about the nature of God" (Habel, *Job*, 50).

42   For the delimitation of this section of the psalm, see Mays, *Psalms*, 344; Konrad Schaefer, *Psalms* (Berit Olam; Collegeville, Minn.: Liturgical Press, 2001), 268. Both these commentators believe that this section of the psalm ends at v. 41. Whether v. 42 is part of the hymn (Fohrer, *Hiob*, 151), or a response to it (Broyles, *Psalms*, 410), v. 43 is certainly set apart as a reflection on what has preceded.

43   Baumgärtel, *Hiobdialog*, 18. Franz Hesse also notices a particular relationship between this hymn and Psalm 107 (Franz Hesse, *Hiob* [ZBK 14; Zürich: Theologischer Verlag, 1978], 53).

44   Beyerlin, *Werden*, 13; Hossfeld and Zenger, *Psalmen 101–150*, 156. Note the repetition of the verb שגב ("to be exalted"). Harry Torczyner considers Ps 107:41 a variant of Job 5:11 (Harry Torczyner, *Das Buch Hiob: Eine kritische Analyse des überlieferten Hiobtextes* [Wien: R. Löwit, 1920], 77).

45   Beyerlin, *Werden*, 13.

46   Fohrer notes the similar conclusions (Fohrer, *Hiob*, 151).

47   Newsom, "Polyphonic," 100.

48   Henning Graf Reventlow, "Skepsis und Klage: Zur Komposition des Hiobbuches," in *Verbindungslinien* (eds. Axel Graupner et al.; Neukirchen-Vluyn: Neukirchener, 2000), 284.

49   The word for "troubles" is masculine singular (צר) in the psalm and feminine plural (צרות) in Job. The same word for "deliver" (נצל) is used in Job 5:19 and in the psalm's first refrain (v. 6). Other synonymous words are used in the later refrains. נצל only appears together with either form of צר in three other verses in the HB: 1 Sam 26:24; Ps 34:17; Ps 54:7.

Thus, over the course of ch. 5, Eliphaz refers to one of the psalm's depictions of distress and deliverance, closely parallels its final hymn, refers to both parts of its refrain, cites an entire phrase, and concludes with a similar admonition, all in support of the same themes of divine reversal and deliverance.[50] The psalm therefore stands behind his attempt to convince Job to turn from the defiance of his opening lament in ch. 3 and instead cry to God and receive deliverance as others had in the past, as Psalm 107 declares. In so doing, Eliphaz emphasizes the positive elements of the psalm. Job, however, takes a different approach.

4.5.2. Job: 12:13–13:2

As in ch. 5, Psalm 107 serves as the major subtext for ch. 12, especially 12:13–25. However, after Eliphaz's use of the psalm, Job's allusions now work on two levels, as he both reinterprets the psalm and incorporates his interpretation into his response to Eliphaz. Thus, as Job parodies Psalm 107, he also mocks Eliphaz. The similarity between 12:13–25 and Eliphaz's hymn in 5:9–16 leads Baumgärtel to claim that both passages are fragments of originally independent psalms that are similar to Psalm 107.[51] Others claim that Job's words are a parody of Eliphaz's creedal hymn in 5:18–26.[52] The extent of the parallels between the two chapters and their common source text will demonstrate that Job likely has both sections of Eliphaz's speech in view.

Job criticizes the friends' wisdom by proclaiming that wisdom, in fact, is with God (v. 13). However, Job's experience colors his presentation of divine wisdom, which he describes "in a one-sided fashion, emphasizing the negative aspects."[53] Thus, though the psalmist portrays God freeing a prisoner by shattering doors of bronze and cutting bars of iron in two in v. 16, Job speaks in v. 14 of God shutting people up with no hope of escape.[54] Whereas the psalmist in vv. 33–37 depicts God both evaporating rivers as a means of judgment and doing the opposite, sending water to provide food for the hungry, Job emphasizes the negative side of this imagery, twists the positive side, and omits the purpose clauses, thereby suggesting that God's actions are arbitrary and universally destructive.[55]

---

50 Several commentators note the shared theme of divine reversal, e.g., Mays, *Psalms*, 344; Schaefer, *Psalms*, 268.

51 Baumgärtel, *Hiobdialog*, 18–19.

52 Andersen, *Job*, 163; Elmer B. Smick, *Job* (The Expositor's Bible Commentary 4; Grand Rapids, Mich.: Zondervan, 1988), 922.

53 Westermann, *Structure*, 73.

54 Driver and Gray, *Job*, 117; Fohrer, *Hiob*, 245 n. 13.

55 Fohrer, *Hiob*, 245 n. 13; Clines, *Job*, 1:299.

He proclaims, "If he withholds the waters, they dry up; if he sends them out, they overwhelm the land" (12:15). This interpretation counters Eliphaz's earlier allusion to only the positive aspects of this description: "He gives rain on the earth and sends waters on the fields" (5:10).[56]

Job's verbatim repetition of the psalm in v. 21 culminates a series of images of God overturning dignitaries, apparently without cause, in vv. 17–20. This includes God loosing the "bonds" (מוסר) of kings, which is an image that likely suggests the loss of their royal power and authority,[57] in contrast with the freedom God provides through breaking the "bonds" (מוסרה) of prisoners (Ps 107:14).[58] Thus, Job takes the words out of Eliphaz's mouth, as it were, when he had claimed that God "takes the wise in their own craftiness" (5:13).[59] Unlike Eliphaz, however, Job gives no indication that these leaders have done anything to deserve their fate, which makes their downfall, like Job's experience, merely tragic.[60]

In v. 22 Job repeats the parallel terms, "darkness" (חשך) and "deep darkness" (צלמות) from Ps 107:10 and 14,[61] to describe not rescued captives as in the psalm, but, Clines argues, the darker side of God, which he has "brought out" (יצא; Job 12:22; Ps 107:14).[62] In v. 23, the positive actions of making nations great and enlarging them found at the beginning of each hemistich are overwhelmed, like the nations themselves, by the negative images of destruction and leading away, presumably into exile, that follow them.[63] Read sequentially, vv. 38–41 of the psalm also tell of the nation increasing and then being led into exile, but they offer hope of restoration, which Job characteristically omits.[64] Here he also presents as threatening God's leading, which twice in the psalm is his means of deliverance (vv. 7, 30[65]). The second half of Job's allusion to Ps 107:40 in v. 24b also alludes to a close parallel within the psalm itself in v. 4, where the first group of sufferers "wandered in desert wastes" before God led them to safety (v. 7), but

---

56   Clines, *Job*, 1:299.

57   Gordis, *Job*, 139; Clines, *Job*, 1:300.

58   Fohrer, *Hiob*, 245 n. 13.

59   Artur Weiser, *Das Buch Hiob* (8th ed.; ATD 13; Göttingen: Vandenhoeck & Ruprecht, 1988), 93–94.

60   Westermann, *Structure*, 75.

61   These two words appear elsewhere in the same verse only in Isa 9:2; Job 3:5; 10:21; 28:3; 34:22.

62   Clines, *Job*, 1:301–2.

63   Westermann, *Structure*, 74; Clines, *Job*, 1:303.

64   For the narrative flow of these verses, see Gerstenberger, *Psalms*, 2:250. Zenger suggests the history of Israel from conquest through exile is retold in vv. 36–41 (Hossfeld and Zenger, *Psalmen 101–150*, 156).

65   In v. 30, the same verb for God's leading is used as in Job, נחה.

Job mentions only their suffering and not their restoration.[66] When, in v. 25, Job elaborates on the fate of the leaders made to wander, he has them grope in the dark like the imprisoned in Ps 107:10–14 and to "stagger like a drunkard" (Job 12:25: וַיְתָעֵם כַּשִּׁכּוֹר; Ps 107:27: יָנוּעוּ כַּשִּׁכּוֹר) like the psalmist's sea-tossed sailors.[67] His "hymn" ends on this note, so this parody, which had began with praise of God's wisdom, "concludes with a pessimistic picture of a world sated with disoriented drunks."[68]

Like Eliphaz at the end of his first speech (Job 5:27) and the psalmist (Ps 107:42–43), Job now reflects on the preceding "hymn," combining verbs of physical and mental perception. Eliphaz had enjoined Job to "hear" (שמע) and "know" (ידע) the "true" ways of God. The psalmist had claimed that the righteous "see" (ראה) God's reversals and are glad; if they are wise, they "attend" (שמר) to them and "consider" (בין) the Lord's "steadfast love." Now Job asserts that his eye has "seen" (ראה) the negative side of God's wisdom, which he has presented in his hymn. His ear has "heard" (שמע) and "understood" (בין) it, and thus he "knows" (ידע) as much as his friends (13:1–2). With Psalm 107 as a subtext for these two speeches, Job has countered Eliphaz's positive version of its reversals by emphasizing their negative aspect.[69] This view accords better with his experience, what he has seen and heard.

4.5.3. Eliphaz: 15:24

When Eliphaz next speaks in ch. 15, he responds to Job's claim to knowledge and understanding by asking, "What do you know [יָדַעְתָּ] that we do not know? What do you understand [תָּבִין] that is not clear to us?" (v. 9). After Job's scathing rejection of Eliphaz's attempt to comfort him in ch. 5, Eliphaz inquires whether "the consolations [תַּנְחֻמוֹת] of God" are "too small" for him (v. 11). He then continues his direct response to Job by demanding that Job "listen" (שמע) to what he himself has "seen" (חזה) (v. 17). He goes on to concede Job's point that God

---

66 Fohrer notes the parallel (Fohrer, *Hiob*, 245 n. 13).

67 Fohrer notes a connection between Job 12:25a and Ps 107:10 (Fohrer, *Hiob*, 245 n. 13). Edgar Gibson sees a parallel between Job 12:25 and Ps 107:27, as does Torczyner, though he claims the similarity results from a variant in the psalm based on Job (Edgar C. S. Gibson, *The Book of Job* [3rd ed.; London: Methuen & Co., 1919], 63; Torczyner, *Hiob*, 77). Driver and Gray note both (Driver and Gray, *Job*, 117). Isa 9:14 and 24:20 are the only other mentions of staggering like a drunkard. The former uses the same verb as Job, while the latter uses the one in the psalm. The verb Job uses for "stagger" (תעה) also recalls the suffering of those who "wandered" (תעה) in the wilderness (Ps 107:4) (Fohrer, *Hiob*, 245 n. 13).

68 Habel, *Job*, 217.

69 Luis Alonso Schökel notes the omission of God's beneficence as a contrast with traditional hymns, as well as the lack of reference to justice (Alonso Schökel and Sicre Díaz, *Job*, 221).

does cause affliction, including "darkness" (חשׁך; vv. 22, 23, 30; cf. 12:25; Ps 107:10) and "wandering" (נדד; v. 23; cf. תעה in 12:24; Ps 107:4, 40), but affirms even more strongly than he had in his first speech (5:12–14) that it is the wicked who suffer these afflictions (v. 20). To underscore his message, as he had in ch. 5, he alludes to the refrain of Psalm 107: "Then they cried to the Lord in their trouble [צר], and he delivered them from their distress [מִמְּצוּקוֹתֵיהֶם]" (v. 6; cf. vv. 13, 19, 28). In v. 24 he claims that "distress" (צר) and "anguish" (מצוקה) terrify the wicked, but instead of them being delivered by God, these powers will "prevail" over them.[70] Following Job, he transforms a positive statement from the psalm into a negative one, but maintains God's justice by directing it at the wicked.

4.5.4. Job: 21:11

Job returns to the psalm again in ch. 21. He begins his speech by demanding his friends "listen carefully" (שׁמעו שׁמוע) to him, so his words might be *their* "consolations" (תנחומת) (v. 2; cf. 15:11).[71] After they bear with him, he gives them permission to "mock on" (לעג) (v. 3). He proceeds to describe the prosperity of the "wicked" (v. 7ff.), once again turning Eliphaz's speech on its head. In so doing, he parodies Psalm 107 again. In v. 11, he mentions the children of the wicked going forth "like a flock" (כצאן), which reverses Ps 107:41, where it was the families of the needy, whom God raised up and made "like a flock" (כצאן).[72] The simile כצאן appears in 18 passages in the HB (e.g., Pss 44:11; 77:20; 2 Chr 18:16), but only in these two passages does the term refer to families. According to Goulder, the allusion to this verse in Job is an example of the "comfort" the psalmist takes from the book of Job.[73] However, Job's application of this image to the wicked makes it unlikely the psalmist would allude to it for that purpose.

---

70 A. F. Kirkpatrick notes the common coupling of these two words in these two passages (Kirkpatrick, *Psalms*, 3:640). The first noun is common, but the second only appears in two other places: Zeph 1:15 and Ps 25:17. In those passages, however, it is paired with צרה, a different form of the former noun.

71 This word only appears here and in 15:11 in the book.

72 The following acknowledge that this similarity suggests a borrowing but all see the psalm as later: J. Barth, *Beiträge zur Erklärung des Buches Hiob* (Leipzig: J.C. Hinrichs'sche Buchhandlung, 1878), 11 n. 2; Delitzsch, *Psalms*, 3:147–48; T. K. Cheyne, *The Book of Psalms* (2 vols.; London: Kegan Paul, Trench, Trübner & Co., 1904), 2:137; Goulder, *Return*, 125.

73 Goulder, *Return*, 125.

4.5.5. Eliphaz: 22:19

Eliphaz recognizes the attack and counters in the next chapter by repeating Job's words in 22:17–18 (cf. 21:14–16) before using the words of Ps 107:42 to reject them in v. 19. According to Eliphaz, the "righteous" see the destruction of the wicked, which he has described (v. 16), and "are glad" (v. 19a). Job's depiction of the prosperity of the wicked in the previous chapter demonstrates that he has not seen their downfall in either a concrete or conceptual sense, and thus, unlike the righteous, he is not glad. Eliphaz then performs his own reversal of the psalm's words by replacing the second clause of Ps 107:42, "injustice shuts its mouth," which he had cited in his first speech (5:16), with the diametrically opposed phrase "the innocent one mocks [יִלְעַג] at them" (v. 19b). In so doing, he associates Job with the wicked and his friends and himself with the righteous and innocent, and even with God, who similarly mocks those who question divine rule (Ps 2:4). The friends, and not Job, rejoice at the destruction of the wicked, and though Job accuses them of mocking him (21:3), they do so in their innocence.

4.6. Holistic Interpretation

Tracing the allusions to Psalm 107 as they recur throughout the dialogue has revealed the psalm's role as a locus for the debate over the role of human experience in the evaluation of God's sovereignty. The argument began with Eliphaz applying the psalm to Job's case in line with the friends' general espousal of a strict doctrine of retribution by emphasizing the divine chastisement of the wicked and deliverance of the righteous, as he hints at the strophe that most clearly sets forth this relation (Ps 107:17–22) and then the positive side of the divine reversals that conclude the psalm.

Job, however, informed by what *he* has seen, balks at the "lopsidedness" of Eliphaz's version of the psalm and, by extension, life, "where everything good happens to the righteous,"[74] which implies he must not be among them. In accordance with his experience, Job parodies both the psalm and Eliphaz's interpretation of it by omitting the purpose clauses and the positive aspects of the psalm's reversals, instead presenting God's sovereignty as threatening and arbitrary (Job 12:13–25).[75] This contrast appears most clearly in their respective allusions to the rain imagery in Ps 107:33–37. Eliphaz only alludes to its positive aspects (5:10),

---

74 Smick, *Job*, 922. Smick is referring explicitly to 5:18–26, but this comment could apply to ch. 5 more generally.

75 Andersen claims that Job is parodying Eliphaz's hymn in 5:18–27 in this way, but, if Eliphaz is alluding to the psalm, both may be true. See Andersen, *Job*, 163. Similarly, Gordis, *Job*, 187.

while Job responds by repeating several words from Eliphaz's version[76] as he alludes to the negative, parodies the positive, and presents both as arbitrary (12:15).

The debate between the two continues through Eliphaz's reassertion of his experience (15:17) and more threatening appeal to the psalm's refrain (15:24), into the third cycle of speeches. Consistent with his earlier allusions, Job turns one of its positive images into a negative one, as the wicked get the procreative blessing promised to the needy (21:11; cf. Ps 107:41), while Eliphaz, after nearly quoting the psalm as he had in 5:16, adopts Job's parodic approach by reversing the following phrase (22:19; cf. Ps 107:42). However, in his allusion, the use of the psalm, like the debate between Job and the friends, degenerates into little more than name-calling.

Beyond merely refuting Eliphaz, however, Job may also be using the psalm as the basis for his accusation against God. William Morrow observes that "argumentative prayer rests on a confidence that God will act as soon as he sees things the way the psalmists do."[77] Job uses these brazen parodies of the psalm to charge God with exercising divine power in a threatening and arbitrary way because he believes that it should be comforting and just and wants God to see this disparity. On the other hand, though Eliphaz presents the psalm in a positive light, he actually uses it with an antagonistic intent to silence Job's complaint by associating him with the wicked in the psalm and affirming a doctrine of retribution that allows no room for lament.

4.7. Reciprocation

Thus, the author of Job draws out a tension that lurks behind the positive message of the psalm. Though the psalm praises God for his deliverance from various afflictions, it also declares him to be responsible for those same hardships. This is implicit in vv. 11 and 17 and explicit in vv. 24–25.[78] Goulder claims that the four scenes of suffering "represent the just punishment for Israel's sins."[79] J. Mejía finds this emphasis on sin "quite remarkable" in a psalm praising YHWH's

---

76   The shared words ארץ ("earth"), שלח ("to send"), and מים ("water") appear in that order in Eliphaz's speech but in the opposite order in Job's (possibly further signaling the parody). Though each common, these words only appear together in four other verses in the Hebrew Bible, but only in one other verse where God is the subject (Amos 8:11).

77   William S. Morrow, *Protest against God: The Eclipse of a Biblical Tradition* (HBM 4; Sheffield: Sheffield Phoenix Press, 2006), 204–5.

78   See Mejía, "Psalm 107," 59; Goldingay, *Psalms*, 3:255.

79   Goulder, *Return*, 117.

saving "steadfast love" (חסד; v. 1).[80] The double-edged nature of divine sovereignty is most evident in the divine reversals in the final section (vv. 33–43), particularly as God both turns fertile fields into desert (vv. 33–34) and dry land into
fecundity (vv. 35–36). Thus, Zenger claims the psalm teaches that everything in
Israel's history is the work of YHWH, "die Unheilsgeschichte ebenso wie die
Heilsgeschichte," but, seen through the hermeneutical lens of the psalm's conclusion (vv. 42–43), all those divine actions should be understood as deeds of divine
love.[81] That the conclusion has such hermeneutical relevance suggests that this
tension in the psalm introduces ambiguity into its interpretation; YHWH's deeds
could be read another way.

The author of Job employs this tension to develop the book's theological dispute by having Job and Eliphaz represent both possible readings. It is little surprise then that the Job poet returns to the rain imagery in vv. 33–36 where that
tension is strongest in both Eliphaz's interpretation of the psalm and Job's (5:10;
12:15). The author exposes the latent ambiguity in the psalm, which has white-
washed the threatening side of divine sovereignty by presenting God's actions
monologically as a source of hope. By personifying the positive and negative
aspects of the psalm in Eliphaz and Job respectively, the Job poet's dialogical
interpretation exposes this tension in God's providence as it reveals the spiritual
anguish experienced by those suffering at God's hands and the emptiness of
pious platitudes in response.

4.8. Historical Implications

By personifying the contrasting views of the psalm's ambiguity, the author of Job
treats Psalm 107 similarly to Psalm 8, which would further support the historical
conclusions made in the last chapter about the authority of texts like this, which
invited dispute over their meaning. But, because of the verbatim citation in 12:21,
24, the use of Psalm 107 in Job has further historical implications. Beyerlin, who
believes the author of the last section of the psalm (vv. 33–43), writing in the
third century B.C.E., was quoting from Job, argues from the exact citation that this
poet wrote when a canon consciousness (*Kanonbewusstsein*) was arising.[82] Since Job
is more likely the quoting text, could the same conclusion be transferred to its
author?

The authoritative status of the psalm, the verbatim citation of Ps 107:40 (Job
12:21, 24), the nearly exact repetition of Ps 107:42 (Job 5:16; 22:19), and the wide-

---

80   Mejía, "Psalm 107," 57.
81   Hossfeld and Zenger, *Psalmen 101–150*, 160.
82   Beyerlin, *Werden*, 107–8.

spread allusions to the psalm all seem to suggest that the author of Job had the text of Psalm 107 before him. Even the slight variations from Ps 107:42 are no argument against this, since the Job poet varies lines he takes from his own work (e.g., 18:5–6 // 21:17), likely for aesthetic or rhetorical reasons. Recent work on the relationship between oral and literary composition in ancient Israel has made such a distinction more complex by indicating that the two indices are not mutually exclusive but poles on a continuum.[83] However, by examining cognitive theories of memory, Cynthia Edenburg has argued that, because of the "complex cognitive process" of making and identifying allusions, certain forms of involved intertextuality would be inaccessible to an oral audience, instead requiring texts fixed in writing that can be perused.[84] The use of Psalm 107 in Job, with the type of extended interaction mentioned above, would fall into this category, which indicates a literary interaction between two texts. Whether the authority accorded to Psalm 107 justifies considering it part of a developing proto-canon is an even more fraught question, but the Job poet's use of the psalm indicates that he at least expected his audience to be familiar with it and agree that it had some sort of normative force in a debate.[85]

4.9. Conclusion

Job and Eliphaz interact with the normative status of the psalm in different ways. Job uses his experience to draw its optimistic depiction of divine deliverance into question and reveal a shadowy side to God's sovereignty. Eliphaz opposes the psalm's positive presentation of divine providence to Job's affliction.[86] Job challenges the norm, while Eliphaz enforces it. And yet, Job's challenge expresses implicit faith in the psalm's accurate presentation of how God interacts with his people. To accuse God of straying from the norm, he must believe that it exists, and his argument for a change in God's behavior requires that a return to that standard is possible. Thus, the book of Job provides insight into the internal

---

83   See, e.g., Susan Niditch, *Oral World and Written Word: Ancient Israelite Literature* (LAI; Louisville, Ky.: Westminster John Knox, 1996); Carr, *Writing*.

84   Cynthia Edenburg, "Intertextuality, Literary Competence and the Question of Readership: Some Preliminary Observations," *JSOT* 35 (2010): 131–48.

85   Certainly by the time the Qumran *Hodayot* were composed, Psalm 107 had become prominent, at least among that community. Among the Psalms, which are alluded to more than any other HB text in that collection, Psalm 107 was "used to a marked degree" (Holm-Nielsen, *Hodayot*, 309).

86   Thus Köhlmoos observes that through the use of psalmic motifs in the dialogue both critical and affirmative receptions of Israel's cult theology appear, with Job depicting God turning "Heil in Unheil" and the friends promising that God is capable of transforming "Unheil in Heil" (Köhlmoos, *Textstrategie*, 129).

struggle of one of the afflicted described in Psalm 107 as Job battles to reconcile his conception of God with his current experience.

4.9.1. Psalms of Praise in Job

Thus, by drawing the praise of Psalms 8 and 107 into the dialogue between Job and his friends, the author of Job reveals their ambiguity by having Job and the friends interpret the tensions in each psalm regarding God's relationship with humanity in opposing ways. Though both psalms present this relationship positively, the undercurrents of human insignificance (Psalm 8) and the destructive side of God's providence (Psalm 107) bubble up to the surface in Job's experience and the friends' response. With Psalm 8, Job complains that his significance is not royal (Job 19:9), as it should be (Ps 8:6), but that the attention God gives him has been transformed from gracious care (Ps 8:5) to oppressive testing (Job 7:17–18). The friends reply that Job is too insignificant to complain (Job 15:14–16; 25:5–6). With Psalm 107, Job argues that God's providence, which the psalm depicts as a testimony to God's steadfast love (Ps 107:1), has become destructive and arbitrary (Job 12:13–25), while Eliphaz maintains that God will deliver the righteous who cry out to him (Job 5; 22:19), just as the psalm says (Ps 107:6, 13, 19, 28). In both cases, Job twists the psalms' praise into accusation by turning positive images of God's care for humanity into negative ones. In response, however, the friends use the negative side of the tension in Psalm 8 (human insignificance) to respond to Job, but the positive side of the tension in Psalm 107 (God's deliverance). The presupposition underlying both psalmic interpretations for the friends appears to be that because God is good and sovereign, Job has no right to question the deity—he cannot be that significant and must trust that God will deliver the righteous. Job, however, seems to presuppose that because God is good and sovereign, he has the right to question divine behavior which seems at odds with at least one of those traits.

Part II

Supplication

5. Ominous Omniscience?: Psalm 139 in Job

But Thou givest leave (dread Lord!) that we
Take shelter from Thyself in Thee;
And with the wings of Thine Own dove
Fly to Thy scepter of soft love.[1]

The use of Psalm 139 in Job is a fitting transition from the consideration of the book's allusions to praise psalms to its use of psalmic supplication. Though, as a whole, Psalm 139 is best considered a psalm of supplication, Job and his friends refer primarily to the praise (vv. 1–18) that grounds the psalmist's request (vv. 19–24). Job's use is particularly similar to his distortion of Psalm 107, as once again he twists the psalmist's praise into a negative presentation of God's action toward him.[2] Like the all-encompassing presence of God Psalm 139 depicts, the similarities between it and the book of Job are inescapable. As Yair Mazor observes, "Even upon *prima vista* of Psalm 139, one can neither deny nor miss some salient affinities between a cluster of verses in the psalm and many verses in the Book of Job."[3] Though verbal and thematic similarities between Ps 139:13–16 and Job 10:8–12, the closest parallel between the texts, have been noted since at least the fourth century C.E.,[4] the extent of these connections and their meaning are rarely addressed.[5] However, once considered, the connections between the

---

1   Richard Crashaw, "Dies iræ, dies illa," in *The English Poems of Richard Crashaw* (ed. Edward Hutton; London: Methuen, 1901), 130.

2   Westermann notes the similarity of Job's manipulation of the praise of God in chs. 9 and 10, the latter of which involves allusions to Psalm 139, and ch. 12, where Job alludes to Psalm 107 (Westermann, *Structure*, 73).

3   Yair Mazor, "When Aesthetics is Harnessed to Psychological Characterization–'Ars Poetica' in Psalm 139," *ZAW* 109 (1997): 267.

4   Julian the Arian, *Der Hiobkommentar des Arianers Julian* (ed. Dieter Hagedorn; PTS 14; Berlin: de Gruyter, 1973), 81.

5   William Brown provides the most thorough consideration of the connections between the two passages. See Brown, *"Creatio,"* 107–24. More limited discussions appear in Mazor, "Psalm 139," 260–71; Christian Frevel, "Schöpfungsglaube und Menschenwürde im Hiobbuch: Anmerkungen zur Anthropologie der Hiob-Reden," in *Das Buch Hiob und seine Interpretationen: Beiträge zum Hiob-Symposium auf dem Monte Verità vom 14.-19. August 2005* (eds. Thomas Krüger et al.; ATANT 88; Zürich: Theologischer Verlag, 2007), 493–95.

two texts inevitably raise the question of dependence,[6] which, once answered, offers the opportunity to explore the interpretive use of the one text by the author of the other.

5.1. Identification

The main parallel which draws these two texts together is between Ps 139:13–16 and Job 10:8–12:

Job 10:8–12	*Ps 139:13–16*
8 Your hands fashioned and made me [וַיַּעֲשׂוּנִי]; and now you turn and destroy me.	13 For it was you who formed my inward parts; you knit me [תְּסֻכֵּנִי] together in my mother's womb.
9 Remember that you fashioned me [עֲשִׂיתָנִי] like clay; and will you turn me to dust again?	14 I praise you, for I am fearfully and wonderfully made. Wonderful are your works; that I know very well.
10 Did you not pour me out like milk and curdle me like cheese?	
11 You clothed me with skin and flesh, and knit [תְּסֹכְכֵנִי] me together with bones [עֲצָמוֹת] and sinews.	15 My frame [עָצְמִי] was not hidden from you, when I was being made [עֻשֵּׂיתִי] in secret, intricately woven in the depths of the earth.
12 You have granted [עָשִׂיתָ] me life and steadfast love, and your care has preserved my spirit.	16 Your eyes beheld my unformed substance. In your book were written all the days that were formed for me, when none of them as yet existed.

The verb סכך ("to knit") in Ps 139:13 and Job 10:11 provides a strong link between the two texts as it only appears in these two passages in the HB, and is used here in the same context of prenatal formation.[7] In addition, the verb עשה (translated as "make," "fashion," and "grant") in Ps 139:15 and Job 10:8, 9, 12 and similar nouns עצם ("frame") in Ps 139:15 and עצמות ("bones") in Job 10:11 provide further lexical connections.[8]

As William Brown remarks, in these passages "comparable terminology and concepts suggest some level of intertextual dependence."[9] It is possible, however,

---

6   Mazor, "Psalm 139," 268.

7   Clines, *Job*, 1:248. The verb may possibly appear in Prov 8:23, as well, though this involves an emendation of the MT. Another verb with the same root סכך ("to cover") is more common.

8   For charts comparing the vocabulary of the entirety of Psalm 139 and Job 10, see Brown, "*Creatio*," 118, 120.

9   Brown, "*Creatio*," 117.

that this dependence is merely a shared reference to a common source. Thus, though Leslie Allen admits that the parallels between the psalm and Job 10:11 "compel dependence," he disputes further links between the texts and then argues that a common tradition may underlie the imagery in Psalm 139 and Job 10:11.[10] In support of his position he quotes Andersen, who hypothesizes, "Perhaps several quite lengthy creation stories lie behind these allusions."[11] Apparently further supporting Allen's contention is Baumgärtel's observation of another close psalmic parallel to Job 10:8 in Ps 119:73:[12]

Job 10:8

יָדֶיךָ עִצְּבוּנִי וַיַּעֲשׂוּנִי יַחַד סָבִיב וַתְּבַלְּעֵנִי   Your hands fashioned and made me,
                                                                and now you turn and destroy me.

Ps 119:73

יָדֶיךָ עָשׂוּנִי וַיְכוֹנְנוּנִי הֲבִינֵנִי וְאֶלְמְדָה מִצְוֹתֶיךָ   Your hands have made and fashioned me;
                                                                     give me understanding that I may learn
                                                                     your commandments.

The lexical and syntactical similarity between the verses is striking, and so, if this is not a formulaic way of expressing divine involvement in personal creation,[13] then dependence is likely.

However, this further parallel need not invalidate a possible allusion to Psalm 139 in Job 10:8–12, since it only overlaps with the parallel between those texts in the shared use of the common word עשה.[14] Thus, the Job poet could be combining language from both texts, as he does elsewhere.[15] Similarly, when Francis Andersen addresses the creation stories that may lie behind Job's imagery, he calls Job's use of Genesis 2 in 10:9 "clear,"[16] which suggests that, to get God's atten-

---

10   Allen, *Psalms*, 259.

11   Andersen, *Job*, 154. Allen cuts off the quotation before Andersen mentions "allusions."

12   Baumgärtel, *Hiobdialog*, 37–38. The midrash similarly mentions the similarity between Ps 119:73 and Job 10:8, 10, 11 (William Gordon Braude, *The Midrash on Psalms* [2 vols.; YJS 13; New Haven: Yale University Press, 1959], 2:265).

13   Culley does not mention this phrase in his adumbration of formulaic language in the psalms, but his list, though extensive, cannot be considered exhaustive. See Culley, *Formulaic Language*. The lexically similar phrase מעשה ידיך ("work of your hands") is common in the HB, appearing forty-four times, often referring to divine creation of humans, e.g., Job 14:15; 34:19; Ps 138:8.

14   This sets this parallel apart from the discussion of stronger or equal connections in a third text, which I earlier argued should draw arguments for allusion into question. See pp. 40–42.

15   See p. 48.

16   Andersen, *Job*, 154. The connection is the common reference to creation from the "dust" (עפר) (Gen 2:7). However, Job only implies creation from the dust through his mention of "returning" (שוב) there. The lexical connection is weak, but the thematic connection indicates a possible allusion.

tion, Job has gathered together several images for creation, drawing them from across the HB.

Beyond Job's apparent collection of previous images of personal creation here, further evidence for dependence lies in the broader connections between the texts. Thus, though Newsom claims that Job is more likely parodying "the complex of religious themes to which Psalm 139 gives expression" than the psalm itself, she claims the argument of Job 10 "is better grasped against the background of a prayer like Psalm 139" and proceeds, like Brown, to identify several parallels with the psalm over the course of the chapter.[17] Though the lexical connections in this primary allusion between Job 10:8–12 and Ps 139:13–16 are weaker than in the allusions to Psalms 8 and 107, these numerous parallels with Psalm 139 across Job 10 and further parallels to other parts of the psalm elsewhere in Job (see below), militate against reading the creation imagery the texts share as the traces of a common source. If there was a shared source, it must have looked very similar to Psalm 139.

5.2. Date

Currently, a postexilic date is generally favored for Psalm 139 on the basis of two main factors. First, the psalm contains several possible Aramaisms, such as מלה ("word"), ארח ("to journey"), and קטל ("to kill"), which suggest to some a postexilic origin.[18] The general value of these purported Aramaisms for dating the psalm has been disputed,[19] and their specific relevance for dating Psalm 139 relative to Job is minimal since many of them occur primarily or exclusively in those two texts. Second, the psalm's affinities with wisdom lead some to date it in a postexilic sapiential milieu.[20] Once again, however, this evidence provides little insight into the relative dates of the two texts because most of the connections the psalm has to wisdom are its similarities to the book of Job, whether the shared emphasis on nature,[21] divine mystery,[22] or reflection on the creature's rela-

---

17 Newsom, "Job," 413–14. See below for further discussion of these parallels.
18 E.g., Delitzsch, *Psalms*, 3:344. For further discussion of Aramaisms in the psalm, see Helen Schüngel-Straumann, "Zur Gattung und Theologie des 139. Psalms," *BZ* 17 (1973): 43; Anderson, *Psalms*, 2:906.
19 Mitchell J. Dahood, *Psalms* (3 vols.; AB 16–17A; Garden City, N.Y.: Doubleday, 1966–1970), 3:287, 297; J. C. M. Holman, "Analysis of the Text of Ps. 139," *BZ* 14 (1970): 43–44, 211–12.
20 E.g., Siegfried Wagner, "Zur Theologie des Psalms 139," in *Congress Volume Göttingen 1977* (VTSup 29; Leiden: Brill, 1978), 373.
21 J. L. Koole, "Quelques remarques sur Psaume 139," in *Studia Biblica et Semitica* (ed. W. C. van Unnik; Wageningen: H. Veenman & Zonen N.V., 1966), 179–80.
22 Schüngel-Straumann, "Gattung," 50–51.

tion to the creator.[23] The alternative conception of the psalm's form as among the "prayers of the accused"[24] could indicate an earlier date, but scholars who take this view rarely take a position on the psalm's date.[25] Thus, the dating of the psalm depends on the date of Job,[26] which makes it impossible to establish the relative date of the works on historical grounds. If the common themes and vocabulary shared by the two texts did not result merely from their sharing a common intellectual milieu, but from one author's familiarity with the work of the other, then an examination of the literary relationship between the two works, which is not excluded in either direction by the historical information available, may provide some insight into their relative dates, and, more importantly, into the role this connection between them may play in the later text.

5.3. Coherence

Mazor, who tries to use the relative dates of the texts to determine the direction of dependence, demonstrates how flimsy such an argument would be. On the basis of Pope's "best guess" of the seventh century B.C.E. for the book of Job[27] and the likely compilation of the Psalter as a whole in the first century B.C.E., with the possible composition of some psalms (he mentions Psalms 27, 44, 74, but, significantly, not 139) in the Hasmonean Period, he concludes, "Thus, generally speaking, the Book of Job would appear to be older than the Book of Psalms (at least, some parts of it)," and therefore that the psalmist is alluding to Job. Unfortunately, he fails to address the relevant question of whether or not Job is older than Psalm 139. His interpretation of the role of the purported allusions to Job in the psalm is illuminating, but because it is merely a comparison in which "the very same division which characterizes the psalmist also characterizes Job,"[28] it could easily go in the other direction.

Brown claims, on the other hand, that Joban dependency is "entirely possible" and that "an equally valid case" can be made for Job's "deconstruction of Ps. 139" as for his parody of Psalm 8 in 7:17–18, but, because this dependence is "difficult to prove conclusively," he focuses on the rhetorical effects of the paral-

23 Wagner, "Theologie," 373–74.
24 Hans Schmidt, *Das Gebet der Angeklagten im Alten Testament* (BZAW 49; Giessen: Töpelmann, 1928), 26 n. 2.
25 E.g., Kraus, who claims the psalm's time of origin is "surely beyond grasp" (Kraus, *Psalms,* 2:513).
26 Dahood, *Psalms,* 3:285. He dates Job to the seventh century B.C.E. and the psalm to the same era.
27 Pope, *Job,* xxxvii.
28 Mazor, "Psalm 139," 269.

lels instead.[29] Though Frevel emphasizes the book's dialogue with the Psalter and considers Job 10:8–12 in particular, he focuses on its possible lexical connection with Prov 8:23 and only gives Psalm 139 three passing references.[30] Nevertheless, by recognizing several other allusions to the psalms in the book of Job, even in ch. 10,[31] and elucidating their "textpragmatische Funktion" as Job's attempt to motivate God to intervene by appealing to the positive image of humanity in the Psalter as a normative standard,[32] Frevel provides a coherent framework in which to understand an allusion to Psalm 139 in Job 10, even if he does not pursue the matter in detail himself.

Because historical investigation cannot definitely establish which of these texts is later than the other, and a lexical comparison gives little indication of which text has priority, a comparison of their external coherence is the best means available to determine the direction of dependence, if one exists. Allen's argument that the two texts are both dependent on a common tradition must remain a possibility, as it cannot be conclusively refuted. However, his suggestion that several creation stories lie behind the passage in Job actually supports Frevel's understanding of Job's use of earlier texts in his case against God. If Job is appealing to the Psalms and their presentation of God's relation to humanity as a normative standard with which to challenge God, allusions to other texts, such as Genesis 2, would only strengthen his case. Thus, combining several of these resources together to get God's attention would not be surprising. On the other hand, the reason the psalmist would choose only the knitting metaphor for God's creation (vv. 13, 15) from Job 10 is less clear.

Considering the context in Job 10 in which this image appears, it is difficult to understand why the psalmist would refer to it at all. Dell observes that in Job 10:8–10 "praise to God as creator is turned into a reproach against him. Job cannot escape God's 'care' but this is seen as a bad thing, not something to be praised."[33] As Job says, "Your hands fashioned and made me; and now you turn and destroy me" (v. 8). Mazor understands Ps 139:13–18, where he claims the psalmist is alluding to Job, to be on the positive pole of the "rhetorical pendulum" he sees in the psalm's ambiguous presentation of relationship with God, as there "the psalmist praises the Lord for creating him, as well as the Lord's prin-

---

29 Brown, *"Creatio,"* 118 n. 33, 122.
30 Frevel, "Schöpfungsglaube," 493–95. He opts for the emendation of נְסַכְתִּי in Prov 8:23 so that it derives from סכך (cf. Ps 139:15; Job 10:11).
31 He refers to an allusion to Ps 1:1 in Job 10:3 (Frevel, "Schöpfungsglaube," 491). See pp. 152–153 below.
32 Frevel, "Schöpfungsglaube," 495.
33 Dell, *Sceptical,* 127–28. Dell considers Job 10:2–12 "a misuse of the kind of form found in Psalm 139." Newsom provides a similar contrast between the psalmist's praise of "God's providential care" and the "more sinister" divine intention Job describes (Newsom, "Job," 414).

cipal power of creation."[34] Yet, how would an allusion to Job's bitter speech, in which he accuses God of wantonly destroying his creation, contribute to the psalmist's praise of God? Once again, the negative nature of Job's complaint would taint the psalmist's intended worship. One might suggest that taking this imagery from Job further contributes to the ambiguity Mazor sees in the psalm, but, though ambiguity is evident in the psalm as a whole, features of the passage in Ps 139:13–18 militate against reading it ambiguously, such as vv. 17–18, in which, as Mazor himself observes, the narrator communicates a feeling of divine protection inspiring meditation on God's marvels.[35]

On the other hand, following Frevel's understanding of the book of Job's inner-canonical dialogue with the Psalms, Job's use of Psalm 139 not only takes the context of the Psalm into account, and, in fact, uses that very message as an appeal against God, it also accords with his practice elsewhere, as allusions to several different psalms appear to undergird his argument at various points. Thus, Job's dependence on Psalm 139 is the most likely explanation of this parallel.

5.4. Use

If Job is alluding to Psalm 139, he has again parodied its positive meaning as he did with Psalms 8 and 107.[36] However, unlike those psalms, where Job was able to play on their ambiguity to give them a negative nuance, this section of Psalm 139 is unambiguously positive, so Job takes the psalmist's unabashed worship and mixes it with accusation in order to turn it from praise to prosecution.[37] Like the psalmist, Job says, "Your hands fashioned and made me," but then he adds, "And now you have destroyed me altogether." Again he betrays the psalmist's sentiment by saying, "Remember that you have made me like clay," before accusing, "And will you return me to the dust?" The extended allusion to the psalmist's worship of God's caring creation in vv. 10–12 of Job's speech, in which he mentions the psalmist's knitting imagery and concludes with one of the most positive representations of his relationship with God in the book ("You have granted me life and steadfast love and your care has preserved my spirit") is followed by an even more extensive repudiation of divine care, which ends in the vitriolic rejection of God's attention in vv. 20–22, in which he says, "Are not the days of my life few? Let me alone, that I may find a little comfort."

---

34   Mazor, "Psalm 139," 263.

35   Mazor, "Psalm 139," 263.

36   Crenshaw and Brown both note the similarity with Job's parody of Psalm 8 (Crenshaw, *Whirlpool*, 61 n. 13; Brown, "*Creatio*," 122).

37   Fohrer claims Job gives hymnic statements the function of lament or accusation in 10:8–12, 13–17 (Fohrer, "Form," 71).

As with Job's parodies of Psalms 8 and 107, Job's parody of Psalm 139 could have a negative purpose as a cynical rejection of the psalmist's praise. Brown, however, suggests that when Job reminds God that he is God's handiwork, he is actually using "the psalmist's rhetoric to further his case against God."[38] Once again, the hope the psalmist finds in relationship with God, this time in the thought of God's creative investment in his life, seems to serve as a paradigm for Job; one he uses in his complaint against God. This would accord with the way the psalmist himself uses the imagery. Unlike Psalms 8 and 107, which I have classified as praise because their primary intent is to encourage others to worship God, Psalm 139 is supplication; its praise is designed to motivate God to intervene on the psalmist's behalf. Thus Brown refers to a covenantal aspect of *creatio corporis*, in which "both Job and the psalmist presume that their personal creation reflects an unconditional commitment on the part of God to preserve and uphold them."[39] This type of argument is made elsewhere in the HB. For example, in Isa 44:2, "Israel's relation to Yahweh as one who has chosen and fashioned her in the womb ensures her of his help and salvation."[40]

5.5. Recurrence

5.5.1. Job: Ch. 10

This appeal to the psalm's language of personal creation does not exhaust the use of Psalm 139 in the book of Job. Brown provides a thorough comparison of Psalm 139 and the entirety of Job 10.[41] After noting the extensive terminological similarities between the two texts' presentations of personal creation, including Job's placement of the womb, which is a positive symbol of God's care for the psalmist, in a negative context in vv. 18–19,[42] Brown turns to the related images of light, darkness, and hiddenness. With the exception of terms related to light, Job expands on the vocabulary in the psalm, as he had when speaking of personal creation. For example, the psalmist uses words derived from the root חשׁך four times in Ps 139:11–12, while Job combines that term with four others in Job

---

38   Brown, "*Creatio*," 117.

39   Brown, "*Creatio*," 124.

40   James Muilenburg, "The Book of Isaiah: Chapters 40–66," in *Ecclesiastes; Song of Songs; Isaiah; Jeremiah* (IB 5; New York: Abingdon, 1956), 502. Similarly, Meira Polliack, "Deutero-Isaiah's Typological Use of Jacob in the Portrayal of Israel's National Renewal," in *Creation in Jewish and Christian Tradition* (JSOTSup 319; London: Sheffield Academic Press, 2002), 98.

41   Brown, "*Creatio*," 118–22.

42   For a similar comparison of womb imagery in Job and Ps 139:13–18, as well as Ps 22:10–11, see Dan Mathewson, *Death and Survival in the Book of Job: Desymbolization and Traumatic Experience* (LHBOTS 450; New York: T&T Clark, 2006), 55.

10:21–22. There, Job puts "an ironic twist" on the psalmist's praise of God's penetration of the darkness (Ps 139:12) by yearning to hide from God in "the land of gloom" that "shines like darkness" (Job 10:22).[43] Similarly, whereas the psalmist praises God's approbatory perception of him even in the womb, Job accuses God of shortsightedness (Job 10:4) and thus arbitrary and false moral judgments, even willfully concealing Job's integrity from himself (Job 10:12–13). In so doing, Brown suggests, Job once again turns the psalmist's praise into accusation, so that "while Job knows himself better than God knows him, the psalmist praises God for knowing him better than he knows himself (Ps 139:1–5)." Thus, in their self-referential language, while the psalmist looks on himself in wonder (Ps 139:14), self-abasement characterizes Job's speech (Job 10:1, 2, 8, 15, 20). Despite their differences, however, Brown maintains that both supplicants share a fundamental belief in the covenantal commitment communicated through their creation. Through their appeals to this belief, both Job and the psalmist hope to motivate God to act on their behalf.[44]

In addition to those Brown mentions, Job 10 includes several more intertextual connections with Psalm 139. First, though Brown sees a "suggestive correlation" between Job 10:1 and the psalmist's indignation against God's enemies (Ps 139:21), which "undercuts the self-referential confidence that pervades the psalmist's rhetoric,"[45] this connection is closer verbally and more significant intertextually than Brown recognizes. The shared verb קוט ("to loathe") only appears six other times in the HB. Clines and Habel both suggest that for Job this cry in 10:1 marks a point of such desperation that he no longer has anything left to lose and may now dare to accuse God.[46] If Job 10:1 is read in light of Ps 139:21, Job's desperate attempt to take God to court, which he hypothetically begins in the following verse, puts him in the position of "those who rise up against [God]" (Ps 139:21).[47] Job's allusion to this verse right before he begins his case against God may represent an internal tension in Job himself. The psalmist indicates his piety

---

43 Brown's translation. Brown claims this longing for darkness explains why Job eschews the many references to light in the psalm. Elihu's assertion that "there is no gloom or deep darkness where evildoers may hide themselves" (Job 34:22) may be an attempt to reinforce the teaching of the psalm against Job's parody. Several scholars note the parallel between this verse and Ps 139:11, e.g., Holman, "Ps. 139," 60; Leslie C. Allen, "Faith on Trial: An Analysis of Psalm 139," *VE* 10 (1977): 13.

44 Brown, "*Creatio*," 123.

45 Brown, "*Creatio*," 122.

46 Habel, *Job*, 188; Clines, *Job*, 1:244.

47 Because of the divergence in tone of the final section of the psalm (vv. 19–24) from what precedes it, some have suggested that these verses (or at least vv. 19–22) are a later addition (e.g., Gunkel, *Psalmen*, 589). However, when the psalm is considered a unity, as it generally is, this section actually appears to express its purpose (e.g., Ernst Würthwein, "Erwägungen zu Psalm 139," *VT* 7 [1957]: 171; J. H. Eaton, *The Psalms* [London: Continuum, 2005], 459).

most prominently by his hatred and loathing of any who oppose God, but Job is attempting to maintain his piety at the same time that he himself opposes God, and even to establish it by that opposition. Because of Job's rare situation as a pious opponent of God, he must reject God even as he worships God and loathe himself even as he defends his life and innocence.[48]

Next, Job 10:2 introduces the theme of knowledge that is so prominent in Psalm 139.[49] The verb ידע ("to know") appears six times in Psalm 139, along with the cognate דעת ("knowledge") and seven synonyms (e.g., חקר, "to search" and בין, "to discern"). With the exception of vv. 6 and 14, God is the subject of each of those verbs, but Job requests knowledge for himself, demanding, "Let me know why you contend against me" (v. 2). Appearing in his opening statement, this demand and the plea that God not "condemn" (רשע) him summarize the demands in Job's suit against God. In v. 7, רשע recurs along with דעת, as Job declares, "you know that I am not guilty." The psalmist's opening statement, "O Lord, you have searched me and known me," has the same meaning.[50] Thus, both Job and the psalmist approach God with the conviction that they are innocent, but whereas the psalmist is content to be known by God, Job desires knowledge of God. This accords with Newsom's analysis of the effect of Job's "recontextualization" of prayer language in legal discourse. She writes, "the one-directional knowledge produced by the divine scrutiny referred to in prayer is displaced in the legal model by a necessity for mutual disclosure."[51]

In the rest of the chapter, Job reverses more imagery from Psalm 139. In v. 3, he presents a similar contrast between "the work of your hands" and "the wicked," which drives the psalmist's appeal to God (Ps 139:13–16, 19–22), as he contrasts God's care for him in creation with the wicked who threaten him.[52] In Job, however, the situation is upended because God appears to "despise" his creation and "favor the schemes of the wicked." In v. 7, Job claims, "there is no one to deliver out of your hand." In so doing he may be negatively portraying the psalmist's conclusion that wherever he goes, God's "hand" will "lead" him and "hold [him] fast" (Ps 139:10). In vv. 14–15, the searching out and testing that Job

---

48   Brown sees a similar tension in Job 9:20–21 (William P. Brown, *Character in Crisis: A Fresh Approach to the Wisdom Literature of the Old Testament* [Grand Rapids, Mich.: Eerdmans, 1996], 72–73). Childs notes that, like the psalmists, Job "intensifies his struggle with the God whom he experienced in judgment and yet one on whose ultimate vindication he relies" (Childs, *Introduction*, 536).

49   Stanley Brice Frost, "Psalm 139: An Exposition," *CJT* 6 (1960): 121.

50   For the parallel, see Anderson, *Psalms*, 2:905. Similarly, referring to Job 10:7, Goulder suggests that God's "profound awareness" of the psalmist's purity of life recalls the book of Job (Goulder, *Return*, 243).

51   Newsom, *Contest*, 159. Newsom refers here primarily to Job's use of questions similar to those in the psalm of complaint (cf. 13:23–24).

52   Newsom, "Job," 414.

identifies as God's true purpose in his creation will lead not to a reformed life (cf. Ps 139:23–24) but to unjust and merciless inspection.[53] In v. 16, Job uses the same root the psalmist had employed to praise God for his "wonderful works" (נפלאים) to reduce those wonders "to God's hunting exploits against pathetic mortal prey."[54] Finally, in light of God's inescapable presence (cf. Ps 139:7–10), which Job considers oppressive, instead of joining in the psalmist's praise, Job requests that God leave him alone (v. 20).

Thus, in Job 10, Job draws the words, images, and hymnic form of the psalm into his parody. However, Job incorporates this parody into his legal case against God, which means that he has a greater purpose than mere rejection of the psalm's message. Instead, his parody of the psalm uses its positive presentation of God's relationship to humans as exhibit A in his accusation against God.[55]

Job's allusions to the psalm unearth tensions within it. First, he magnifies the ambiguity of the psalm's descriptions of the divine-human relationship by casting a negative shadow on even the most positive of them. The psalmist's marveling depiction of God's personal creation is joined with accusations of divine destruction (Job 10:8–9; cf. Ps 139:13–16). Even God's granting of life and loyalty is presented as intended for a malicious purpose (Job 10:12–14). It would have been better if they had never been given at all (Job 10:18–19). In Job's speech, God's omniscience, praised by the psalmist, takes on a threatening aspect. Though Job affirms that God knows his character (Job 10:7; cf. Ps 139:1–4), he accuses God of both shortsightedness (Job 10:4; cf. Ps 139:16) and willful distortion of the truth, focusing on Job's faults while ignoring his integrity (Job 10:14–15; cf. Ps 139:24). Accordingly, Job finds God's omnipresence oppressive and longs to be left alone (Job 10:20; cf. Ps 139:7–10). Because God's brutal behavior forces him to oppose his God, Job loathes his life as the psalmist loathes the wicked (Job 10:1; cf. Ps 139:21).

Second, a tension between intimate subjectivity and abstract objectivity also informs Job's speech. Throughout, he addresses God directly, as does the psalmist, but this address is characterized by an accusation of God's lack of intimacy with Job's true self, which he claims to know better than God does. This being the case, Job would prefer God's personal attention to be removed (Job 10:20), which would leave the deity only as an abstraction. The intimacy of God's creation of Job with his own "hands" (Job 10:3, 8) is paired with images of

---

53 Newsom, "Job," 414.

54 Habel, *Job*, 200.

55 Though Newsom recognizes that "the motifs and language of prayer seep into" Job's speech, due to Job's return to the categories of legal language in vv. 13–17, she claims, "Job bitterly repudiates the possibility that such language could provide the basis for an appeal to God" (Newsom, "Job," 439). Attending to the allusions to the psalms throughout Job's appeal to God indicates that the interplay between the roles of prayer and legal language may be more complex.

destruction (Job 10:8–9). God's position as judge, which the psalmist depends on, is questioned (Job 10:2, 6–7, 13–15), and his knowledge is impugned (Job 10:4, 6–7). Thus, Job maligns the objective truths about God, which had given the psalmist hope in his subjective situation. Because Job questions the purpose behind God's omniscience and omnipresence these abstract traits inspire despair rather than hope when applied to him personally.

5.5.2. Zophar: 11:7–9

It appears that Zophar has recognized Job's allusions to Psalm 139, because he returns to the psalm in the following speech:

Job 11:7–9

7 הַחֵקֶר אֱלוֹהַ תִּמְצָא אִם עַד־תַּכְלִית שַׁדַּי תִּמְצָא
   Can you find out the deep things of God?
   Can you find out the limit of the Almighty?

8 גָּבְהֵי שָׁמַיִם מַה־תִּפְעָל עֲמֻקָּה מִשְּׁאוֹל מַה־תֵּדָע
   It is higher than heaven—what can you do?
   Deeper than Sheol—what can you know?

9 אֲרֻכָּה מֵאֶרֶץ מִדָּהּ וּרְחָבָה מִנִּי־יָם
   Its measure is longer than the earth, and broader than the sea.

Ps 139:7–10

7 אָנָה אֵלֵךְ מֵרוּחֶךָ וְאָנָה מִפָּנֶיךָ אֶבְרָח
   Where can I go from your spirit?
   Or where can I flee from your presence?

8 אִם־אֶסַּק שָׁמַיִם שָׁם אָתָּה וְאַצִּיעָה שְּׁאוֹל הִנֶּךָּ
   If I ascend to heaven, you are there;
   if I make my bed in Sheol, you are there.

9 אֶשָּׂא כַנְפֵי־שָׁחַר אֶשְׁכְּנָה בְּאַחֲרִית יָם
   If I take the wings of the morning and settle at the farthest limits of the sea,

10 גַּם־שָׁם יָדְךָ תַנְחֵנִי וְתֹאחֲזֵנִי יְמִינֶךָ
   even there your hand shall lead me, and your right hand shall hold me fast.

The notable similarity between these texts stems from affinities in form, context, and vocabulary.[56] Both begin with rhetorical questions. Though Zophar's questions could be indicators of a disputation (*Disputationsfrage*),[57] comparing them to Pss 113:5–6; 139:7, Clines claims they are also "reminiscent of hymnic traditions, in which also the form of the rhetorical question is used to extol the majesty of

---

56   For a discussion of some of these similarities, see J. Krašovec, "Die polare Ausdruckweise im Psalm 139," *BZ* 18 (1974): 238.

57   Horst, *Hiob*, 169.

God."[58] Further parallels between this passage and Psalm 139 support Clines's observation. The noun in the first of Zophar's questions translated "deep things" is חקר, which is derived from the root חקר ("to search") that appears in Ps 139:1, 23, as part of the inclusio which holds the psalm together.[59] The noun indicates an "object of searching,"[60] and thus, by using this word, Zophar creates a stark contrast with the psalm, where it is the psalmist who invites God's searching instead of attempting to search God and his purposes, as Job desires (cf. Job 10:2, 13). This contrast between God's knowledge of humanity and humanity's ignorance of God in these two passages is picked up in the midrash on Psalm 139. To explain Ps 139:1 it cites Job 11:7–9 with the comment, "No man can understand the purpose of the Almighty."[61] Also, in v. 7, Zophar uses the word תכלית ("limit"), which appears elsewhere only in Ps 139:22 and three other passages (Job 26:10; 28:3; Neh 3:21).[62]

Many commentators have noted the similarity between Zophar's reference to the "four regions of the cosmos" and Ps 139:8–9.[63] Both passages begin with a vertical totality stretching from "heaven" (שמים) to "Sheol" (שאול), and then move to a horizontal totality ending with the "sea" (ים). The third term differs, with Zophar referring to the "earth" (ארץ) and the psalmist the "wings of the morning" (כנפי־שחר).[64] Though "heaven" and "Sheol" are both fairly common words, they only appear in the same verse on one other occasion, Amos 9:2, though there Sheol appears first. That verse appears in a passage (Amos 9:1–4), which, like Psalm 139, deals with fleeing from God, and also includes "sea" in the next verse, though in contrast with "the top of Carmel," which repeats the vertical totality instead of extending it horizontally.[65] Ps 135:6 has three of the terms mentioned in Job 11 (heaven, earth, and sea), but there, heaven is contrasted with earth, and "sea" is in the plural, and Hag 2:6 shares those same three terms, though with "sea" in the singular. Neither of the latter two passages deals with the presence of God in these extremities of the cosmos. Thus, in terms of vocabulary, Job 11:7–9 is the closest parallel to Ps 139:7–10 in the HB, with the possi-

58 Clines, *Job*, 264. Fohrer also notes that these verses in Job reflect a hymnic form (Fohrer, "Form," 66).
59 For the inclusio, see G. A. Danell, "Psalm 139," *Uppsala Universitets Årsskrift* 1 (1951): 21–22; Würthwein, "Psalm 139," 170.
60 HALOT.
61 Braude, *Midrash on Psalms*, 2:342, on 139:1.
62 Schüngel-Straumann, "Gattung," 45.
63 Newsom, "Job," 420. See, also, e.g., Kissane, *Psalms*, 2:294; Schüngel-Straumann, "Gattung," 47.
64 The phrase "wings of the morning" likely refers to the sun's rising in the east, while, from an Israelite perspective, the sea would be the west.
65 See Alonso Schökel and Sicre Díaz, *Job*, 200.

ble exception of Amos 9:1–4.[66] This similarity, as the texts depict a fourfold cos-
mic totality, also sets them apart from any found in the ANE.[67]

Whereas the psalmist used this imagery to emphasize the inescapable intimacy of a God who is with him no matter where he goes, Zophar uses it to
depict God's omnipresent eye of judgment.[68] In vv. 10–11 he makes his point:

> 10 If he passes through, and imprisons [סגר]
>   and assembles for judgment, who can hinder him?
> 11 For he knows [ידע] those who are worthless [שוא];
>   when he sees iniquity [און], will he not consider it?

The psalmist had praised God's ever-present care because wherever he imagined
going, as he says, "Even there your hand shall lead me, and your right hand shall
hold me fast [אחז]" (Ps 139:10). The verb אחז could carry either negative or positive connotations (cf. "seize" in Job 16:12[69]). Zophar therefore replaces it with
one that makes clear the message he wants to get across to Job, that no one can
escape this limitless God if the deity chooses to "imprison" (סגר). He thus
emphasizes the negative aspect of the ambiguous image from the psalm, as Eliphaz and Bildad did with Psalm 8. He then continues his interpretation of the
psalm in the next verse by referring to the crucial concepts of knowing (ידע) and
discerning (בין), which appear in Ps 139:2. However, instead of speaking of God's
knowledge of one's innocence, as the psalmist and Job do (10:7), he threateningly
applies these verbs to God's knowledge of worthlessness (שוא; cf. Ps 139:20) and
iniquity (און). Again, the ambiguity is resolved negatively as God's knowledge
becomes threatening.

Thus, Zophar replies to Job's interpretation of Psalm 139 with one of his
own.[70] Referring primarily to the imagery of God as personal creator, Job had
parodied the positive view of God's care, contrasting it with his current experi-

---

66 Greenstein points to Deut 30:11–13 and Jer 31:36 (though he likely means Jer 31:37) as further
     parallels, however, the former only mentions "heaven" and "sea" and is not describing horizon-
     tal and vertical totalities, and the latter only creates a vertical totality through contrasting
     "heavens" and "earth." See Greenstein, review of Pyeon.

67 For a response to Greenstein's further suggestion (see previous note) that an even closer parallel
     can be found in two ANE texts, see pp. 43–45.

68 Though Clines claims that these verses refer to God's knowledge, and Habel suggests they refer
     to his wisdom, the spatial imagery suggests תכלית is best translated "limit," and the most
     straightforward reading of the passage suggests the omnipresence of God is in view. See Habel,
     Job, 208; Clines, *Job*, 1:255.

69 Mitchell Dahood, who notes this "semantic rapprochement" as evidence Job and Psalm 139
     stem from a shared literary provenance, argues for a hostile meaning to the verb in the psalm
     (Dahood, *Psalms*, 3:290).

70 Pyeon observes that 11:7–9 is an "echo" of Ps 139:7–12, but he does not discuss the earlier allu-
     sions to the psalm in Job 10 so he misses much of its significance. See Pyeon, *Intertextuality*, 186–
     88.

ence in order to affirm his innocence and "jolt God's memory ... and compel God to act."[71] Now Zophar emphasizes God's omniscience and omnipresence, similarly building on imagery from the psalm, to counter Job's argument and press him to confess that his affliction is a result of his sinfulness. As Westermann, noting the similarity between 11:7–9 and Psalm 139, observes, "Obviously Zophar intends to strip Job of the illusion that he might be able to elude God by concealing his sin."[72]

Zophar's interpretation of the psalm takes the tension between abstraction and personal intimacy and throws it completely toward the former pole. In his presentation, God is inaccessible and inapproachable. Job cannot hope to affect him with direct address. Zophar asks, "What can you do? ... Who can turn him back?" (v. 8, 10). Further, because of God's transcendence, Zophar claims Job's desire to know the reason for God's antagonism (10:2) will go unfulfilled, as he asks, "What can you know?" (11:8). The intimate relationship with God that characterizes the psalm is impossible in Zophar's view. The omnipresence and omniscience of God become threats that Zophar uses to warn Job of continuing to maintain his innocence. Additionally, he cuts through the ambiguity of God's relation to Job by implicitly placing Job with the wicked—"Know then that God exacts of you less than your guilt deserves" (v. 11). But in applying the psalm's imagery to Job in this way Zophar is actually guilty of objectifying God, and, according to Schüngel-Straumann, this would put *him* in the position of the wicked in the psalm, as God later declares (42:7–8).[73]

5.5.3. Job: 23:8–10

Job will not let Zophar have the last word on the meaning of Psalm 139, so to further emphasize the contrast between the way things are and the way they should be, in 23:8–9 Job parodies both the psalm and Zophar's interpretation of it. Once more Job in ch. 23 speaks of his "case" against God (v. 4). He longs to "know" (ידע) what God would answer him and to "understand" (בין) what he would say to him (v. 5; cf. Ps 139:2; Job 11:10). But before he can bring his case before God, he has to find him (v. 3). This he declares impossible. Countering the friends' certainty of knowing God's ways,[74] he again alludes to Psalm 139:

---

71   Brown, *"Creatio,"* 123.

72   Westermann, *Structure,* 76.

73   Schüngel-Straumann, "Gattung," 50.

74   Dell, *Sceptical,* 182.

Job 23:8–9	*Ps 139:5, 7–10*
8 If I go forward [קֶדֶם], he is not there; or backward [וְאָחוֹר], but I cannot perceive him;	5 You hem me in, behind and before [אָחוֹר וָקֶדֶם], and lay your hand upon me. …
9 on the left he hides, and I cannot behold him; I turn to the right, but I cannot see him.	7 Where can I go from your spirit? Or where can I flee from your presence?
	8 If I ascend to heaven, you are there; if I make my bed in Sheol, you are there.
	9 If I take the wings of the morning and settle at the farthest limits of the sea,
	10 even there your hand shall lead me, and your right hand shall hold me fast.

In contrast to the psalmist, who is hemmed in "behind and before" (אחור וקדם) whether Job goes "forward" (קדם) or "backward" (אחור), he does not find God.[75] These two words only occur elsewhere in the same verse in Isa 9:11 and Ezek 8:16. In addition, Job's use of a fourfold representation of totality also reflects both Zophar's speech and the psalm.[76] But Job has reversed the image so that instead of being omnipresent, God is completely absent, making his unfulfilled search "an ironic contrast to the psalmist's imaginary flight from God in Ps 139:7–12."[77] Thus, Mettinger claims that in Job's intertextual dialogue with tradition, which he uses to "undermine and deconstruct the tradition's ideas about God," he here inverts the theme of God's omnipresence in Psalm 139, speaking instead of an "omni-absent God."[78] However, Job's parody of Psalm 139 does not necessarily imply that Job has rejected the psalmist's view of God. In fact, he is more likely presenting it as the norm from which his current experience of God has departed, as "Job continues to contend that God is graspable, perceivable,

---

75 George Savran similarly argues that here the Job poet "converses" with Psalm 139 (George Savran, "Seeing is Believing: On the Relative Priority of Visual and Verbal Perception of the Divine," *BibInt* 17 [2009]: 352).

76 Newsom, "Job," 508, 509. D. A. Templeton calls Psalm 139 the "pretext" for Job 23 (D. A. Templeton, "A 'Farced Epistol' to a Sinking Sun of David. *Ecclesiastes* and *Finnegan's Wake*: The Sinoptic [sic] View," in *Text as Pretext: Essays in Honour of Robert Davidson* [ed. R. Carroll; JSOTSup 138; Sheffield: JSOT Press, 1992], 284). Augustine (354–430) also compares Job's search for God in Job 23:8–9 with Ps 139:8 (Augustine, *Adnotationum in Job liber unus* [PL 34], 849). Similarly, Calvin, *Job*, 417.

77 Newsom, "Job," 509. Similarly, Dell, *Sceptical*, 182.

78 Tryggve N. D. Mettinger, "The Enigma of Job: The Deconstruction of God in Intertextual Perspective," *JNSL* 23 (1997): 6–7.

even visible."[79] Once again, Job's antithetical allusion to the psalm involves a desire to see its depiction of intimate relationship with God actualized. And thus, he searches for the God who is no longer there (23:3), reversing roles with the God of the psalm, whose pursuit was inescapable.[80]

After this scathing parody of the psalm, Job apparently finds hope in the words with which it ends:

Job 23:10

כִּי־יָדַע דֶּרֶךְ עִמָּדִי בְּחָנַנִי כַּזָּהָב אֵצֵא

But he knows the way that I take;
when he has tested me, I shall come out
like gold.

Ps 139:23–24

חָקְרֵנִי אֵל וְדַע לְבָבִי בְּחָנַנִי וְדַע שַׂרְעַפָּי 23 Search me, O God, and know my heart;
test me and know my thoughts.

וּרְאֵה אִם־דֶּרֶךְ־עֹצֶב בִּי וּנְחֵנִי בְּדֶרֶךְ עוֹלָם 24 See if there is any wicked way in me,
and lead me in the way everlasting.

The words "know" (ידע), "way" (דרך), and "test" (בחן) only appear within two verses in three other passages (Jer 6:27; 17:9–10; Ps 95:9–10). This allusion is not particularly strong, if it exists at all,[81] but, after the allusion to Psalm 139 in the previous verses, the resonance with that psalm is suggestive. Job is so confident of his integrity that he can long for God's scrutiny, just like the psalmist.[82] It may seem ironic for Job, whether he is alluding to the psalm here or not, to end up in the same place as the psalmist after repeatedly parodying his sentiments, but this would be consistent with the view that his parodies are intended only to sharpen his accusation against God for departing from the psalmic paradigm for which Job actually yearns.

5.6. Holistic Interpretation

In the Job poet's allusions to Psalm 139, Zophar takes his turn at sparring with Job over the interpretation of a psalm. Once again Job parodies the psalm's positive presentation of relationship with God. In particular, he capitalizes on the ambiguity of its presentation of God's omniscience and omnipresence. He first

---

79   Savran, "Seeing," 353. Savran also suggests there may be an allusion to the way "God's hand holds the psalmist fast (אחז), while Job is unable to grasp/see God (אחז)" (353). The homophone is certainly there, but the verb in Job 23:9 is actually חזה ("to see"). See Clines, *Job*, 2:578.
80   Savran, "Seeing," 352.
81   In fact, Job 23:10 has a closer connection to Ps 1:1, 6, but it could be a conflation of both. See pp. 155–157.
82   Newsom, "Job," 509. See also Terrien, *Psalms*, 879.

presents them in their threatening aspect, as he suggests that God has willfully distorted his knowledge of him and expresses a desire to be left alone in ch. 10. He then turns the tables by suggesting that because God knows the truth of Job's righteous character, God is avoiding him, turning the divine omnipresence into omni-absence in ch. 23. Job even introduces tension into the psalm where none originally existed by placing images of God's destructive power alongside the psalmist's praise of God's personal creation. However, as his search for God (23:8–9) and longing to be tried by the deity (23:10) indicates, Job is not rejecting the psalmist's depiction of relationship with God, but using parody to emphasize how far his experience has departed from it, in order to motivate God to rectify apparently aberrant divine behavior. Thus, though Job presents the psalm's imagery antithetically, his intent accords with the psalmist's desire to remind God of the deity's beneficent attributes and commitment to creation, so that God will deliver him from trouble and continue to lavish divine blessing on him.[83]

Zophar, however, consistent with the other friends' interpretations of the psalms, turns the promise of divine relationship into empty dogma. He also plays on the ambiguity of divine omniscience and omnipresence and, like Job, presents it negatively. As with the friends' use of Psalm 8, this negative presentation seems to be a response to the underlying positive hope in Job's parody, as the friends "reject Job's right to protest against God."[84] Zophar denies that Job can dare to expect the type of intimacy with God the psalmist describes. Instead, because humans are divided by such a great gulf from the omnipresent God, their knowledge of the deity is impossible and their hopes to draw God to their cause futile (11:7–9). God's omnipresent ability to judge and omniscient knowledge of human worthlessness and iniquity cannot be escaped. Like the other friends, Zophar's interpretation of the psalm intends to deny Job's appeal to it and silence his supplication. Thus, commenting on Zophar's use of imagery which appears in Psalm 139, Westermann remarks, "Once again praise of the majesty of God is totally subservient to the ulterior motives of the friends. ... [P]raise of God, which sentence for sentence could just as conceivably stand in the mouth of Job, receives a completely different slant when placed in the context of the speeches of the friends."[85] In Zophar's opposition to Job, he acts like the psalmist who loathes those who rise up against God (v. 21), but Job's experience demonstrates that things are more complex than a simple division between the pious who agree

---

83   This accords with the complaint psalms, "which charge God with failing certain traditions normally expressed as praise," though their aim "is never simply to complain, for this protest is always directed toward the purpose of summoning God to conform to his promises, as contained in these traditions" (Craig C. Broyles, *The Conflict of Faith and Experience in the Psalms: A Form-Critical and Theological Study* [JSOTSup 52; Sheffield: JSOT Press, 1989], 221).

84   Morrow, *Protest*, 139.

85   Westermann, *Structure*, 76.

with God and the wicked who oppose God. Sometimes piety involves holding God to the standard of God's own character. As Abraham says, "Shall not the Judge of all the earth do what is just?" (Gen 18:25).

5.7. Reciprocation

Beyond nuancing the psalm's conclusion, this reading also has wider implications for our understanding of Psalm 139. Referring to Job's use of the psalm in ch. 10 as an example, Newsom suggests that the Job poet "fragments and recombines motifs from traditional psalms of supplication, re-presenting them in ways that expose repressed aspects of their meaning."[86] When the use of the psalm across the course of the dialogue is taken into account, two tensions in the psalm become evident. The first is between God's intimate creative care, to which Job appeals in ch. 10, and the potential threat of his omniscience and omnipresence as Zophar employs it to chasten Job. The second is between the psalm as a subjective witness to God's intimacy versus as an abstract depiction of divine attributes

Mazor recognizes the first tension in the psalm, as it presents, in his view, the "dual nature of the psalmist's attitude towards his Creator," in which he fluctuates between admiration and complaint or even recoil, as if his attitude toward God were a pendulum swinging between positive and negative poles, as the psalmist's praise is punctuated by the complaint of God laying his hand upon him (v. 5), the contemplation of escaping from God (vv. 7–9), and the thought of darkness "crushing" him (v. 11).[87] Mazor is not alone in recognizing the possibility of a negative connotation in these images, yet others defend the positive meaning of each.[88] This leads to two levels of ambiguity in the psalm as both the import of the images themselves and the psalmist's attitude to God as a whole are open to debate. Samuel Terrien even suggests that the psalmist himself reflects on this ambiguity in v. 23, when he uses the word שׂרעפים, which, according to Terrien, could be translated as "divided opinions" or even "doubts" and may indicate that "this poet has come to understand ... an ambivalence on his part that threatens the devotion of his fidelity."[89]

The resolution of this ambiguity depends on the perspective from which the images are viewed. Alexander MacLaren declares, "'Thou God seest me' may

---

86   Newsom, *Contest*, 131.

87   Mazor, "Psalm 139," 260, 262–64.

88   E.g., Anderson, *Psalms*, 2:906–8. Ewald claims the psalmist thinks of God "with endless refreshment and content" and ever-increasing wonder (Heinrich A. Ewald, *Commentary on the Psalms* [trans. E. Johnson; 2 vols.; TTFL 23–24; London: Williams and Norgate, 1880–1881], 2:218).

89   Terrien, *Psalms*, 879.

either be a dread or blessed thought."[90] T. Booij observes that the images of God's nearness in vv. 5–7 are only threatening if spoken by an arbitrary person. If spoken by one with faith in God's guidance, "they can scarcely stem from negative feelings with regard to God's presence," as the psalm as a whole indicates.[91] But, as Ernst Würthwein notes, one whose relationship with YHWH is not in order finds no security before him.[92] Thus, the interpretation of these images depends on one's perception of the psalmist's personal integrity. This seems to be the crux of the issue in the use of Psalm 139 in Job, as well: whether Job is righteous, and deserves more care from God than he has received, as Job argues, or is tainted by sin, and should feel threatened by God's omnipresent omniscience, as Zophar proclaims.

The second tension between intimacy and abstraction questions whether the psalm should be read primarily as an intimate personal interaction or a string of abstract doctrinal statements about God's nature. Thus, while A. F. Kirkpatrick claims, "The consciousness of the intimate personal relation between God and man which is characteristic of the whole Psalter reaches its climax in Ps 139,"[93] Edward Kissane argues, "[The psalmist] gives us the finest presentation of the doctrine of the omniscience of God to be found in the Old Testament."[94] Helen Schüngel-Straumann makes this tension intrinsic to the meaning of the psalm. She asserts that the relationship between YHWH and the psalmist is in question throughout the psalm, and therefore, reading the psalm as commentary on the book of Job, she considers it a sapiential polemic against those who, like Job's friends, objectify God by thinking they can explain him completely while overlooking the mystery that surrounds him.[95] The allusions to Psalm 139 in Job suggest its author was aware of these tensions and incorporated them into the dispute between Job, his friends, and God, and that the polemic Schüngel-Straumann observes actually becomes evident through the Job poet's commentary on the psalm.

---

90 Alexander MacLaren, "The Psalms," in *Psalms–Isaiah* (ExB 3; Hartford, Conn.: S. S. Scranton Co., 1904), 325. Goldingay discusses the possibility that the psalm could be perceived either as "good news" or "bad news" (Goldingay, *Psalms*, 3:639–40).

91 T. Booij, "Psalm cxxxix," *VT* 55 (2005): 2–3. Similarly Mays, *Psalms*, 429.

92 Ernst Würthwein, "Erwägungen zu Psalm 73," in *Wort und Existenz: Studien zum Alten Testament* (Göttingen: Vandenhoeck & Ruprecht, 1970), 178.

93 Kirkpatrick, *Psalms*, 3:785.

94 Kissane, *Psalms*, 2:291.

95 Schüngel-Straumann, "Gattung," 46, 50–51. In a similar contrast of the abstract and intimate in the psalm, Siegfried Wagner argues that the solution to the speaker's feeling of enclosure in the first half of the psalm is not to remain transfixed by the omniscience, omnipotence, and ubiquity of God, but to press forward to YHWH, the "you" of the psalm, in a personal encounter (Wagner, "Theologie," 367).

5.8. Historical Implications

This incorporation of the psalm into Job reflects a phenomenon that Judith Newman calls "scripturalization," in which prayer in the Second Temple period was shaped by earlier "scripture" through the reuse of biblical texts and interpretive traditions.[96] She defines prayer as non-conversational human-initiated address to God that predominantly speaks to the deity in the second person, though it may describe God in the third person.[97] This definition would include sections of Job's speeches, such as ch. 10.[98] Thus, the repeated allusions to earlier texts and imitation of established forms in Job accord with the increasing tendency toward the scripturalization of prayer in the Second Temple period. This helps explain the prevalence of allusions in Job and serves as further evidence for a postexilic date for Job.

5.9. Conclusion

As the use of Psalm 107 in Job had demonstrated the difficulty of evaluating divine sovereignty according to human experience, the use of Psalm 139 delves into the conflict between divine and human knowledge. Is God's intimate knowledge of humans, stretching back to their formation in the womb, any guarantee of divine care? In ch. 10 Job uses Psalm 139 to challenge God to prove that it is. More than that, he turns the tables by demanding to know the reasons for God's actions (10:2). Is God's omniscient knowledge of humanity comforting or threatening? Zophar molds the message of the psalm to warn Job of divine chastisement (11:7–9). Can humans have any knowledge of the divine? Job complains that God eludes his grasp (23:8–9), and yet, spurning Zophar's counsel, yearns for God to know him because he is confident of his vindication (23:10). In my view, the latent ambiguity of Psalm 139 allows the author of Job to manipulate its emphasis on knowledge to explore these different questions. The psalm has become a resource for theological dispute even as it contributes to the scripturalization of Job's prayers.

---

96   Judith H. Newman, *Praying by the Book: The Scripturalization of Prayer in Second Temple Judaism* (SBLEJL 14; Atlanta: Scholars Press, 1999), 12–13.

97   Newman, *Scripturalization*, 6–7.

98   See Dale Patrick, "Job's Address of God," *ZAW* 91 (1979): 269.

6. Harassed Hope: Psalm 39 in Job

I kept my faith, even when I said, "I am greatly afflicted" (Ps 116:10).

Klaus Seybold calls Psalm 39 a "Hiob-Psalm," not only because of the many verbal connections between the texts, but also because the narrative of Job illuminates the situation of the psalmist.[1] Both Job and the psalmist have suffered at the hand of God (Ps 39:10; cf. Job 1:11–12; 2:5–6; 3:23; 19:8–9; 42:11) and at first respond in submissive silence to avoid sinning with their tongues (Ps 39:2–3; cf. Job 1:22; 2:10).[2] Eventually their pain overwhelms their resolve to control their speech and they lash out at God (Ps 39:4; cf. Job 3).[3] They complain of the brevity of human life (Ps 39:5–7; cf. Job 7:7, 16; 10:20; 14:1–6)[4] and of God's implacable wrath (Ps 39:11; cf. Job 9:34). In so doing, they evoke the ire of their companions (Ps 39:2, 9; cf. Job 16:10–11; 17:6; 30:1, 9–11). With hearts torn between their dependence on God and their rejection of God's current antagonistic appearance, they long for the deity both to hear them (Ps 39:13; cf. Job 9:16; 31:35) and to leave them alone (Ps 39:14; cf. Job 7:19; 10:20–21), as they warn God that they will soon be out of God's reach (Ps 39:14; cf. Job 7:8, 21; 10:21–22). However, the narratives differ in Job's consistent declaration of his innocence (e.g., Job 10:17; 31:1–40), whereas the psalmist confesses his sin (Ps 39:9).[5]

Many of these parallels involve lexical as well as thematic links, leading Heinrich Ewald to proclaim that, in light of the "great and not accidental resemblance" between the speeches of Job 3–31 and the psalm, "either [the author of Psalm 39] has read the book of Job, or the poet of the book of Job was determined by the complaints of this song to attempt a higher solution."[6] Scholars

---

1   Seybold, *Psalmen*, 162. He also calls it a "Qohelet-Psalm" because of its discussion of the transience of humanity using the word הבל ("vanity").

2   Ernst Hengstenberg claims Ps 39:2 and Job 1:22; 2:10 are "exactly parallel" (Hengstenberg, *Psalms*, 2:54).

3   Hengstenberg suggests the words of Ps 39:4 are related to those of v. 2 "precisely as" those in Job 3:1 are related to Job 2:20 and 1:22 (Hengstenberg, *Psalms*, 2:56).

4   Calvin comments on Ps 39:5: "Of this, and similar complaints, the discourses of Job are almost full" (Calvin, *Psalms*, 2:77).

5   Christine Forster, *Begrenztes Leben als Herausforderung: Das Vergänglichkeitsmotiv in weisheitlichen Psalmen* (Zürich: Pano, 2000), 245; Schaefer, *Psalms*, 97–98.

6   Ewald, *Psalms*, 1:205.

have particularly noted the similarity between Job 10:20–22 and Ps 39:14.[7] Several commentators around the turn of the twentieth century considered the parallel close enough to serve as evidence of the psalmist's dependence on Job.[8] However, Hengstenberg argued that dependence was in the other direction, with the author of Job clearly acquainted with the psalm.[9] Nonetheless, over the course of the twentieth century this connection between the two texts was relegated to a mere cross reference in commentaries on the Psalms and nearly forgotten in the interpretation of Job. In fact, I have yet to find significant discussion of the parallel in a commentary on Job, and even mention of the parallel is rare and generally restricted to attempts to solve the difficult textual issues in the Job passage.[10]

6.1. Identification

Ps 39:14 is particularly relevant for determining whether one of these texts is dependent on the other, and, if so, in which direction, because, as Kirkpatrick comments, "Parallels for every phrase in the verse are to be found in Job."[11] This linguistic confluence was what convinced Hengstenberg that the Job poet was acquainted with the psalm. Most of those common words are found in Job 10:20–21:

Job 10:20–21

20 הֲלֹא־מְעַט יָמַי יֶחְדָּל [וַחֲדָל] יָשִׁית [וְשִׁית]   Are not the days of my life few?
מִמֶּנִּי וְאַבְלִיגָה מְּעָט   Let me alone, that I may find a little
                                                  comfort

21 בְּטֶרֶם אֵלֵךְ וְלֹא אָשׁוּב אֶל־אֶרֶץ חֹשֶׁךְ וְצַלְמָוֶת   before I go, never to return,
                                                   to the land of gloom and deep
                                                        darkness …

Ps 39:14

הָשַׁע מִמֶּנִּי וְאַבְלִיגָה בְּטֶרֶם אֵלֵךְ וְאֵינֶנִּי   Turn your gaze away from me, that I may
                                                     smile again,
                                                 before I depart and am no more.

Textual corruption leaves Job's exact words in doubt, but because determining them affects the strength of the allusion, they are worth pursuing in detail.

---

7   E.g., Delitzsch, *Psalms*, 2:37; Dahood, *Psalms*, 1:242; Dhorme, *Job*, 155.

8   Duhm, *Psalmen*, 116; Cheyne, *Psalms*, 1:170; Charles Augustus Briggs, *The Book of Psalms* (2 vols.; ICC; Edinburgh: T&T Clark, 1906–1909), 1:345, 349.

9   Hengstenberg, *Psalms*, 2:63.

10   E.g., Delitzsch, *Job*, 1:172; Driver and Gray, *Job*, 66; Dhorme, *Job*, 154–55.

11   Kirkpatrick, *Psalms*, 1:207.

Observing that the LXX and Syriac witness to the original wording יְמֵי חֶלְדִי ("the days of my life") in 10:20a,[12] Dhorme suggests the confusion in the MT stems from 7:16, where the more common word חדל is used, which led the rare word חלד to be transposed in agreement.[13] The possibility that חדל may be a metathesis for חלד, and mean "life" without a change of consonants (cf. Isa 38:11; Ps 39:5),[14] could also easily have led to confusion with the verb חדל. Fohrer claims the *yod* at the end of ימי was repeated at the beginning of חדל/חלד and the *yod* serving as the first person suffix of that word was erroneously attached to the imperative שית.[15] This gave rise to the *kethib* forms יֶחְדָּל and יָשִׁית, which were later transformed into the *qere* forms וְחֶדָל and וְשִׁית. The *qere* forms make the third person imperfect verbs into imperatives preceded by *waw*, which better fits the context, in which Job is addressing God directly, but the *waw* conjunctions, particularly the one before חדל, are awkward. Since the *qere* וְשִׁית may have developed secondarily to account for the dislocation surrounding חדל, it should not be used to establish the original form of חדל, as Pope and Clines attempt to do.[16] By reading the *kethib*, moving the *yod* at the beginning of יָשִׁית back to the end of חדל/חלד, and removing the extra *yod* at the beginning of that word, the text becomes הֲלֹא־מְעַט יְמֵי חֶדְלִי שִׁית מִמֶּנִּי ("are not the days of my life few? Withdraw from me"). This version, proposed by the editors of BHS (with the more common spelling חֶלְדִי), makes more sense than the possibilities in the MT and only involves removing a single *yod*.[17]

These textual difficulties and the parallel's extension across a verse division in Job may have contributed to the striking similarity between Job 10:20b–21a and Ps 39:14 often being overlooked. Set side by side, the extent of the parallel becomes more apparent:

Job 10:20b–21a: שִׁית מִמֶּנִּי וְאַבְלִיגָה מְעָט בְּטֶרֶם אֵלֵךְ וְלֹא אָשׁוּב

Ps 39:14: הָשַׁע[18] מִמֶּנִּי וְאַבְלִיגָה בְּטֶרֶם אֵלֵךְ וְאֵינֶנִּי

---

12   The LXX is actually ὁ βίος τοῦ χρόνου μου ("the life of my time"). See Joseph Ziegler, *Iob* (Septuaginta: Vetus Testamentum Graecum XI, 4; Göttingen: Vandenhoeck & Ruprecht, 1982), 257. However, Gordis claims this is "an inner Greek error" for "the time of my life" (Gordis, *Job*, 115).

13   Dhorme, *Job*, 154–55. חדל also appears in the imperfect in 14:6.

14   See D. Winton Thomas, "Some Observations on the Hebrew Root חדל," in *Volume du Congrès* (VTSup 4; Leiden: Brill, 1957), 13–14. Similarly, Gordis, *Job*, 115. Clines takes issue with this in Job because, he claims, the combination of "days" with חלד occurs nowhere else (Clines, *Job*, 1:223). However, the word only appears five times in the HB, which is too few to make compelling generalizations, and in Ps 39:6 the words do appear together, though a *waw* intervenes.

15   Fohrer, *Hiob*, 201. Dhorme only discusses the second of these changes.

16   Pope, *Job*, 81; Clines, *Job*, 1:223.

17   Gordis also comes to this conclusion (Gordis, *Job*, 115).

18   Some suggest reading the Hebrew verb here as a form of שעע ("to seal over, paste over")

This nearly verbatim correspondence strongly suggests dependence.[19] First, like the psalmist, Job begins with an imperative directed at God. These two imperatives, הֶשַׁע ("look") in Psalm 39, and שִׁית ("set") in Job, sound similar, and, though Job's use of שִׁית without an object is unusual, the context suggests that they both communicate a desire for freedom from God (cf. Job 10:17), as the word that follows in both texts, מִמֶּנִּי ("from me"), indicates. Both texts continue with the rare word בלג ("to become cheerful") in exactly the same form prefixed with a *waw* (וְאַבְלִיגָה).[20] Though Job has one word intervening, both texts move on to motivate God's action with the phrase בטרם אלך ("before I depart").[21] These are the only two places in the HB where those words appear together in that order.[22] Both speakers intensify this motivation with synonymous statements of imminent absence from the world, as Job warns, "and I will not return" (ולא אשוב), and the psalmist says, "and I am no more" (וְאֵינֶנִּי).[23]

6.2. Date

A historical evaluation does little to determine the direction of dependence of this likely allusion. Because of the lack of "firm clues" for the date of Psalm 39,[24] interpreters are left to conjecture at its origin based on its tone, religious ideas, and likely allusions to other texts.[25] In each of these categories, connections with Job have played a prominent role.[26] This, along with similarities with Ecclesiastes, has led scholars who venture a guess at the psalm's date to place it in the Persian

---

instead of שעה ("to look, gaze"), e.g., HALOT. Others emend the text to שָׁעָה (cf. Job 7:19, 14:6). See Moses Buttenwieser, *The Psalms: Chronologically Treated with a New Translation* (LBS; New York: Ktav, 1969), 551. Delitzsch, however, explains the odd vocalization as an imperative apocopated *hiphil*, which is pronounced like the imperative *hiphil* of שעע in Isa 6:10 (Delitzsch, *Psalms*, 2:37).

19 John Mason Good, who notes the "verbatim" repetition, attributes it to the psalmist (Good, *Job*, 124).

20 The word only appears elsewhere in the HB in Job 9:27 and Amos 5:9, though in the latter reference, it appears to mean "to cause to flash" (HALOT).

21 Forster, *Vergänglichkeitsmotiv*, 57.

22 Gen 45:28 is the only other verse where the two words appear together at all.

23 Luis Alonso Schökel, "Todo Adán es Abel: Salmo 39," *EstBib* 46 (1988): 279.

24 Kraus, *Psalms*, 1:417.

25 For shared language with Gen 1:28; 4:4–5, see Alonso Schökel, "Salmo 39," 272. For 1 Chr 29:15 and the word הבל in Ecclesiastes, see Goldingay, *Psalms*, 1:555, 563–64

26 For the similarity in language, see Robert Alter, *The Art of Biblical Poetry* (Edinburgh: T&T Clark, 1990), 68. For similarity in thought, see F. Stolz, "Der 39. Psaim," *WD* 13 (1975): 32; Manfred Oeming, *Das Buch der Psalmen: Psalm 1–41* (NSKAT 13/1; Stuttgart: Verlag Katholisches Bibelwerk GmbH, 2000), 214.

period (fifth to third century B.C.E.),[27] though those who consider it dependent on Ecclesiastes place it even later.[28] Because the evidence for dependence on Ecclesiastes is weak,[29] arguments for this date must be based primarily on the psalm's location in a sapiential milieu. However, scholars debate whether Psalm 39 should even be considered a "wisdom psalm," with most following Gunkel in labeling the psalm a "lament of the individual."[30] Even if the psalm were from a late sapiential milieu in the Persian period, this would not determine its date relative to Job, which likely comes from the same era.

6.3. Coherence

With a consideration of the dates of the two texts providing little insight into the direction of dependence, a comparison of the coherence of the allusions may shed some light, though it only flickers faintly because the texts are so similar thematically. The differences between the two passages open a limited vista into both their meaning and direction of dependence. The first difference, Job's use of the transitive verb שִׁית to begin the passage instead of the psalmist's שָׁעָה, is difficult to interpret because שִׁית lacks a direct object. As a result, some have suggested replacing שִׁית with a form of שָׁעָה, either שָׁעָה (cf. Job 7:19)[31] or הָשַׁע (cf. Ps 39:14).[32] This is possible, but Dhorme's proposal, following Rashi, that שִׁית be retained and a reflexive pronoun be understood remains closer to the text as it appears and is therefore preferable.[33] If this is the case, Job's version expresses an even stronger aversion to God than the psalmist's. Whereas the psalmist implores God to remove the divine gaze from him, Job demands that God leave him com-

---

27   E.g., Anderson, *Psalms*, 1:308; Hossfeld and Zenger, *Psalmen*, 1:247; Otto Kaiser, "Psalm 39," in *Von Gott reden: Beiträge zur Theologie und Exegese des Alten Testament* (Neukirchen-Vluyn: Neukirchener Verlag, 1995), 138.

28   Stolz, "39. Psalm," 31; Oeming, *Psalmen*, 214.

29   The evidence is primarily the shared comparison of life to הבל, which is not strong enough to merit dependence in either direction, in my view. The same word and idea appear in Job 7:7, 16. Thus, Crenshaw, when discussing the intertextual connections between the psalm and Ecclesiastes, refrains from asserting literary dependence. See James L. Crenshaw, "The Journey from Voluntary to Obligatory Silence (Reflections on Psalm 39 and Qoheleth)," (forthcoming in a Festschrift for Douglas A. Knight).

30   Gunkel, *Psalmen*, 163. E.g., Hossfeld and Zenger, *Psalmen*, 1:246; Walter Brueggemann, "Voice as Counter to Violence," *CTJ* 36 (2001): 25.

31   Fohrer, *Hiob*, 201.

32   Driver and Gray, *Job*, 66.

33   Dhorme, *Job*, 155. The Targum agrees with the MT, and though the LXX uses the same verb (ἐάω) with which it translates שָׁעָה in Job 7:19, this verb also is used in 9:18 to translate נתן, which has a similar meaning to שִׁית, so the evidence it provides is inconclusive.

pletely. The second difference between the texts is Job's addition of "a little" to the cheer both supplicants seek, thereby making his cry even more pessimistic than the psalmist's. The most he can hope for is "a *little* cheer." The third difference extends beyond the psalmist's words. Though the psalmist breaks off dramatically with the words "no more," in Job's speech, as Dhorme puts it, this "terse formula" is "amplified" as Job continues for a verse and a half describing where he will go: "the land of gloom and deep darkness, the land of gloom and chaos, where light is like darkness" (Job 10:21b–22).[34]

In light of these differences, it is more reasonable to consider the longer text in Job the result of later additions by its author rather than subtractions by the psalmist. Though, admittedly, the difference between the first verbs in the two texts may suggest that Job is earlier because שׁית without an object in Job 10:20b is the more difficult reading, which one could imagine the psalmist later clarifying, the garbled text there in Job does not support firm conclusions. In fact, as mentioned above, some form of שׁעה may actually be original in Job.

A comparison of the external coherence of the two passages is more suggestive though still not conclusive. The psalmist's abbreviated version lacks some of the pathos of Job's cry. If the psalmist was alluding to Job's words, it seems unlikely that he would cite them in a way that made them less forceful, since the slight modifications would lessen the impact of the imagery if it was intended to agree with Job's sentiment, but they are not significant enough to mitigate his endorsement of their message, if that were their purpose.[35] It is the implicit endorsement which such an allusion would communicate that makes the possibility that the psalmist is alluding to Job's words particularly problematic from the standpoint of external coherence. As will be demonstrated below, the parts of Job's speeches that share words and imagery with the psalm are consistently even darker than the psalmist's gloomy grumbling, as Job consistently denies the hope which the psalmist partially preserves (and which appears to preserve him). Denial like Job's better follows affirmation like the psalmist's than precedes it, even if that affirmation is only partial. By rejecting the psalmist's hope, Job intensifies his lament, but an appeal to Job's denial (as in Job 6:8–11; see below) would invite his hopelessness into the psalm, threatening to undercut the psalmist's avowal of hope (Ps 39:8). However, even here, the conflicted nature of the psalm prevents this argument from being definitive.

---

34   Dhorme, *Job*, 155. Though Job's elaborate description of the underworld could be evidence of theological development from the psalmist's apparent denial of post-mortem existence, Nicholas Tromp argues that "traces of mythological language about Death and the Beyond are found throughout the OT" and thus should not be labeled late (Nicholas J. Tromp, *Primitive Conceptions of Death and the Nether World in the Old Testament* [BibOr 21; Rome: Pontifical Biblical Institute, 1969], 3).

35   This is not a theological correction because the rejection of God's attention is the same.

Further evidence for Job's dependence on Psalm 39 appears in Job 10:20a, where another parallel with the psalm appears:

Job 10:20a

הֲלֹא־מְעַט יָמַי חֲדָלִי   Are not the days of my life few?

Ps 39:5–6

הוֹדִיעֵנִי יְהוָה קִצִּי וּמִדַּת יָמַי מַה־הִיא אֵדְעָה   5 LORD, let me know my end,
מֶה־חָדֵל אָנִי   and what is the measure of my days;
                                        let me know how fleeting my life is.

הִנֵּה טְפָחוֹת נָתַתָּה יָמַי וְחֶלְדִּי כְאַיִן נֶגְדֶּךָ אַךְ   6 You have made my days a few
כָּל־הֶבֶל כָּל־אָדָם נִצָּב סֶלָה   handbreadths,
                                        and my lifetime is as nothing in your
                                          sight.
                                        Surely everyone stands as a mere breath.
                                        Selah

It makes little difference whether the consonants in the MT of Job are emended to חֶלְדִּי ("my life") or maintained with the understanding that חדל may be a metathesis for חלד, as suggested above. Either way, and even if the verb חדל of the MT of Job is original, Job's words have an affinity with Ps 39:5–6 because the psalm likely uses both the roots which may lie behind the corrupted word in Job. The adjective חדל in Ps 39:5 is from the same root as the verb חדל used in the MT of Job,[36] and the psalm twice repeats the phrase "my days" (ימי) which appears there as well.[37] Job's rhetorical question assumes a shared knowledge of the brevity of his life with his addressee, God, while the psalmist, consistent with the psalm as a whole, is more conflicted, asking to be informed of his lifespan before declaring it inconsequential. An allusion to Job's assertion by the psalmist would undercut this progression, while Job's allusion to the results of the psalmist's inner debate supports his confident proclamation, making Job's dependence on the psalm here more likely, and, as a result, increasing the probability that he is alluding to Ps 39:14 in 10:20b–21a also.

Job's dependence on Ps 39:14 encounters two objections. First, addressing the internal coherence of the allusion, Charles Briggs argues that the psalmist must, in fact, be dependent on Job at this point because Ps 39:14 is "not altogether in keeping with the original [psalm]."[38] Several scholars have argued on the basis of this incongruity that both vv. 13 and 14 are later additions.[39] However,

---

36 If חדל in Ps 39:5 is a metathesis or transposition for חלד, this would not be the case, but it would also strengthen the argument for a metathesis in Job.

37 The word יום only appears with either the verbal or adjectival form of this root in seven other passages, and of those only in Job 7:16 and 14:6 with a possessive suffix, both of which may be further allusions to Psalm 39. See below.

38 Briggs, *Psalms*, 1:349.

39 Briggs, *Psalms*, 1:344–45. Duhm thinks vv. 13–14 are from another poem, along with vv. 9, 11

others have claimed that the verses, especially v. 14, play a crucial role in the text's unified message as they tie together its themes and bring them to a "climactic" conclusion.[40] In addition, the sudden swing from crying to God to demanding his departure between vv. 13 and 14 actually appears to be in keeping with the tenor of the psalm as a whole, which includes several such reversals (cf. vv. 7–8).[41]

Moses Buttenwieser raises a second objection by claiming that the similarities do not result from dependence but from the same writer dealing with an identical subject.[42] Though he is alone in attributing the two works to the same author, the possibility he raises that the shared terminology is simply a coincidence resulting from the common subject matter should be addressed. In the case of this parallel, however, the level of agreement between the two texts, including the similarity of structure, the number of repeated words in the same order, and the common use of the rare word בלג, is too great to dismiss as coincidence. The verbal and thematic agreement between these two passages strongly indicates dependence and Job's intensification of the psalmist's plaintive request suggests that Job is the later text, though the evidence is not definitive.

The lack of definitive evidence leaves open the possibility that here, the dialogue between Job and the Psalms begins with the opposite partner, as a psalmist alludes to Job. It is conceivable that this psalmist has undertaken a slightly mollified form of Job's complaints to advocate a more cautious piety. The narrative similarities between the psalm and the final form of Job, including parallels with the prologue, might then support this direction of dependence (though the psalm's implied narrative might also have inspired the juxtaposition of Job's initial submissive response with his later complaints in Job). This chronological indeterminacy thus invites exploration of the meaning of the intertextual connection in either direction. However, because I believe the evidence tips slightly in the direction of Job's dependence on the psalm, and because allusions to other psalms create a cumulative case which also legitimately predisposes interpretation of other

---

(Duhm, *Psalmen*, 113). And Otto Kaiser suggests that a later author added vv. 2–4, 13–14 to a lament on human transience (Kaiser, "Psalm 39," 142).

40   J. Clinton McCann, Jr., "The Book of Psalms," in *1 & 2 Maccabees, Introduction to Hebrew Poetry, Job, Psalms* (NIB 4; Nashville: Abingdon Press, 1996), 837. Similarly, E. Baumann claims the final verses draw together the themes of vv. 5–7 and 8–12 and communicate the unconquered dejection of the whole song (E. Baumann, "Struktur-untersuchungen im Psalter I," *ZAW* 61 (1945–1948): 147). Similarly, Alter, *Poetry*, 72.

41   Kraus, *Psalms*, 1:419. For the various oppositions held in tension in the psalm, see Alter, *Poetry*, 69–72.

42   Buttenwieser, *Psalms*, 546.

psalmic parallels in that direction unless compelling evidence suggests otherwise, it is reasonable to interpret this connection as Job's intensification of Psalm 39.[43]

6.4. Use

This intensification means that, unlike his allusions to the psalms previously discussed, Job does not parody Ps 39:14.[44] As with his allusions to Psalm 139, Job has the same purpose as the author of Psalm 39, to motivate God to intervene. However the author of Psalm 139 used praise to remind God of his commitment to his creation, which Job turned into accusation. In Psalm 39, the psalmist, like Job, uses complaint and the threat of absence. However, though both threaten in the hope of eliciting a divine response, Job's threat is slightly more forceful than the psalmist's, and by superseding the complaint of one of the most despairing psalms in the Psalter, one of the few laments that does not end in praise,[45] Job demonstrates the extreme depths of his sorrow.

6.5. Recurrence

6.5.1. Job: 6:8–11

Job builds up to the marked allusion at the end of ch. 10 through several earlier allusions to Psalm 39, which begin in his first response to Eliphaz:

Job 6:11

מַה־כֹּחִי כִי־אֲיַחֵל וּמַה־קִצִּי כִּי־אַאֲרִיךְ נַפְשִׁי   What is my strength, that I should wait?
                                                        And what is my end, that I should be
                                                        patient?

Ps 39:5, 8

הוֹדִיעֵנִי יְהוָה קִצִּי וּמִדַּת יָמַי מַה־הִיא אֵדְעָה   5 LORD, let me know my end,
מֶה־חָדֵל אָנִי   and what is the measure of my days;
                                                        let me know how fleeting my life is.

---

43   Indeed, as will become apparent below, the majority of the few recent interpreters who address
       this possible allusion agree on this direction of dependence, though none discuss their reasons
       for doing so in any detail.

44   Job does exaggerate the psalm's imagery, which could be an indicator of parody. See Morson,
       "Parody," 67. However, the exaggeration in parody must be taken to such a length that it over-
       turns the original because antithesis is essential to parody, and that is not the case here. For the
       essential role of antithesis in parody, see Kynes, "Parody," 290–91.

45   The other is Psalm 88. See Brueggemann, "Voice," 25.

8 וְעַתָּה מַה־קִּוִּיתִי אֲדֹנָי תּוֹחַלְתִּי לְךָ הִיא   And now, O Lord, what do I wait for?
                                                                                  My hope is in you.

The word קֵץ ("end") receives a first person singular suffix only in these two passages in the HB. The shared use of that rare phrase along with the common question of life's duration have led many commentators to note the similarity between
these texts.[46] Interpreters debate about what "end" means in these verses,[47] but
Hengstenberg makes the cogent suggestion that the psalmist, like Job, despairing
salvation from God, "looks for the end of his sufferings only with the end of his
life" (cf. Job 6:8–9).[48] However, whereas the psalmist's tone is cautious and humble, Job's is sharp and despairing.[49] Once again, he intensifies the psalm's
message.

Clines takes the exegesis of these parallel passages a step further by observing
the common use of the root יחל ("to wait, hope?"), as well. He notes that Job's
use of the word as a verb to express his despair contrasts with the psalmist's affirmation of his "hope," which Clines translates "patience," in Ps 39:8. Clines
remarks that, though the psalmist may be able to find patience in God, "Job has
not the strength for patience; nor can he break through his limitations to hope
that his life should be prolonged."[50]

Job's rejection of the psalmist's hope is even more devastating than Clines
presents it. A few verses earlier, Job had said,

8   O that I might have my request,
        and that God would grant my desire [תִקְוָתִי];
9   that it would please God to crush me,
        that he would let loose his hand and cut me off! (Job 6:8–9)

In so doing, he uses a word from the same root קוה as the psalmist in Ps 39:8,
when he asks "And now, O Lord, what do I wait for [קִוִּיתִי]?" Whereas in v. 11,
Job replaces the psalmist's noun with a verb from the same root, here he

---

46   E.g., Gunkel, *Psalmen*, 164, 166; Dhorme, *Job*, 83; Habel, *Job*, 148; Hossfeld and Zenger, *Psalmen*,
     1:250.
47   In Job, some argue it means "purpose" or "goal" (Fohrer, *Hiob*, 171; Tur-Sinai, *Job*, 121), but
     others, based on the parallel with the psalm, claim it refers to the limit of Job's life (Dhorme, *Job*,
     83; Habel, *Job*, 148). In the psalm, Richard Clifford argues, based on the context of the psalm
     and ANE parallels, that "end" actually refers to the cessation of the psalmist's suffering, not his
     life (Richard J. Clifford, "What Does the Psalmist Ask for in Psalms 39:5 and 90:12?" *JBL* 119
     [2000]: 59–66).
48   Hengstenberg, *Psalms*, 2:57.
49   Forster, *Vergänglichkeitsmotiv*, 39.
50   Clines, *Job*, 1:175. Clines thinks that by "end" both speakers are referring to their "limitations" as
     human beings. Though this meaning is there since transience is a sign of limitation, the parallel
     with "my days" in Ps 39:5 indicates duration of life is the primary meaning.

exchanges a verb for a noun. As the psalmist's response, "My hope is in you," demonstrates, this word carries the connotation of hopeful anticipation,[51] which Job then applies to his "hope" for death, thereby suggesting "the bankruptcy of any real human hope."[52] With this antithetical use of a word normally applied to positive expectations, Job returns to his characteristic parodic use of the psalms.

Thus, though both Job and the psalmist express concern about their "ends," the psalmist's "hope" is able to emerge afresh—as Hengstenberg says, "A new David steps forth"[53]—whereas Job explicitly denies such a possibility. Instead, he sighs, "In truth I have no help in me, and any resource is driven from me" (Job 6:13). Job magnifies the psalmist's despair and denies the positive aspect of the psalmist's fluctuating attitude toward God. Job's use of the psalm contributes to Job's "surprising and highly critical argument against the phenomenon of hope and the possibility of a hope for man."[54] And yet, he still proclaims, "I have not denied the words of the Holy One" (6:10). As Clines remarks, the content of these "words of the Holy One" is uncertain. He suggests the phrase refers to "the range of divine commands by which [Job] as a godly man has lived,"[55] but if it were to include the psalms to which I have argued Job alludes, this passage would be a strong indication that, rather than rejecting them, Job is alluding to them as authoritative paradigms.[56]

6.5.2. Job: Ch. 7

Later in the same speech, Job returns to his lack of hope as his end approaches. According to Luis Alonso Schökel, "Job 7 functions as an authorized commentary on Psalm 39."[57] Alonso Schökel lists several verses that share the same or equivalent terminology with the psalm and claims this accumulation speaks for itself as evidence that the psalm was the inspiration for the Job poet.[58] Those parallels begin in vv. 6–8, where Job says,

---

51   See HALOT.

52   Walther Zimmerli, *Man and His Hope in the Old Testament* (SBT 2/20; London: SCM Press, 1971), 19. Zimmerli notes the use of both roots related to hope in Job 6:8, 11.

53   Hengstenberg, *Psalms*, 2:60.

54   Zimmerli, *Hope*, 16.

55   Clines, *Job*, 1:174. See also his argument for translating כחד as "denied" (1:159).

56   Fohrer claims the phrase is a gloss, in part because wisdom teaching is not a divine word (Fohrer, *Hiob*, 161). But if the Psalms had already gained a scriptural status when Job was written, they may be the divine words to which Job is referring. See p. 140 below.

57   "Job 7 funciona como comentario autorizado de Sal 39" (Alonso Schökel, "Salmo 39," 278).

58   Alonso Schökel, "Salmo 39," 277–78.

6 My days [יָמַי] are swifter than a weaver's shuttle,
>   and come to their end [וַיִּכְלוּ] without hope [תִקְוָה].[59]
7 Remember that my life is a breath [רוּחַ];
>   my eye will never again see good.
8 The eye that beholds me will see me no more;
>   while your eyes are upon me, I shall be gone [וְאֵינֶנִּי]. (Job 7:6–8)

Though Job uses the verb כלה and not the noun קץ to express his "days" coming
to an "end," the idea is similar to Ps 39:5. As in 6:11, Job combines an allusion to
Ps 39:5 with one to the theme of "hope" in Ps 39:8 by once again using the same
root used there, though now in noun form. The psalmist had asked, "And now,
O Lord, what do I wait for [קִוִּיתִי]?" before responding, "My hope is in you."
Now Job declares that his days are without "hope" (תקוה), again snuffing out the
psalmist's flicker of faith.

Job picks up another theme from the psalm in the next verse (v. 7), as he
asks God to "remember" that his life is a "breath" (רוח).[60] The psalmist twice
repeats that everyone is a "breath," though he uses a different word (הבל) (Ps
39:6, 12).[61] Job personalizes the psalmist's despairing refrain and then heightens it
by adding, "my eye will never again see good."

He then continues with ocular imagery in v. 8, claiming first that his friends
will no longer see him and then that he will disappear from before the eyes of
God himself (the "you" in v. 8b is singular). In so doing, he concludes, like the
psalmist in Ps 39:14, with the phrase ואיני ("and I shall be gone" or "and I am no
more").[62] אין occurs with a first person singular suffix prefixed with a *waw* three
times in the HB. The others are in Ps 39:14 and later in Job 7.[63] The combination
of this phrase with the anthropomorphic image of God's eyes also resonates with
the psalmist's demand that God turn away his "gaze" from him in the same verse.
As he will do again at the end of ch. 10, Job elaborates on the psalmist's threat-

---

59   There is some debate about whether תקוה should be translated "hope" or "thread" here since it
     can mean either. However, this may be a wordplay in which the author intends both meanings
     (e.g., Pope, *Job*, 60; Gordis, *Job*, 80; Habel, *Job*, 159).

60   For the parallel, see Kissane, *Psalms*, 1:175; Anderson, *Psalms*, 1:310.

61   The parallel to Ps 78:39 is even closer. There the psalmist declares, "He remembered that they
     were but flesh, a wind [רוּחַ] that passes and does not come again." See Clines, *Job*, 1:186. Thus,
     this may not be a direct allusion to Psalm 39, but in light of the repeated references to the psalm
     in this chapter, that psalm's use of this imagery likely informs this passage, though it may be
     mixed with words from another psalm or a common formula.

62   Kirkpatrick, *Psalms*, 207; Kissane, *Psalms*, 1:175; Dhorme, *Job*, 102.

63   Without the *waw*, the phrase appears another nine times, but not to describe personal absence.
     The other uses, such as Deut 4:12 and Isa 1:15, involve the negation of a nominal clause. See
     Joüon and Muraoka, *Grammar*, 2:604. Deut 1:42 is an exception, but even there God adds a
     prepositional phrase, אינני בקרבכם ("I am not in the midst of you"), which suggests relative and
     not absolute absence.

ened absence with an extended description of Sheol in the following verses (vv. 9–10), this time focusing on the impossibility of a return from the land of the dead instead of on its darkness.

Job returns to the psalm several verses later when he demands of God, "Let me alone, for my days are a breath [חֲדַל מִמֶּנִּי כִּי־הֶבֶל יָמָי]" (v. 16). Here he combines an imperative directed at God followed by ממני asking for the removal of divine attention, just as the psalmist does in Ps 39:14 (השע ממני), with the theme of life as "breath," now using the same word הבל the psalmist uses three times (vv. 6, 7,[64] 12),[65] and the reference to "my days" (ימי), which is repeated twice in Ps 39:5, 6. In so doing, Job uses at least one word from each of the verses of the psalm he has alluded to so far, and in five words summarizes the negative aspect of the psalm's message.

He then turns to his parody of Psalm 8 in vv. 17–18 before returning to Psalm 39 in v. 19. He follows the author of Psalm 39 in reversing the common psalmic question of how long God will ignore the supplicant's plight,[66] by complaining of God's constant afflictive attention.[67] In this allusion to Ps 39:14,[68] Job again surpasses the psalmist's sentiment, as he replaces the psalm's reverent tone with the sardonic question, "Will you not look away from me for a while [כַּמָּה לֹא־תִשְׁעֶה מִמֶּנִּי], let me alone until I swallow my spittle?"[69] Once again, Job elaborates on the psalm, this time taking it to comical lengths. Besides this verse and Ps 39:14, a form of שעה only occurs with מן in two other places: Isa 22:4, where the imperative is not directed at God, and Job 14:6 (see below).[70]

Job concludes his speech with one more allusion to the psalm. Like the psalmist (Ps 39:14), he finishes by threatening his absence from the world, proclaiming, "For now I shall lie in the earth; you will seek me, but I shall not be [וְאֵינֶנִּי]," and then dramatizing his warning by lapsing into silence.[71] By repeating

---

64   In his next speech, Job uses the word הבל in the sense of "vanity" as the psalmist does in Ps 39:7, as he wonders why he continues to "labor in vain" (הבל איגע) (9:29), thereby recalling the psalmist's claim that everyone is "in turmoil for nothing" (הבל יהמיון) (Ps 39:7).

65   See, e.g., Newsom, "Job," 396; Schmid, "Schriftdiskussion," 259.

66   E.g., "How long, O LORD? Will you hide yourself forever?" (Ps 89:47).

67   Mandolfo, "Renegade," 55. See also Fredrik Lindström, *Suffering and Sin: Interpretations of Illness in the Individual Complaint Psalms* (ConBOT 37; Stockholm: Almqvist & Wiksell International, 1994), 269.

68   Newsom refers to the interaction between these passages as an example of how Job "fragments and recombines motifs from traditional psalms of supplication" (Newsom, *Contest*, 131). Schmid also notes the allusion (Schmid, "Schriftdiskussion," 259).

69   For the contrasting tones, see Mandolfo, "Renegade," 55.

70   Clines notes that such a wish for God to look away is only expressed in Ps 39:14 outside Job, though "Job's rejection of God's gaze is in its context much more categorical" (Clines, *Job*, 1:193).

71   Newsom, "Job," 396; Schaefer, *Psalms*, 97.

the phrase "I shall not be" (וְאֵינֶנִּי) in this chapter and giving it the same prominent place as his final words, Job marks his allusion to the psalm.

Newsom claims that comparing his words with those of the psalm under-
scores "Job's alienation from the traditional language of prayer."[72] Like the
psalmist, Job requests that God look away (v. 19; cf. Ps 39:14) and pleads for
relief from divine anger because human existence is "mere breath" (v. 16; cf. Ps
39:12) and he will soon "be no more" (v. 21; cf. Ps 39:14). However, unlike the
psalmist, who pleads with God to deliver him from all his transgressions, Job
denies the legitimacy of divine anger, maintaining that his sin, if it exists,[73] cannot
have harmed God (v. 20) and should simply be pardoned (v. 21). As Newsom
observes, in this speech, which she calls "Job's anti-psalm," he replaces prayer
with parody.[74]

Carleen Mandolfo similarly suggests Job is "drawing on Ps 39, or at least the
spirit of it," in this passage.[75] Both supplicants request God remove their transgressions and thereby improve their situations, but, she observes, although the
psalmist holds to his hope in YHWH, Job has no hope. Most significantly,
although the psalmist addresses his prayer to God (v. 13a), Job's speech lacks any
formal acknowledgement of supplication. Though Mandolfo correctly notes this
interplay between the two texts, when Job's allusions to Psalm 39 are considered
in light of his broader dispute with God and his friends and his use of other
psalms, the implicit nature of both his hope and his supplication become evident.

6.5.3. Job: 13:28–14:6

When Job alludes to Psalm 39 in 10:20–21, he combines the themes of the
brevity of life from Ps 39:5–6, the threat of absence from Ps 39:14,[76] and even the
rare word בְּלַג used in the same form as the psalmist (9:27)[77] from earlier

---

72 Newsom, "Job," 396.

73 Interpreters generally consider v. 20 to be hypothetical, e.g., Driver and Gray, *Job*, 74; Habel, *Job*,
    165. Andersen disagrees (Andersen, *Job*, 138).

74 Newsom, "Job," 396. Similarly, Alonso Schökel says Job's words are not a prayer, as in the
    psalm, but a legal controversy (Alonso Schökel, "Salmo 39," 278).

75 Mandolfo, "Renegade," 56.

76 The connection between the allusion to Ps 39:14 in 10:20–21 and his earlier allusion in 7:7–10
    may explain why he says, "and I shall not return," instead of "and I am no more" in 10:21, dif-
    fering from the psalm. In his description of Sheol in that earlier passage, Job had focused on the
    impossibility of return, claiming that those who go there "shall not return" (לֹא יָשׁוּב).

77 Another possible allusion to Psalm 39 appears several verses later in ch. 9. In v. 34, Job says, "If
    he would take his rod away from me [יָסֵר מֵעָלַי שִׁבְטוֹ]." The psalmist similarly pleads, "Remove
    your stroke from me [הָסֵר מֵעָלַי נִגְעֶךָ]" (v. 11). Buttenwieser claims the first two words of both
    verses are "practically identical" (Buttenwieser, *Psalms*, 547). Others note the parallel, e.g.,
    Kirkpatrick, *Psalms*, 1:206; Gunkel, *Psalmen*, 165; Anderson, *Psalms*, 1:312. This combination of

speeches, so that they are already freighted with meaning. However, Job is not done with the psalm. It continues to reverberate at the juncture of chs. 13 and 14. Alonso Schökel notes several lexical connections between Job 13:28–14:6 and Psalm 39, though he admits that the relation is more thematic than verbal. Though both texts use the rare word עָשׁ ("moth")[78] to describe the moth-eaten nature of existence (Job 13:28; Ps 39:12),[79] Alonso Schökel remarks that the link between the Job 14:6 and Ps 39:14 is the most significant.[80] There Job says, "Look away from them, and desist, [שְׁעֵה מֵעָלָיו וְיֶחְדָּל] that they may enjoy [יִרְצֶה], like laborers, their days." After describing the brevity of life (Job 14:5; cf. Ps 39:5–7),[81] Job combines the desire for God to look away (cf. Ps 39:14)[82] with the request for him to "desist" (חדל; cf. Ps 39:5, where the same root appears) so that humankind may "enjoy" (רצה; cf. בלג in Ps 39:14) their fleeting days. By applying the same imagery to humankind, Job universalizes his experience as the psalmist does (cf. Ps 39:6–7, 12).[83]

6.6. Holistic Interpretation

Psalm 39 is "permeated by two sensations that are at war with each other."[84] On one hand, the psalmist hopes in God and longs for the deity to hear his prayer; on the other, he accuses God of dooming humanity to a brief, transient existence and desires to be left alone. Job interacts with both aspects of the psalmist's bellicose consciousness and manipulates them to his purpose of gaining God's attention and entreating the deity to see the world from his perspective. Job magnifies the psalmist's complaint, adding extended descriptions of Sheol to the psalmist's threat of absence, while subverting his affirmation of hope, and thus submerging the entire psalm in darkness. Instead of parodying praise, Job

---

the verb סור with the combined prepositions מן and על and a suffix appears sixteen times in the HB, but elsewhere only in Exod 10:17 and Num 21:7 with God as the subject of the verb and with a negative object. The two words that differ in the two phrases, נגע and שבט, may be synonymous based on their parallel use in 2 Sam 7:14 and Ps 89:33.

78   The word only appears five other times in the HB (Isa 50:9; 51:8, Hos 5:12, Job 4:19; 27:18), though its meaning in the other passages in Job is debated. Gordis suggests it means "bird's nest" in both instances (Gordis, Job, 50).

79   Fohrer claims the Job poet has borrowed this image from the psalmic style (Fohrer, Hiob, 253). Others note the parallel, e.g., Ewald, Psalms, 1:208; Gunkel, Psalmen, 167; Hossfeld and Zenger, Psalmen, 1:251. However, the lexical and syntactic similarity with Isa 51:8 is closer.

80   Alonso Schökel, "Salmo 39," 278. Similarly, Forster, Vergänglichkeitsmotiv, 57, 244.

81   For the parallel theme, see Hengstenberg, Psalms, 2:57; Delitzsch, Job, 1:226; Habel, Job, 240.

82   Gunkel, Psalmen, 165, 167; Buttenwieser, Psalms, 548.

83   Baumann, "Struktur-untersuchungen," 152–53.

84   Kraus, Psalms, 1:419.

employs a second interpretive approach, the intensification of lament.[85] Even so, his use of Psalm 39 is similar to his treatment of the theme of divine reversal in Psalm 107, where he also accentuated the negative and omitted or subverted the positive.

His choice of Psalm 39 is significant because it is one of the bleakest songs in the Psalter. In fact, by simply ending with a request that God look away, the psalm leaves the restoration of the psalmist's relationship with God open to question.[86] By exceeding even this psalm's dismal presentation of relationship with God, Job suggests to God that his suffering is beyond anything to which God has previously subjected his people.[87]

However, though Job has drawn the psalmist's sentiments deeper into despair, the possibility still remains that he has done so motivated by an underlying hope that his psalmic allusions will draw God out of hiding to act on his behalf. Job's impending death (7:21; 10:21–22) is a threat, and, as such, it intends to motivate changed behavior.[88] The extreme form of this threat, in which Job even denies the possibility of hope, is reminiscent of the death-wish found in several lament psalms.[89] In his analysis of the argumentative function of this motif and Job's use of it in 6:8–10 and 7:15–21, Frevel argues that it serves as an implicit accusation against God. Though Frevel does not mention Psalm 39, he proposes that Job uses the death-wish theme, like his parody of Psalm 8 in 7:17–18, to appeal to God to live up to the standard given in the tradition.[90] Neither

---

85 For Job's elaboration on other texts from Jeremiah (e.g., Jer 20:14–18 // Job 3), see Greenstein, "Jeremiah," 98–110.

86 Forster, *Vergänglichkeitsmotiv*, 59. Forster claims this makes the message of the psalm more forceful than the book of Job. Though the psalm provides less sure hope than the book of Job as a whole, Job's speeches that use the psalm present his situation as more despairing than the psalmist's without even the hint of hope the psalmist affirms. See Zimmerli, *Hope*, 38.

87 Thus, Alonso Schökel claims the author of Job had Psalm 39 very much in mind as he had his protagonist take the tragic sentiment of the psalm and resolve it on a higher plane (Alonso Schökel, "Salmo 39," 279).

88 Zuckerman reads Job's use of the death-wish theme as a parodic attempt to undercut its conventional intent to motivate God to intervene on the supplicant's behalf. Therefore, he paraphrases Job 7:21 in a way that removes its threatening aspect. However, tellingly, he then calls it "an illogical and disjunctive turn in Job's discourse" (Zuckerman, *Job*, 265 n. 393). I prefer to interpret this verse as a threat because it maintains the logic of Job's argument.

89 Zuckerman gives examples of this motif in Psalm 88 and ANE texts, such as *Ludlul*. However, the nearly verbatim repetition of its expression in Psalm 39 in Job 10 supports my contention elsewhere that an author can allude to a specific literary representation of a broader theme, and that the disjunction between allusions either to texts or to formulaic language is a false one. See pp. 45, 65–65.

90 Christian Frevel, "'Dann wär' ich nicht mehr da: Der Todeswunsch Ijobs als Element der Klagerhetorik," in *Tod und Jenseits im alten Israel und in seiner Umwelt* (eds. Angelika Berlejung and Bernd Janowski; Tübingen: Mohr Siebeck, 2009), 36–37. Dan Mathewson even claims that the threat of imminent death in 7:20–21 continues the parody of Psalm 8 in 7:17–18 (Mathewson, *Death*, 100).

resignation nor a cynical hope for death as a better alternative, the death-wish is a dramatic stylistic means in Job's defense of his lament, which sharpens the tension between Job's righteousness and God's, so that God can only maintain God's own righteousness if the deity treats Job in a way that corresponds with Job's righteousness.[91] Thus, Frevel claims Habel is both right and wrong when he represents a widespread understanding of Job's death-wish in 7:11–16 by saying, "Though Job does not plan suicide, he prefers death to an endless life of oppression at the hands of an arbitrary God (7: 11–16)."[92] Indeed, Job does not plan suicide and refuses to accept his life as it currently is.[93] He even, undoubtedly, prefers death to *this* life, but, Frevel argues, Job's argument does not presuppose an arbitrary God, and therefore does not intend death to be an escape. Instead he presupposes a God who will respond to the charge of unrighteousness, and thus the death-wish is a rhetorical weapon in the struggle for life and the reestablishment of righteousness, both Job's and God's.[94] This is precisely what Job seems to be doing with his allusions to Psalm 39.

Unlike the other psalms in this study, Job appears to be alone in alluding to Psalm 39. Though the friends may personify the cautionary voice that God will deliver from confessed sin (e.g., Job 5:19), which the psalmist has "internalized" (Ps 39:9),[95] they do not seem to interact directly with the psalm, leaving Job to employ it unchallenged.[96] Given the Job poet's use of other psalms, in which he dialogically divides the psalmic tension to have its contrasting poles represented by Job and the friends, the friends' silence in response to Job's allusions to Psalm 39 is surprising. Both the need for God to hear the supplicant's prayer and the transience of humanity are themes to which they repeatedly appeal, and for which the psalm would have offered them ample resources. Job's impudent intensification of the psalmist's lament to accuse God of injustice would also seem just the type of theological affront to draw their ire. Authorial omission is harder to explain than authorial action, but, given the friends' apparent desire to silence

---

91 Frevel, "Todeswunsch," 39.

92 Habel, *Job*, 63.

93 Thus, Zuckerman, though he understands Job's death-wishes to be genuine, and not an invitation for God to rectify his relationship with Job, observes that though it would seem to make sense for Job to take his own life given his expressed desire to die (6:9–10), "there is really only one *logical* reason why Job does not kill himself but rather continues complaining—because he wants his afflictions lifted" (Zuckerman, *Job*, 122; emphasis original).

94 Frevel, "Todeswunsch," 39–40. Frevel points out that Job has no advantage in death, but God has a disadvantage, in that God's unrighteousness would be established irreversibly (37). Similarly, Mathewson claims 7:20–21 and 10:20 are charges of divine immorality (Mathewson, *Death*, 101–2).

95 Forster, *Vergänglichkeitsmotiv*, 245.

96 In 4:19, Eliphaz uses the rare word עָשׁ ("moth") that appears in Ps 39:12, but no clear thematic relationship exists between the two passages, so an allusion is unlikely.

Job's lament, they may have been uncomfortable appealing to such a stark lament psalm as an authority, since it would undercut their argument. Additionally, since Job's use of the psalm is more elaboration than parody, they may not have felt the same need to reestablish their understanding of the psalm against his.

6.7. Reciprocation

Without the friends to embody part of the psalm's tension, Job represents it all himself, and to such a degree that his allusions highlight the faint faith flickering in its words. Alter elucidates the tension in Psalm 39, claiming the psalmist "flounders in a world of radical ambiguities where the antithetical values of speech and silence, existence and extinction, perhaps even innocence and trans-gression, have been brought dangerously close together."[97] The tensions he identifies between silence and speech and between existence and extinction are facets of what Walter Brueggemann calls the "terrible ambiguity of life with God,"[98] which characterizes the psalm as, according to J. Clinton McCann, it "articulates despair and hope *simultaneously*" and leaves them unresolved standing side by side at the end.[99] Though interpreters have attempted to parse these con-flicting attitudes into layers of development, the psalm contains no actual break in form or content to make any of these theories compelling,[100] as the differences between the proposals indicate. Thus, it seems preferable to conclude with Hans-Joachim Kraus that this ambivalence toward God is characteristic of the psalm itself, so it would be wrong to attempt to neutralize it.[101] Doing so would muzzle the psalmist's cry of faith, which combines both the silence of submission and the scream of exasperation, as he wrestles with the fact that the only place he has to turn is to the very God who has turned on him (v. 11; cf. v. 8).[102]

By taking the hope and accusation in Psalm 39 to their extreme through foregrounding the threat of death and burying the hope of vindication into the depths of implication—affirming it only through denying it should God continue in his apparent injustice, Job's use of the psalm makes even its superlative dark-ness in the Psalter a little brighter. His allusions place an even blacker shade next to the psalmist's dusky hues of depression, thus making them lighter in compari-son. Thus, Job's allusions to Psalm 39 support Brueggemann's contention, when

---

97   Alter, *Poetry*, 69.

98   Brueggemann, "Voice," 32.

99   McCann, "Psalms," 837, 839. Emphasis original. Similarly, Forster, *Vergänglichkeitsmotiv*, 244.

100 Forster, *Vergänglichkeitsmotiv*, 27.

101 Kraus, *Psalms*, 1:419. Similarly, Forster, *Vergänglichkeitsmotiv*, 27.

102 See Brueggemann, "Voice," 28, 33. Similarly, Artur Weiser, *The Psalms: A Commentary* (OTL; Philadelphia: Westminster Press, 1962), 330–31.

he says, "I dare imagine that Psalm 39 affirms that both sides of the ambiguity voiced here are acts of faith. The trusting affirmation is an act of faith; but so is the abrasive accusation an act of faith."[103]

6.8. Historical Implications

Because it mixes aspects of individual lament, particularly that motivated by sickness (*Krankenpsalm*), with elements of reflective wisdom, a cultic setting for Psalm 39 is uncertain.[104] However, through the allusions to this psalm, as well as the other psalms in this study, the book of Job demonstrates how, at least by the postexilic period when Job was likely written, these psalms had gone through a process of moving from their original setting, whether cultic or not, to being considered "Scripture."[105] Though we should not read back into their status a modern canonical understanding of that term,[106] the allusions in Job show that the Psalms, freed from the cult, had gained "a significance in themselves" and could therefore be used in new contexts and "reworked and rearranged in a different situation without losing their meaning."[107] This enabled the author of Job to take the psalm from the Israelite cult and put it into a debate over the proper response to suffering in a very different situation.

6.9. Conclusion

Whether or not the psalmist's words were originally voiced in the temple, Job puts them to new use in the context of his suffering. Thus, whereas the psalmist displays faith through the tension between hope and accusation, Job accuses by denying hope, but, paradoxically, does so because he hopes God will live up to a divine standard of justice. Despite his dark brooding, somewhere deep within him

---

103   Brueggemann, "Voice," 33.

104   See Stolz, "39. Psalm," 23–34.

105   James L. Kugel, "Topics in the History of the Spirituality of the Psalms," in vol. 1 of *Jewish Spirituality: From the Bible through the Middle Ages* (ed. Arthur Green; 3 vols.; New York: SCM Press, 1985), 136. He calls this "scripturalization," but he means it in a different sense than Newman. See p. 121 above.

106   Donald Harman Akenson, *Surpassing Wonder: The Invention of the Bible and the Talmuds* (Chicago: University of Chicago Press, 1998), 60.

107   Childs, *Introduction*, 514–15. Childs argues that this process is evident in the anthological citation of portions of several psalms in Chronicles. He observes that this transformation involved the Psalms, words of humans to God, becoming God's word to humans (513–14; similarly, Kugel, "Topics," 136).

there is the conviction that "if God really desires to have dealings with man, as Job knows he does, then there must yet be hope even for a Job, even for a man deep in the night of tribulation."[108] Just like the psalmist, Job experiences God both as the one who has afflicted him and as his only hope.[109]

6.9.1. Psalms of Supplication in Job

How can mortals motivate the Almighty to act on their behalf? Psalms 139 and 39 offer two opposing possibilities: praise or complaint and threat. Job demonstrates a third: argument. For his case against God, he uses a variety of resources, including the petitions of earlier sufferers, manipulating them to make his suit more persuasive. Adapting acclamation into accusation and surpassing sorrowful supplication, Job takes these psalms in a direction that allows the friends little opportunity for response. Zophar's appeal to the ominous implications of God's omniscience in Psalm 139 only supports Job's point: things are not as they should be, and God must change them. Whether reminding God of how good things can be (Psalm 139) or complaining about how bad they have become (Psalm 39), this is the message of psalmic supplication, one that Job uses these psalms to express.

---

108 Zimmerli, *Hope*, 22.
109 Forster, *Vergänglichkeitsmotiv*, 244–45.

Part III

Instruction

7. From Didactic to Dialogic: Psalm 1 in Job

Job! Job! Job! Job! … a faithful witness to the distress and grief a heart can harbor, a trustworthy advocate who dared to complain "in anguish of spirit" and to contend with God.[1]

So far, I have argued that the author of Job alludes to both psalms of praise (Psalms 8 and 107) and supplication (Psalms 139 and 39), but his use of the Psalter extends to several psalms that do not fit well into these two formal categories that dominate the collection. Among these outliers are psalms generally identified by their content as "wisdom" or by their intent as "didactic." Since "praise" and "supplication" primarily suggest intent, I prefer the label "instruction," which conveys this aspect and agrees with the other terms better.[2] Two psalms, 1 and 73, often included in this disputed category figure prominently in the Job dialogue.[3] In this chapter, I will consider the contribution the former may make to the dispute between Job and the friends. Though the message of Job is often contrasted with that of Psalm 1, rarely is the possibility of an intentional intertextual dialogue between the texts considered.

7.1. Identification

This intertextual relationship between Job and Psalm 1 is most evident in Job 21. In the midst of his discourse on the prosperity of the wicked, Job interjects his rejection of their "counsel," using the phrase עצת רשעים ("counsel[4] of the wicked") which only appears outside Job in Ps 1:1:

---

1   Søren Kierkegaard, *Repetition* (trans. W. Lowrie; Princeton: Princeton University Press, 1941), 110–11.

2   See p. 36 n. 99.

3   For a recent discussion of the debate surrounding this category, which includes Psalms 1 and 73 within it, see J. Kenneth Kuntz, "Reclaiming Biblical Wisdom Psalms: A Response to Crenshaw," *CBR* 1 (2003): 145–54.

4   Roland Bergmeier and Dahood argue that עצה in עצת רשעים means "council" and not "counsel," however G. W. Anderson responds that the "obvious meaning" of the phrase X בעצת הלך is "to follow the advice (adopt the principles) of X" as 2 Chr 22:5 indicates. See Dahood, *Psalms,* 1:1; Roland Bergmeier, "Zum Ausdruck עצת רשעים in Ps 1:1, Hi 10:3, 21:16 und 22:18," *ZAW* 79 (1967): 229–32; G. W. Anderson, "A Note on Psalm i 1," *VT* 24 (1974): 232.

Job 21:16

הֵן לֹא בְיָדָם טוּבָם עֲצַת רְשָׁעִים רָחֲקָה מֶנִּי   Is not their prosperity indeed their own
                                                  achievement?
                                                  The plans of the wicked are repugnant to
                                                  me.

Ps 1:1

אַשְׁרֵי־הָאִישׁ אֲשֶׁר לֹא הָלַךְ בַּעֲצַת רְשָׁעִים וּבְדֶרֶךְ   Happy are those
חַטָּאִים לֹא עָמָד וּבְמוֹשַׁב לֵצִים לֹא יָשָׁב   who do not follow the advice of the
                                                  wicked,
                                                  or take the path that sinners tread,
                                                  or sit in the seat of scoffers …

Two verses later, Job uses the same imagery of wind-blown chaff as the psalmist.
This image is more common, appearing six times in the HB:

Job 21:18

יִהְיוּ כְּתֶבֶן לִפְנֵי־רוּחַ וּכְמֹץ גְּנָבַתּוּ סוּפָה   How often are they like straw before the
                                                  wind,
                                                  and like chaff that the storm carries away?

Ps 1:4

לֹא־כֵן הָרְשָׁעִים כִּי אִם־כַּמֹּץ אֲשֶׁר־תִּדְּפֶנּוּ רוּחַ   The wicked are not so,
                                                  but are like chaff that the wind drives
                                                  away.

Ps 35:5

יִהְיוּ כְּמֹץ לִפְנֵי־רוּחַ וּמַלְאַךְ יְהוָה דּוֹחֶה   Let them be like chaff before the wind,
                                                  with the angel of the LORD driving them
                                                  on.

Ps 83:14

אֱלֹהַי שִׁיתֵמוֹ כַגַּלְגַּל כְּקַשׁ לִפְנֵי־רוּחַ   O my God, make them like whirling dust,
                                                  like chaff before the wind.

Isa 17:13

לְאֻמִּים כִּשְׁאוֹן מַיִם רַבִּים יִשָּׁאוּן וְגָעַר בּוֹ וְנָס   The nations roar like the roaring of many
מִמֶּרְחָק וְרֻדַּף כְּמֹץ הָרִים לִפְנֵי־רוּחַ וּכְגַלְגַּל לִפְנֵי   waters,
סוּפָה   but he will rebuke them, and they will flee
                                                  far away,
                                                  chased like chaff on the mountains before
                                                  the wind
                                                  and whirling dust before the storm.

Hos 13:3

לָכֵן יִהְיוּ כַּעֲנַן־בֹּקֶר וְכַטַּל מַשְׁכִּים הֹלֵךְ כְּמֹץ יְסֹעֵר   Therefore they shall be like the morning
מִגֹּרֶן וּכְעָשָׁן מֵאֲרֻבָּה   mist
                                                  or like the dew that goes away early,
                                                  like chaff that swirls from the threshing
                                                  floor
                                                  or like smoke from a window.

Job 21:18 and Ps 1:4 share the rare word מץ ("chaff"), which only appears eight times in the HB. The combination of this word with רוח ("wind") is rarer still, appearing a mere four times. However, the other two texts which share these words are linguistically closer to Job than Ps 1:4. The first half of Ps 35:5 is almost exactly the same as the first half of Job 21:18, though the word תבן ("straw"), is replaced with מץ from the second half of the verse in Job. Though without this degree of syntactical similarity, Isa 17:13 also shares the word סופה ("whirlwind") with Job and is the only other verse to combine those three nouns. Ps 83:14 uses another word for "chaff" (קש), but is still closer syntactically to Job than Ps 1:4 and mentions a "whirlwind" (סופה) two verses later (v. 16).

In light of the relatively common use of this imagery in the HB,[5] one might conclude that Job is simply using a typical formula to express his frustration at how the wicked elude the destruction they deserve. If Job is alluding to a specific passage, it would seem that those with closer lexical parallels, such as Ps 35:5 or Isa 17:13, would be better candidates. However, despite this, several scholars have argued that Job is alluding to a specific passage, and they all suggest the passage he has in mind is Psalm 1.[6] To justify this view, Dhorme, Clines, and Gerald Wilson all appeal to the proximity of Job's reference to the "counsel of the wicked" two verses before. Two more commentators, who stop short of affirming Job's dependence on the psalm, still claim that Job is questioning the statement in Psalm 1.[7] In a sense, Job is disputing all the passages, but Psalm 1 stands out because it alone addresses the wicked generally, as does Job, instead of the psalmist's enemies (Pss 35:5; 83:14), the nations (Isa 17:13), or Israel (Hos 13:3). In fact, the word רשעים ("wicked") does not appear anywhere in the vicinity of the other verses.

Because Job 21:18 does not agree completely with any one of these passages but shares different lexical components with several of them, it is unlikely that the author copied this image from any one of them specifically. His word choice is probably informed by several of the passages. However, because of the thematic similarity of this passage in Job and Psalm 1 and the combination of the chaff imagery with the phrase "counsel of the wicked" unique to Job and Psalm 1, it seems fair to conclude that, though the exact wording is not what the Job poet had in mind, he is primarily alluding to the image as it was used in Psalm 1. In

---

5   See Gustaf Hermann Dalman, *Arbeit und Sitte in Palästina* (7 vols.; SDPI; Hildesheim: Georg Olms, 1964), 3:138.

6   See Friedrich Umbreit, *Das Buch Hiob* (2nd ed.; Heidelberg: Mohr, 1832), 211; Dhorme, *Job*, 16; Clines, *Job*, 2:529; Gerald Henry Wilson, *Job* (NIBCOT; Peabody, Mass.: Hendrickson, 2007), 231. Ambrose noted this similarity between the two passages in the fourth century C.E., as did Luther in the sixteenth (Ambrose, "Prayer," 364; Martin Luther, *Selected Psalms* [3 vols.; Luther's Works 12–14; St. Louis: Concordia, 1955–1958], 3:306).

7   Delitzsch, *Job*, 1:407; Rowley, *Job*, 149.

fact, the verse between these two possible allusions to Psalm 1, Job 21:17, in which Job freely adapts language from Bildad's speech in 18:5, indicates the loose manner in which Job often alludes to earlier texts.[8]

7.2. Date

As it now stands, Psalm 1 serves as an introduction to the compiled Psalter. If it was composed for this position, as some believe, it would be quite late, possibly in the first century B.C.E.[9] However, if the psalm was merely chosen for this position,[10] it could have been composed significantly earlier in Israel's history. Just how much earlier depends primarily on two aspects of the psalm: its parallels to other texts in the HB,[11] and its possible indications of late Israelite thought, primarily those related to torah and wisdom.[12] However, no general consensus has been reached on the first issue,[13] and the widespread agreement on the latter does little to determine a definitive date, since the diachronic development of these ideas is uncertain.[14] If an interest in these topics did only develop late in Israel's history, then E. Lipinski's suggestion of a date as late as the fourth or third century B.C.E. would be reasonable.[15] However, even Lipinski acknowledges that the psalm likely had some existence in the oral culture of Israel long before it was written down.[16] Therefore, though a postexilic date may be more likely, Kraus

---

8   See p. 47.

9   Duhm, *Psalmen*, 5.

10   Weiser, *Psalms*, 102; Craigie, *Psalms*, 59.

11   These parallels include: Deut 6:4–6 and 2 Chr 22:5 // Ps 1:1; Josh 1:8 and Mal 3:22 // Ps 1:2; Ps 52:10, Ps 92:13–15, Ezek 47:12 and Josh 1:7 // Ps 1:3; and Jer 17:5–8 // Ps 1:3–4.

12   E.g., Gunkel, *Psalmen*, 3; Anderson, *Psalms*, 1:57.

13   The parallel with Jeremiah, which is the strongest, has received the most discussion, but the direction of dependence and even its existence remain inconclusive. See E. Lipinski, "Macarismes et psaumes de congratulation," *RB* 75 (1968): 336; Robert P. Carroll, *Jeremiah: A Commentary* (OTL; London: SCM Press, 1986), 351; William L. Holladay, *Jeremiah* (2 vols.; Hermeneia; Philadelphia: Fortress Press, 1986–1989), 490; Jerome F. Creach, "Like a Tree Planted by the Temple Stream: The Portrait of the Righteous in Ps 1:3," *CBQ* 61 (1999): 38. Most scholars who address the issue seem to assume, with the exception of 2 Chr 22:5, that the psalmist is alluding to the other texts, but generally because they have already concluded that the psalm is late for other reasons, e.g., Briggs, *Psalms*, 1:3; Phil J. Botha, "Intertextuality and the Interpretation of Psalm 1," in *Psalms and Mythology* (ed. Dirk J. Human; JSOTSup 462; New York: T&T Clark, 2007), 72.

14   For skepticism toward a linear diachronic development of wisdom thought, see Dell, "Development," 135–51.

15   Lipinski, "Macarismes," 338. Similarly, P. Auvray, "Le Psaume 1. Notes de grammaire et d'exégèse," *RB* 53 (1946): 371.

16   In Lipinski's view, the psalm is a paraphrase of an ancient chant of blessing (Lipinski,

judiciously concludes that the psalm's time of composition "can hardly be determined."[17]

7.3. Coherence

If the similarity between Job 21:16, 18 and Ps 1:1, 4 is the result of an allusion from one to the other, external coherence is once again the best indicator of the direction of dependence. Job's questioning of God's consistency in actually carrying out this punishment on the wicked (cf. 21:17) demonstrates that his text is likely later. If the psalmist were to refer to this passage from Job, in which he complains that the wicked often prosper, he would undercut his argument entirely. Consequently, Friedrich Umbreit claims that Job is responding to "eine einseitige und lieblose" interpretation of Psalm 1.[18] The lack of internal coherence between the words taken from Ps 1:1 in Job's affirmation, "The plans of the wicked are repugnant to me," which has led many to attempt to remove the phrase as a pious gloss[19] or emend the statement "from me" (מני) at the end of the verse to "from him," referring to God,[20] further supports this direction of dependence as it highlights the foreign element within it which likely results from the allusion to another text.

7.4. Use

In ch. 21, Job subjects the ruinous fate of the wicked, a favorite argument of his prosecutorial friends, to a blistering cross-examination. In ch. 18, Bildad had called the experience of the wicked to the witness stand and stated that their light is surely extinguished (Job 18:5). With a possible contrasting allusion to the image

---

"Macarismes," 330). Similarly, Terrien suggests the oral form of the psalm "may go back to early Yahwistic wisdom or the courts of Solomon and Hezekiah" (Terrien, *Psalms*, 75).

17   Kraus, *Psalms*, 1:114.

18   Umbreit, *Hiob*, 211.

19   E.g., C. J. Ball, *The Book of Job* (Oxford: Clarendon Press, 1922), 291; Fohrer, *Hiob*, 338; Pope, *Job*, 159. Clines, however, prefers to avoid this "counsel of despair" and instead attempt to understand the verse in its context (Clines, *Job*, 2:509).

20   This would make the original Hebrew agree with the LXX. See, E.g., Kissane, *Psalms*, 136; Dhorme, *Job*, 316; Clines, *Job*, 2:510. The orthography (מני instead of the expected ממני) is admittedly unusual, but it may be an archaic and rare form of the word (Gordis, *Job*, 230). With its implicit accusation of God, "from me" is the *lectio difficilior*, which provides further reason to prefer the MT over the possible theological correction in the LXX, which shows a proclivity to soften Job's attacks against God.

of the healthy, well-watered tree of Ps 1:3, he added, "their roots dry up beneath, and their branches wither above" (Job 18:16).[21] In response, appealing to both the posterity (Job 21:8, 11) and general prosperity (v. 13) of the wicked, Job progresses toward a direct refutation of Bildad's argument, which comes in a series of rhetorical questions: "How often is the lamp of the wicked put out? How often does calamity come upon them? How often does God distribute pains in his anger?" (v. 17). He then takes on Psalm 1: "How often are they like straw before the wind, and like chaff that the storm carries away?" (v. 18; cf. Ps 1:4).[22] Because Job has experienced this affliction, which the wicked deserve,[23] as Delitzsch says, he "puts in the form of a question what Ps. 1. maintains."[24]

When Job appends a question mark to the affirmation of Ps 1:4, is he rebutting the psalm in the same way that he is disputing the belief of the friends, particularly Bildad, in the wicked's destruction? Job's allusion to Ps 1:1 two verses earlier indicates that, as Wilson puts it, "the retributive theology of Ps. 1 may lurk behind Job's comments."[25] But, can Job reject his friends' narrow understanding of that theology without discarding it altogether? Wilson thinks so.[26] He believes that despite Job's confusion, frustration, anger, and near despair at things not working out according to his expectations based on the accepted wisdom tradition, he remains faithful. And thus, in this speech, Job struggles with Psalm 1, but he does not reject it. Instead, in Job's parody of the psalm,[27] Wilson claims, "Job is contesting a naïve reading of that psalm in light of his own experience." Job longs for "comfort," but, since his experience seems to be the exception to the retributive rule, a strict application of the doctrine is an "empty nothing" (21:34). However, no doctrine of justice in the world would be just as hollow.

This interpretation of Job's allusion to Ps 1:4 in 21:18 helps explain his allusion to Ps 1:1 two verses earlier. Though some attempt to remove or emend Job's apparent *non sequitur*, "the plans of the wicked are repugnant to me," read in the context of Psalm 1, this verse becomes an affirmation of Job's righteousness. The prosperity of the wicked, which Job has just described and which is *far from* his current experience, indicates things are the opposite of the way the psalm depicts them. However, not only is Job far from the counsel of the wicked in relation to their respective fates, he is also far from it in terms of his rejection of it. The

---

21   Bildad may have already alluded to Ps 1:3 in 8:11–13. See p. 154 n. 50.

22   Andersen notes how Job questions the affirmations of both Bildad and the psalmist (Andersen, *Job*, 200).

23   Habel, *Job*, 328.

24   Delitzsch, *Job*, 1:407.

25   Wilson, *Job*, 229.

26   Wilson, *Job*, 228–29.

27   Clines, following Fohrer, suggests ch. 21 may be a "parody of a traditional form of wisdom instruction, the poem on the blessedness of the pious" (Clines, *Job*, 2:520).

phrase is most commonly understood as a disavowal of the wicked and their ways,[28] even as an expression of Job's piety.[29] Set in this wider context, it also becomes a declaration of his righteousness because, even though he has seen that the wicked actually prosper, he acts like the blessed person in Ps 1:1, who does not walk in the "counsel of the wicked."[30] His piety is therefore not for gain; it is the type of חנם ("for nothing") piety the Satan thought was impossible (1:9).[31] With this allusion, Job even suggests he is more righteous than God, who seems to favor the "counsel of the wicked" (10:3).[32]

7.5. Recurrence

7.5.1. Eliphaz: 5:13–14

The type of one-sided and uncharitable interpretation of Psalm 1 to which Umbreit claims Job is responding is evident in Eliphaz's allusions to the psalm. The first appears in his opening speech:

Job 5:13–14

לֹכֵד חֲכָמִים בְּעָרְמָם וַעֲצַת נִפְתָּלִים נִמְהָרָה 13 He takes the wise in their own craftiness;
and the schemes of the wily are brought
to a quick end.

יוֹמָם יְפַגְּשׁוּ־חֹשֶׁךְ וְכַלַּיְלָה יְמַשְׁשׁוּ בַצָּהֳרָיִם 14 They meet with darkness in the daytime,
and grope at noonday as in the night.

Ps 1:1–2

אַשְׁרֵי־הָאִישׁ אֲשֶׁר לֹא הָלַךְ בַּעֲצַת רְשָׁעִים 1 Happy are those
וּבְדֶרֶךְ חַטָּאִים לֹא עָמָד וּבְמוֹשַׁב לֵצִים לֹא יָשָׁב who do not follow the advice of the
wicked,
or take the path that sinners tread,
or sit in the seat of scoffers

כִּי אִם בְּתוֹרַת יְהוָה חֶפְצוֹ וּבְתוֹרָתוֹ יֶהְגֶּה יוֹמָם 2 but their delight is in the law of the
וָלָיְלָה LORD,
and on his law they meditate day and
night.

---

28 E.g., Delitzsch, *Job*, 1:405; Davidson, *Job*, 156; Habel, *Job*, 328.
29 Gordis, *Job*, 230; Janzen, *Job*, 159. Newsom believes he is actually mimicking piety (Newsom, "Job," 492).
30 Wilson, *Job*, 229. Dhorme also believes this to be an allusion to Psalm 1 (Dhorme, *Job*, 315). Both Alonso Schökel and Clines think an allusion is possible (Alonso Schökel and Sicre Díaz, *Job*, 74; Clines, *Job*, 2:528).
31 See Rowley, *Job*, 156.
32 See pp. 152–153.

To accentuate his warning to Job, Eliphaz expresses the psalm's message negatively, describing the downfall of the "schemes of the wily" (עצת נפתלים). Eliphaz
intends to entreat Job to avoid them like the blessed person in Psalm 1 does.[33]
This shared combination of עצה in construct with either a participle or adjective
representing a negative group of people does not appear elsewhere in the HB,[34]
and neither do the three words עצה, יומם, and לילה in such close proximity.[35]
Eliphaz uses the latter two words to reinforce his message by presenting the negative equivalent of the image that follows in the psalm of the continual meditation on the law of the Lord both day (יומם) and night (לילה). He keeps his focus
on the wicked, who, instead of meditating, meet with darkness by day (יומם) just
as if it were night (לילה).[36] Though Eliphaz transforms the positive image in the
psalm into a negative one, he only does so to underscore the psalm's message: the
righteous prosper while the wicked are destroyed.

7.5.2. Job: 10:3

However, the message of Psalm 1 directly contradicts Job's experience. He is one
of the righteous, and yet, instead of experiencing God's blessing, he suffers. In
his life, everything is backward, so he responds to Eliphaz's allusion to Ps 1:1
with one of his own, in which he reverses the psalm's imagery. In 10:3, he asks
God, "Does it seem good to you to oppress, to despise the work of your hands
and favor the schemes of the wicked [עֲצַת רְשָׁעִים]?"[37] With this word combination, which is unique to Job and Psalm 1, Job's allusion expresses in a few words
the exact opposite of what is said in Psalm 1, for not the pious but the godless
receive God's approbation.[38] Job's use of this phrase does not merely refute Eliphaz's by suggesting that instead of bringing the "schemes of the wily" (עצת
נפתלים) to a quick end (5:13), God chooses to "favor" them, it also attacks God
for this unjust behavior.[39] This allusion contrasts God with pious wise men who,

---

33   Fohrer, *Hiob*, 151.

34   The closest parallel is the "plans of the poor" (עצת עני) in Ps 14:6, but "poor" represents a posi-
     tive group there.

35   אשרי ("blessed"), the first word of Psalm 1, also appears for the only time in Job three verses
     later (5:17).

36   This combination of Hebrew words is common, appearing forty times in the HB, but its prox-
     imity to the previous image suggests that Eliphaz still has Psalm 1 in view.

37   Several scholars note the similarity between the passages without further comment, e.g., Gunkel,
     Psalmen, 4; Kissane, *Psalms*, 1:2.

38   Bergmeier, "Ausdruck," 231.

39   Clines notes the "deliberate irony" in applying to the wicked the verb יפע, which is used in
     psalmic language of "God's self-manifestation in order to bring salvation (cf. Deut 33:2; Ps 50:2;
     80:3 [2]; 94:1)" (Clines, *Job*, 1:245).

unlike God, do not follow the "counsel of the wicked."[40] However, Job's parody does not condemn the psalm itself, because the force of Job's argument relies on God agreeing with the psalmist that favoring the wicked's counsel is wrong.

Job's use of these few words to respond to Eliphaz and draw Psalm 1 into this accusation of God indicates that they are not "rather lame" and worthy of omission,[41] but a powerful contribution to his case against God. The suggestion that the phrase is a gloss[42] does indicate, though, that it fits the text uncomfortably, which could result from the importation of this phrase from Psalm 1.

7.5.3. Job: 13:25

In ch. 13, Job's words continue to bristle with irony and parody, and another allusion to Psalm 1 contributes to his case against God. Again the dagger at the end of his accusation is curled into a question mark, as he asks, "Will you frighten a windblown leaf and pursue dry chaff?" (Job 13:25). Like David, who asks Saul, "Against whom has the king of Israel come out? Whom do you pursue? A dead dog? A single flea?" (1 Sam 24:15),[43] Job appeals to the "dizzying lack of proportion" of God exerting divine might against a creature as fragile as himself.[44]

Job sharpens the point of his divinely directed rhetorical dagger with a parody of Ps 1:3–4:

Job 13:25

הֶעָלֶה נִדָּף תַּעֲרוֹץ וְאֶת־קַשׁ יָבֵשׁ תִּרְדֹּף   Will you frighten a windblown leaf
                                                            and pursue dry chaff?

Ps 1:3–4

וְהָיָה כְּעֵץ שָׁתוּל עַל־פַּלְגֵי מָיִם אֲשֶׁר פִּרְיוֹ יִתֵּן   3 They are like trees
בְּעִתּוֹ וְעָלֵהוּ לֹא־יִבּוֹל וְכֹל אֲשֶׁר־יַעֲשֶׂה יַצְלִיחַ   planted by streams of water,
                                                            which yield their fruit in its season,
                                                            and their leaves do not wither.
                                                            In all that they do, they prosper.

לֹא־כֵן הָרְשָׁעִים כִּי אִם־כַּמֹּץ אֲשֶׁר־תִּדְּפֶנּוּ רוּחַ   4 The wicked are not so,
                                                            but are like chaff that the wind drives
                                                            away.

According to Ps 1:3, the righteous should expect to be like a tree whose leaf does not wither, but by reversing the image, Job contrasts his experience with what the

---

40   Frevel, "Schöpfungsglaube," 491.
41   Driver and Gray, *Job*, 98.
42   E.g., Fohrer, *Hiob*, 200.
43   Dhorme, *Job*, 191; Newsom, "Job," 439.
44   Clines, *Job*, 1:320.

psalm teaches.[45] As Pope observes, the withering leaf is a rather common image for the destruction of the wicked (he mentions Isa 1:30; 34:4; 64:6; Jer 8:13; Ezek 47:12; Ps 1:3), and windblown chaff is also used several times with the same meaning (Pope notes Pss 1:4; 83:14,[46] but the other passages which refer to chaff listed above could be included: Isa 17:13; Hos 13:3; Ps 35:5; Job 21:18). However, Pope concludes with respect to Job 13:25, that "the use of both leaf and chaff in the sense of a helpless and insignificant victim of such overwhelming power occurs nowhere else in the [Old Testament]."[47] But he has just mentioned both Ps 1:3 and Ps 1:4 as parallels to each of these images;[48] though it does not describe the power imbalance so starkly, there *is* one other place where the images are combined: Psalm 1. In fact, Job 13:25 and Ps 1:3–4 are the only two passages in the HB in which the word עלה ("leaf") and either word for "chaff" (קש or מץ) appear together. Beyond that, both Job and the psalm use the rare verb נדף ("to drive away"), which only appears nine times in the HB. Job plays on that verb in the second half of the verse by using the aurally similar word רדף ("to pursue").

In the psalm, vv. 3 and 4 are connected by the contrast they together create between the righteous person as a tree solidly planted by streams of water and the wicked as chaff defenseless against the wind.[49] It is natural for Job to appeal to both at once.[50] However, as he does so, he associates himself with the wicked, and, by attributing the wicked's punishment to God, even goes further than the psalm, which leaves divine agency in judgment unmentioned.[51] This corresponds with the previous verse, in which Job asks why God considers him an "enemy" (13:24).

---

45   See Clines, *Job*, 1:320.

46   The latter, like Job 13:25, uses the word קש, which may be better translated "straw," but still communicates the same idea of insignificance. See Dalman, *Arbeit*, 3:137; Rowley, *Job*, 101; HALOT.

47   Pope, *Job*, 102.

48   Alonso Schökel also notes the parallel to Ps 1:3 and C. J. Ball notes the parallel to Ps 1:4 (Alonso Schökel and Sicre Díaz, *Job*, 229; Ball, *Job*, 226).

49   Thus, the midrash on Psalm 1 claims the verb שתל used to describe the tree's planting emphasizes that "even if all the winds come and blow at the righteous man, they will be unable to budge him from his place" (Braude, *Midrash on Psalms*, 1:14).

50   This allusion may also be a response to a possible allusion to the tree imagery in Psalm 1 by Bildad in 8:11–13, where he refers to the need plants have for water to grow and then states that "the hope of the godless will perish," a phrase that has syntactical and lexical affinities with Ps 1:6, where the way of the wicked perishes (cf. also Prov 10:28). See Pyeon, *Intertextuality*, 151–52; Botha, "Psalm 1," 69.

51   "Explicit judgment by Yahweh is conspicuously absent in Ps 1" (Botha, "Psalm 1," 62 n. 14).

7.5.4. Eliphaz: 22:18

In the chapter after Job's allusion to Ps 1:1, 4 in 21:16, 18, Eliphaz co-opts Job's allusion to Ps 1:1 by repeating it exactly in 22:18, likely with heavy emphasis on the word "me" at the end: "but the plans of the wicked (עצת רשעים) are repugnant to *me*" (22:18).[52] Because of the disputative context of the statement, Eliphaz likely intends this allusion, not to mean the same thing as Job's disavowal of the wicked, as is sometimes suggested,[53] but to respond to Job's argument in ch. 21 that the wicked often prosper by associating Job himself with the wicked (v. 5).[54] He asserts, alluding to Job's own affliction, that it is, indeed, the wicked who suffer,[55] and the truly righteous person will enjoy this judgment that Job denies (v. 19).[56] Thus, Eliphaz attempts once again to reaffirm the strict retributive understanding of the psalm, as both Job 22:18 and Ps 1:1 "assume that the duty of the righteous is to avoid association with those self-focused persons who deny the power of God in their lives."[57] Whereas 21:16b is "Job's mimicking of a typical pious platitude," Eliphaz "restores it to its non-ironic, non-sarcastic meaning."[58]

7.5.5. Job: 23:10–11

Job, however, refuses to submit to Eliphaz's interpretation of the psalm because it contradicts his experience. In his response in the next chapter, he makes a final allusion to Psalm 1:

Job 23:10–11

כִּי־יָדַע דֶּרֶךְ עִמָּדִי בְּחָנַנִי כַּזָּהָב אֵצֵא	10 But he knows the way that I take; when he has tested me, I shall come out like gold.
בַּאֲשֻׁרוֹ אָחֲזָה רַגְלִי דַּרְכּוֹ שָׁמַרְתִּי וְלֹא־אָט	11 My foot has held fast to his steps; I have kept his way and have not turned aside.

---

52   This also includes the unusual form of "from me" (מֶנִּי). Some commentators emend the text to
     "from him" here, as well, e.g., Dhorme, *Job*, 334; Clines, *Job*, 2:543. Others consider this passage
     a gloss also, e.g., Ball, *Job*, 300; Fohrer, *Hiob*, 351.
53   E.g., Heinrich A. Ewald, *Commentary on the Book of Job* (trans. J. Frederick Smith; TTFL 28; Lon-
     don: Williams & Norgate, 1882), 234; Gordis, *Job*, 248; Clines, *Job*, 2:560.
54   Delitzsch, *Job*, 1:439; Wilson, *Job*, 246.
55   Driver and Gray, *Job*, 196.
56   Andersen, *Job*, 204.
57   Wilson, *Job*, 247.
58   Newsom, "Job," 492, 502.

Ps 1:1, 6

אַשְׁרֵי־הָאִישׁ אֲשֶׁר לֹא הָלַךְ בַּעֲצַת רְשָׁעִים   1   Happy are those
וּבְדֶרֶךְ   who do not follow the advice of the
חַטָּאִים לֹא עָמָד וּבְמוֹשַׁב לֵצִים לֹא יָשָׁב   wicked,
                                                      or take the path that sinners tread,
                                                      or sit in the seat of scoffers …

כִּי־יוֹדֵעַ יְהוָה דֶּרֶךְ צַדִּיקִים וְדֶרֶךְ רְשָׁעִים תֹּאבֵד   6   for the LORD watches over the way of
                                                       the righteous,
                                                       but the way of the wicked will perish.

Job 23:10a and Ps 1:6a share lexical ("to know" [ידע]; "way" [דרך]), semantic
(similar word order and opening כי), and thematic similarities (God's knowledge
of the way of the righteous).[59] Job's repetition of the word דרך in the following
verse reflects its repeated use in the psalm, and his use of עמדי, which may mean
"with me" or "my standing,"[60] combined with דרך harkens to Ps 1:1, where the
blessed do not "stand" (עמד) in the "way" (דרך) of "sinners."[61] Job's use of the
word אשר ("step") also recalls Ps 1:1 as it is aurally and possibly etymologically
linked to אשרי ("blessed") in that verse.[62] Thus, in the clear influence of psalmic
models in Job's depiction of his piety here,[63] Psalm 1 plays a prominent role.

    This allusion to Psalm 1 carries a double meaning. In a parody of Ps 139:5,
7–10, Job has just accused God of avoiding him (vv. 8–9). Now, he suggests why:
the divine judge knows Job would win his case against him.[64] As Saadiah trans-

---

59   Though ידע and דרך are both common Hebrew words and appear together frequently, in only
     two other passages is the phrase כי ידע combined with דרך (Gen 18:19; Deut 31:29), but in nei-
     ther case are the words so closely connected.

60   For a discussion of the interpretive options, see Clines, *Job*, 2:578.

61   Hartley appeals to the combination of "stand" and "way" in Ps 1:1 as support for reading עמד as
     the infinitive "to stand" in Job (Hartley, *Job*, 339 n. 3). Fohrer also notes the general similarity
     between the two passages (Fohrer, *Hiob*, 366).

62   Goldingay and Schaefer note the wordplay, with the latter appealing to Job 23:11 as an example,
     where the word means "step" (Schaefer, *Psalms*, 3 n. 1; Goldingay, *Psalms*, 1:81–82). See also
     Norman Henry Snaith, "The Language of the Old Testament," in *General Articles on the Old Testa-
     ment* (IB 1; New York: Abingdon Press, 1952), 225. However, James Barr criticizes the purported
     etymological connection between the words because it was "almost certainly unknown and
     unknowable to [the psalmist] and his contemporaries" (James Barr, *The Semantics of Biblical Lan-
     guage* [Oxford: Oxford University Press, 1961], 116). Aaron Rubin claims אשרי actually derives
     from the root שרי (Aaron D. Rubin, "The Form and Meaning of Hebrew *ašrê*," *VT* 60 [2010]:
     366–72). However, even if there is no etymological connection, the aural link between the two
     words still remains.

63   Clines, *Job*, 2:592. See also the use of Ps 139:5, 7–10, 23–24 and Ps 73:2 discussed on pp. 115–
     117, 173–174.

64   Edwin M. Good, *In Turns of Tempest: A Reading of Job* (Stanford, Calif.: Stanford University Press,
     1990), 277.

lates v. 10, "For He knoweth that the way of judgment is with me."[65] Job is sure of his success in a divine trial because he believes what Psalm 1 teaches: the righteous will be blessed. He may have decried the failure of the doctrine of retribution in his previous speech, appealing to the prosperity of the wicked as a compelling counterexample against his friends' strict application of it, but he still trusts in it to some degree as his only hope for justice. So now, ironically, he turns the promise of God in the psalm into an accusation against God for not living up to it. This irony is accentuated by the meaning of the word ידע in the context of Ps 1:6, where, in contrast to the destruction of the wicked, it suggests God's loving protection.[66] Job, however, feels he has experienced exactly the opposite, and sarcasm seethes through his use of the term.

7.6. Holistic Interpretation

In the allusions to Psalm 1 over the course of the dialogue (with Eliphaz again playing a prominent role), the author practices a similar interpretive technique as in his use of Psalms 8, 107, and 139. The friends interpret the psalm woodenly, drawing from it a strict doctrine of retribution to attack Job's attempt to maintain his innocence. This interpretation of the psalm is reflected in several commentators, especially those around the turn of the twentieth century, who also read the psalm as a legalistic replacement of confidence in God with dedication to the law.[67]

In response, Job appeals to the psalm and its implied promise of blessing for the righteous as an accusation against God for apparent injustice. Job parodies retribution to criticize God for not living up to it. However, this cannot be a rejection, because then Job would have no grounds for complaint.[68] As James Crenshaw recognizes, "Job has no case at all against God apart from an operative principle of reward and retribution."[69] Instead, Job's experience pushes him beyond a naive understanding into a more nuanced conception of retribution; one that can allow for the affliction of a righteous man like himself. He comes to grasp that the blessing of the righteous and destruction of the wicked cannot be

---

65   Saadiah, *Job*, 312.

66   For this connotation of the verb in the psalm, see Dahood, *Psalms*, 1:5; Anderson, *Psalms*, 1:63; Craigie, *Psalms*, 57–58.

67   D. Rudolph Kittel, *Die Psalmen* (KAT 13; Leipzig: A Deichertsche Verlagsbuchhandlung, 1914), 5; Gunkel, *Psalmen*, 2; Buttenwieser, *Psalms*, 851.

68   Heckl, *Hiob*, 208.

69   Crenshaw, *Whirlpool*, 62. He goes on to remark that Job's attack against retribution and "eventual rejection of its fundamental premise render his argument highly suspect." But, if his attack is intended to motivate God to rectify this injustice, then Job's arguments are coherent.

as immediate as his friends believe, but must be deferred to some future time
when the hidden God finally comes to judge (23:8–11). And thus, because he
knows he is righteous (e.g., ch. 31), he pleads for that judgment (e.g., 31:35).[70]

7.7. Reciprocation

The psalm's message may at first seem straightforward, so that, as Brueggemann
remarks, it presents no middle ground and "does not bargain or allow for ambiguity."[71] The psalmist depicts life as a simple binary opposition: the righteous are
blessed and the wicked destroyed. But when considered in light of the Psalter's
laments, the disparity between the just portrait of life in Psalm 1 and the injustice
which makes other psalmists wail, "Why?" (Pss 10:1; 22:2; 42:10, etc.), is glaring,
inviting the charge of naivety. However, the psalm's mention of coming judgment
and its internal tension both suggest it is not as naive as it seems, which corresponds with Job's allusions.[72]

Like Job, the psalmist actually appears to believe retribution can be delayed,
which reconciles his message with the laments. This delay is reflected in some
interpretations, both ancient and modern, of Ps 1:5: "Therefore the wicked will
not stand in the judgment, nor sinners in the congregation of the righteous." The
LXX claims the wicked will not "rise" (ἀναστήσονται) in the judgment, which
may express an eschatological perspective. In the Targum, "the judgment"
becomes "the great day of judgment,"[73] which alludes to the "day of the Lord" so
prominent in prophetic literature. Ewald claims the end of the psalm is "quite
prophetical, indeed Messianic," expressing "the hope of a Divine judgment," and
Dahood also believes "the final judgment" which "will take place in the heavenly
council" is in view.[74] And though some would disagree with this eschatological
reading of the psalm,[75] it need not be so theologically well-defined to correspond
with Job's argument. It need only hold out the promise of a judgment to come

---

70 In this he is similar to the author of Psalm 86, who in vv. 2–3 appeals to his righteousness as a
    reason why God in his justice should deliver him. See Hayyim Angel, "The Differences Between
    the Wise and the Foolish in Psalms: Theodicy, Understanding Providence, and Religious
    Responses," *JBQ* 38 (2010): 158–59.

71 Walter Brueggemann, *The Message of the Psalms: A Theological Commentary* (AOTS; Minneapolis:
    Augsburg, 1984), 39.

72 For defenses of the psalm against the charge of naivety, see McCann, "Psalms," 684; C. J. S.
    Lombaard, "By Implication: Didactical Strategy in Psalm 1," *OTE* 12 (1999): 507; Oeming,
    Psalmen, 52.

73 Stec, *Targum of Psalms*, 29.

74 Ewald, *Psalms*, 1:320; Dahood, *Psalms*, 1:4.

75 E.g., Craigie, *Psalms*, 61; Goldingay, *Psalms*, 1:87.

some day, some way to right the scales of justice. Thus, Goldingay considers the psalm a "preemptive strike" on the suffering and lament in the Psalter, as it "invites the godly to set such experiences in the context of its promise."[76]

In fact, whether final or not, as long as the judgment mentioned in Ps 1:5 is not immediate, it demonstrates that on closer consideration, particularly as the psalm is applied to Job's case by Job and Eliphaz, the external tension the psalm has with other psalms in the Psalter may be internal as well. Despite its explicit declaration of retributive justice, it implicitly acknowledges exceptions to this rule. For some indefinite amount of time before their judgment, the wicked may prosper. Additionally, the promise that the leaf of the righteous will not wither "smuggles in a threatening aspect to the psalm" by tacitly recognizing some threat to the righteous precisely because of their righteousness.[77] Similarly, the proclamation of the wicked's wind-driven fate does not guarantee the righteous exemption from the blustery vicissitudes of life, just assurance of withstanding them.[78]

The psalm, therefore, does not promise immediate punishment for the wicked or freedom from suffering for the righteous, but eventual justice and the power to persevere. In this way, instead of being naive and legalistic, Psalm 1 has a "consolatory character," as Hengstenberg describes it, enlivening the hope of the righteous and filling them with confidence, "that every thing which now appears contrary to their hope, shall come to an end; the judgment of God shall remove the offences, which were caused by the temporal prosperity of the wicked, and the troubles thence accruing to them."[79] Thus, if Job, who perseveres to see justice eventually, does indeed appeal to Psalm 1 against God, he demonstrates how Eliphaz's wooden and legalistic interpretation of the psalm may itself be naive, when, actually, "The words of the psalm are words of faith."[80]

7.8. Historical Implications

In his study of the diachronic development of the doctrine of retribution, Samuel Adams traces how its focus progressed from the earthly in Egyptian instructions to the eschatological in 4QInstruction.[81] Along the way, Ecclesiastes countered

---

76   Goldingay, *Psalms*, 1:90.

77   Goldingay, *Psalms*, 1:85.

78   The midrash acknowledges this. See p. 154 n. 49.

79   Hengstenberg, *Psalms*, 1:2.

80   Luther, *Psalms*, 3:291. Thus, Angel summarizes the message of Psalm 1 as "In the end, all will be righted, so be patient" and calls it a "confident declaration of faith" (Angel, "Differences," 160, 163).

81   Samuel L. Adams, *Wisdom in Transition: Act and Consequence in Second Temple Instructions* (JSJSup 125; Leiden: Brill, 2008).

the confidence in retribution found in Proverbs with the argument that death denies significance to human action and Ben Sira mounted an apologetic response to individual immortality in order to defend God's justice without resorting to post-mortem possibilities. Because Job is "not a formal instruction," Adams does not discuss the book in depth, but he does claim its author "was aware of the changing modes of discourse."[82] Adams argues that Job, Ecclesiastes, and Ben Sira demonstrate that "various figures began to see weaknesses in the standard retributive model."[83] Whether Job shares the rejection of an afterlife that Adams suggests is evident in the other two books is open to debate, but the way Job waits for God's vindicating judgment (23:10–11; cf. 31:35), a delayed retribution only implied in Psalm 1, at least provides a step on the path from the earthly to the otherworldly in Second Temple instruction that Adams has identified.

7.9. Conclusion

Once again, the dialogical nature of the author of Job's interpretation of a psalm prizes open the tensions within it. By embodying the naive interpretation of Psalm 1 in Eliphaz and causing Job to counter it through his own experience, the author displays the psalm's potential to offer hope in the midst of affliction. Job joins in the cries of the psalmic laments, and thus a naive understanding of Psalm 1 would be a natural target for his animus. However, Job would accomplish little by rejecting the psalm's vision of life. What he wants is for its "promise," to use Goldingay's term, to apply to his life, since he believes his righteousness entitles him to the blessing the psalm describes, just as he had formerly experienced (Job 1:2–3; 29:1–25). Therefore, though he parodies the psalm, as with other psalms (e.g., Psalms 8, 107, 139), he does so not to reject its message but to appeal to it as an accusation against God. Through his reinterpretation of retribution, Job's experience parallels that of the author of Psalm 73, the psalm to which we now turn.

---

82   Adams, *Wisdom*, 135 n. 107.
83   Adams, *Wisdom*, 274.

8. Re-interpreting Retribution: Psalm 73 in Job

Contre Dieu, Job convoque Dieu. C'est un défi à la logique.[1]

Because of its common struggle with the message of Psalm 1, Gunkel calls Psalm 73 a "Hiob-Psalm."[2] Similarly, Kissane observes that the two texts address the same theme: "How can the doctrine of the justice of God be reconciled with the facts of experience?"[3] However, despite Hubert Irsigler's proclamation that, "It is unmistakable and uncontested that Psalm 73 shows a special proximity to the book of Job,"[4] the possibility of direct dependence between them has not been fully pursued.[5] Buttenwieser, who considers the texts so closely related that he suggests the same author wrote them both, claims that similar passages in Job "may serve as the most illuminating commentary on the psalm."[6] On the other hand, after tracing the lexical connections between the two texts, Luyten states that if Schüngel-Straumann can suggest that Psalm 139 is a commentary on Job, "the same is true to an even greater extent of Ps., 73."[7] A detailed study of the parallels between the two texts will suggest that, just as with Psalm 139, the Job poet is commenting on the psalm and that the interaction is even more direct than Buttenwieser imagines it, as imagery from Psalm 73 informs the dialogue between Job and his friends, especially Job's final clash with Eliphaz.

---

1   Bernard Sarrazin, "Du rire dans la Bible: La théophanie de Job comme parodie," *RSR* 76 (1988): 50.

2   Hermann Gunkel, "Die Psalmen," in *Zur Neueren Psalmenforschung* (ed. Peter H. A. Neumann; WdF 192; Darmstadt: Wissenschaftliche Buchgesellschaft, 1976), 53.

3   Kissane, *Psalms*, 2:1.

4   Hubert Irsigler, "Quest for Justice as Reconciliation for the Poor and the Righteous in Psalms 37, 49 and 73," *ZABR* 5 (1999): 265.

5   Jos Luyten has made the fullest investigation to date, but his intent is primarily to justify the classification of Psalm 73 as "wisdom," not to interpret the intertextual connections between the texts, and he stops short of affirming dependence in one direction or the other. See Jos Luyten, "Psalm 73 and Wisdom," in *La Sagesse de l'Ancien Testament* (ed. Maurice Gilbert; Gembloux: J. Duculot, 1979), 59–81.

6   Buttenwieser, *Psalms*, 528.

7   Luyten, "Psalm 73," 81; cf. Schüngel-Straumann, "Gattung," 51. Luyten takes a step back from this suggestion in the next sentence: "Whatever their mutual relations may be, Job and Ps., 73 betray the same cultural and spiritual climate and perhaps the times of their composition are not so greatly separated."

8.1. Identification

Though several words and images from Psalm 73 prepare the reader along the way, the most marked allusion to the psalm does not appear until ch. 22. There Eliphaz puts the words of the wicked in Psalm 73 into Job's mouth:

Job 22:13

וְאָמַרְתָּ מַה־יָּדַע אֵל הַבְעַד עֲרָפֶל יִשְׁפּוֹט   Therefore you say, "What does God know? Can he judge through the deep darkness?"

Ps 73:11

וְאָמְרוּ אֵיכָה יָדַע־אֵל וְיֵשׁ דֵּעָה בְעֶלְיוֹן   And they say, "How can God know? Is there knowledge in the Most High?"

The first halves of both verses are nearly identical with the exception of the change from third to second person for the verb אמר ("to say") and the use of the interrogative מה ("what?") instead of איכה ("how?" or "what?"; cf. 2 Kings 6:15[8]) in Job. Eliphaz's reference to God's height in the previous verse, where he asks, "Is not God high in the heavens?" possibly attributing this question to Job,[9] also recalls the psalmist's reference to God as "the Most High" (עליון). As Crenshaw observes, the wicked's use of this divine appellation in the psalm suggests God's distance from and disinterest in humanity.[10] Further drawing the two passages together, in vv. 15–16, Eliphaz asks Job if he will "keep to the old way that the wicked have trod?" and then describes their quick and utter demise similarly to the psalmist in Ps 73:19, though without repeating any of the same words:

Job 22:16

אֲשֶׁר־קֻמְּטוּ וְלֹא־עֵת נָהָר יוּצַק יְסוֹדָם   They were snatched away before their time; their foundation was washed away by a flood.

Ps 73:19

אֵיךְ הָיוּ לְשַׁמָּה כְרָגַע סָפוּ תַמּוּ מִן־בַּלָּהוֹת   How they are destroyed in a moment, swept away utterly by terrors!

Dependence on a shared source or common phrase is a possible explanation of the similarity between Job 22:13 and Ps 73:11 that must be considered. Baumgärtel notes that Ps 94:7 is also similar.[11] There the psalmist writes:

---

8   See HALOT. In fact, since Ps 73:11b uses the noun דעה ("knowledge") and lacks a verb, the content (i.e., what) and not the means (i.e., how) of God's knowledge seems to be at issue.

9   Gordis, *Job*, 240, 247.

10   Crenshaw, *Whirlpool*, 101. Similarly, Irsigler, "Quest," 268; Goldingay, *Psalms*, 2:407.

11   Baumgärtel, *Hiobdialog*, 144.

Ps 94:7

וַיֹּאמְרוּ לֹא יִרְאֶה־יָּהּ וְלֹא־יָבִין אֱלֹהֵי יַעֲקֹב   And they say, "The LORD does not see;
the God of Jacob does not perceive."

Thematically, the verse does resonate with Job 22:13, but lexically, the two verses only share the common word אמר, though, in the next verse in Job, the words לֹא ראה ("he does not see") do appear. Eliphaz may be conflating the two verses; one need not choose between them as the source for Job 22:13 since they only overlap in the initial word.

Habel claims Job 22:13 is simply using a "standard cry attributed to the wicked."[12] He appeals to Isa 29:15 as another example. To this we could add Ezek 8:12 and Ps 10:11:

Isa 29:15

הוֹי הַמַּעֲמִיקִים מֵיהוָה לַסְתִּר עֵצָה וְהָיָה בְמַחְשָׁךְ   Ha! You who hide a plan too deep for the
מַעֲשֵׂיהֶם וַיֹּאמְרוּ מִי רֹאֵנוּ וּמִי יֹדְעֵנוּ   Lord,
         whose deeds are in the dark,
         and who say, "Who sees us? Who knows
           us?"

Ezek 8:12

וַיֹּאמֶר אֵלַי הֲרָאִיתָ בֶן־אָדָם אֲשֶׁר זִקְנֵי   Then he said to me, "Mortal, have you seen
בֵית־יִשְׂרָאֵל עֹשִׂים בַּחֹשֶׁךְ אִישׁ בְּחַדְרֵי מַשְׂכִּיתוֹ   what the elders of the house of Israel are
כִּי אֹמְרִים אֵין יְהוָה רֹאֶה אֹתָנוּ עָזַב יְהוָה   doing in the dark, each in his room of
אֶת־הָאָרֶץ   images? For they say, 'The Lord does not
         see us, the Lord has forsaken the land.'"

Ps 10:11

אָמַר בְּלִבּוֹ שָׁכַח אֵל הִסְתִּיר פָּנָיו בַּל־רָאָה לָנֶצַח   They think in their heart, "God has
         forgotten,
         he has hidden his face, he will never see
           it."

Each of these verses combines the *verbum dicendi* and the verb ראה as does Ps 94:7, and Isa 29:15 adds the verb ידע ("to know"), which appears in both Ps 73:11 and Job 22:13. Comparing these verses to Job 22:13 and Ps 73:11 only demonstrates how close the latter two passages actually are. Though a belief in God's ignorance and blindness may have commonly been attributed to the wicked, the phrases used to represent it elsewhere in the HB differ, while Job and the author of Psalm 73 have presented them almost exactly the same, thus suggesting a direct allusion.

---

12   Habel, *Job*, 340.

8.2. Date

Similar evidence is used to attempt to date Psalm 73 as the other psalms in this study, and it has similarly led to a postexilic date for the psalm, but, once again, the evidence is tenuous and does little to establish its date relative to Job. First, linguistic factors, such as possible Aramaisms (מוק, v. 8; שׂגה, v. 12), could suggest a late date,[13] but need not do so,[14] and would do little to differentiate the psalm chronologically from Job, which includes similar linguistic features. Second, theologically, many appeal to the psalm's witness to a perceived postexilic "crisis of Wisdom,"[15] but again, the same argument could be made for Job. Finally, appeal is made to indications of a socio-historical setting, but this evidence is also inconclusive. McCann associates the psalm's message with the exile, but Irsigler argues it fits better in the Persian period, and Goldingay observes that it could apply to several threats to the nation across its history.[16] Thus, as with the other psalms in this study, it seems best to conclude that the psalm, though likely postexilic based on the evidence now available to us, was composed at an unknown date.[17]

8.3. Coherence

Though neither a comparison of internal nor external coherence gives a strong indication of direction of dependence for this allusion, the former is more suggestive. Whereas a hypothetical quotation from the generalized wicked fits naturally in the psalm, Job never actually says what Eliphaz accuses him here of saying. Despite the *verbum dicendi*, Eliphaz is not actually quoting Job's words, nor even a position he has presented in the dialogue thus far.[18] According to Clines, "Not for a moment did Job suggest that God was unaware of what was going on among humans, that he did not 'know'; he simply said that God did not care (cf. also

---

13   Gunkel, *Psalmen*, 316. For an overview of the distinctive linguistic features of the psalm, see Goldingay, *Psalms*, 2:400–401.

14   They could also be evidence of a northern dialect. See Gary A. Rendsburg, *Linguistic Evidence for the Northern Origin of Selected Psalms* (SBLMS 43; Atlanta: Scholars Press, 1990), 73–81.

15   E.g., Irsigler, "Quest," 258–59; Terrien, *Psalms*, 534. However, a similar complaint of the wicked's prosperity also appears in Jer 12:1–3, which might suggest an exilic date. See Terry L. Smith, "A Crisis in Faith: An Exegesis of Psalm 73," *ResQ* 17 (1974): 167; Seybold, *Psalmen*, 282.

16   See McCann, "Psalms," 968; Irsigler, "Quest," 266, 258; Goldingay, *Psalms*, 2:400.

17   See, e.g., Weiser, *Psalms*, 508; Luyten, "Psalm 73," 81; Anderson, *Psalms*, 2:529.

18   Admittedly, there is also no evidence that the wicked in the psalm actually said what the psalmist attributes to them, but the psalm is a short text that is not a dialogue between different speakers, so this would not be expected.

19:7)."[19] Job has repeatedly affirmed God's knowledge of him (e.g., 7:19; 10:6, 14; 14:3, 6), and he will go on to appeal to it for his vindication (23:10). Noting this disparity, and the similarity of Job 22:13 to Pss 73:11; 94:7, Baumgärtel suggests the verse has probably been inserted from elsewhere.[20] Considering the close lexical similarity between this passage and Ps 73:11 and the Job poet's allusions to the Psalms throughout the dialogue, this external source is likely Psalm 73 itself.

The shared use of this phrase to characterize improper behavior toward God makes a comparison of external coherence inconclusive. However, it does lean toward Job as the later text. Though it makes sense for Eliphaz to use this phrase to associate Job with the wicked as they are depicted in the psalm, it is unclear why the psalmist would want to associate the wicked with Eliphaz's representation of Job's opinion of God. In so doing, the psalmist would be endorsing Eliphaz's accusation that Job is speaking wrongly by giving words purported to have come from Job's mouth to the wicked to say. But, given that the psalmist's experience and message are so similar to Job's, this seems unlikely. Thus, comparing the internal and external coherence of the passages, Job's dependence on the psalm seems more probable.

8.4. Use

Observing that Job has not said what Eliphaz accuses him of in 22:13–14, Westermann[21] argues that the verses should "be understood solely on the basis of their origin," which he is certain is "the description of the ungodly" that appears in individual lament psalms. Noting the similarity between the Job passage and Ps 73:11, along with several other psalms, he argues that "we are here dealing with precisely this motif from Psalms."[22] However, instead of removing these verses as secondary because of this similarity, he claims the speech "*must* come here" (emphasis original) as it culminates the friends' progressive identification of Job with the wicked. "That Eliphaz should conceal his accusation of Job at this decisive juncture, relying totally on traditional descriptions of the ungodly," Westermann claims, "corresponds perfectly to the structure of the whole." As Newsom observes, since Eliphaz has concluded that Job is among the wicked, he "can only see him in the stereotyped image of the sinner that tradition describes."[23]

---

19   Clines, *Job*, 2:558. Similarly, e.g., Driver and Gray, *Job*, 195; Pope, *Job*, 166.
20   Baumgärtel, *Hiobdialog*, 144.
21   Westermann, *Structure*, 24–25.
22   Similarly, Delitzsch, *Job*, 2:434.
23   Newsom, "Job," 501.

If the origin of Eliphaz's accusation is not merely the generalized description of the ungodly in lament, but the actual description in Psalm 73, then it sharpens Eliphaz's attack even more. By using the words the psalmist attributed to the wicked against Job,[24] Eliphaz's allusion then draws in the terrifying fate that the psalm affirms for the wicked (Job 22:16; Ps 73:19). At the same time, Eliphaz uses the allusion to cloak his animus, not only in traditional words as Westermann suggests, but in the words of another text.

8.5. Recurrence

8.5.1. Job: 7:18

Further allusions to the psalm as they appear throughout the dialogue, especially as Job and Eliphaz confront one another with its words in the third cycle, will further suggest that the Job poet has Psalm 73 particularly in mind. First, in Job's first reply to Eliphaz, he uses imagery of wrathful divine visitation in the morning, unique to Ps 73:14 in the Psalms,[25] to intensify his parody of Ps 8:5,[26] demonstrating the great disparity between God's loving care presented in the latter passage and his current afflicted experience:

Job 7:18

... visit them every morning,   וַתִּפְקְדֶנּוּ לִבְקָרִים לִרְגָעִים תִּבְחָנֶנּוּ
          test them every moment?

Ps 73:14

For all day long I have been plagued,   וָאֱהִי נָגוּעַ כָּל־הַיּוֹם וְתוֹכַחְתִּי לַבְּקָרִים
          and am punished every morning.

The context in Job already indicates that פקד ("to visit") and בחן ("to test") are intended to have negative connotations, but their correspondence with נגע ("to plague") and יכח ("to punish") in the psalm magnifies their threatening significance. "Every moment" in Job also parallels "all day long" in the psalm. Discip-

---

24   "His friends go so far as to attribute to him not only the behaviour, but the language of the godless … as is expressed in Ps., 73,11" (Luyten, "Psalm 73," 76). In Psalm 73, it is unclear whether the wicked or a group of apostate followers they have gathered from the people (v. 10) are speaking in v. 11. However, the distinction makes little difference in terms of Eliphaz's accusation against Job because even the apostates are now among the wicked, though, considering the fall Eliphaz considers Job to have taken from his former state (e.g., Job 4:3–4), the latter would be especially appropriate.

25   Clines, *Job*, 1:193. Clines observes that in the Psalms, the morning is usually described as a time for God's deliverance (192).

26   Habel notes this modification of Ps 8:5 through "expressions of temporal intensification" (Habel, *Job*, 165).

line at dawn is found only in these two passages,[27] which further contributes to their "conspicuous similarity."[28] Kraus imagines the psalmist asking with this verse, "Is this suffering God's answer to the obedient walk?"[29] Job uses the imagery because he wonders the same thing.

8.5.2. Job: 9:29–31

In his next speech, Job elaborates on the psalmist's complaint of the vanity of his attempts at purity:

Job 9:29–31

אָנֹכִי אֶרְשָׁע לָמָּה־זֶּה הֶבֶל אִיגָע 29   I shall be condemned;
                                                why then do I labor in vain?

אִם־הִתְרָחַצְתִּי בְמוֹ־[בְמֵי־]שָׁלֶג וַהֲזִכּוֹתִי בְּבֹר 30   If I wash myself with soap
כַּפָּי   and cleanse my hands with lye,

אָז בַּשַּׁחַת תִּטְבְּלֵנִי וְתִעֲבוּנִי שַׂלְמוֹתָי 31   yet you will plunge me into filth,
                                                and my own clothes will abhor me.

Ps 73:13

אַךְ־רִיק זִכִּיתִי לְבָבִי וָאֶרְחַץ בְּנִקָּיוֹן כַּפָּי   All in vain have I kept my heart clean
                                                and washed my hands in innocence.

There are psalmic parallels to washing one's hands in innocence (Ps 26:6) and clean hands and a pure heart as prerequisites for entrance into the temple (Ps 24:4), but only in these two passage are these rituals declared "vain" (הבל in Job; ריק in Psalm 73).[30] In addition, Job employs the same words for "to wash" (רחץ) and "hands" (כף), similar syntax,[31] a by-form also meaning "to be clean or pure" (זכך in Job; זכה in Psalm 73), and the word בר, which, if translated "purity" or "cleanness" as it must be in Job 22:30 instead of "lye" (cf. Isa 1:25),[32] would be synonymous with נקיון ("innocence") in Ps 73:13.[33]

John Mason Good claims the authors of both Psalms 26 and 73 have "closely copied" the verse from Job.[34] The dependence of the former text on Job

---

27   Luyten, "Psalm 73," 76.

28   Buttenwieser, *Psalms*, 529. Other scholars note the similarity, e.g., Delitzsch, *Psalms*, 2:362; Wolfers, *Job*, 165.

29   Kraus, *Psalms*, 2:88.

30   In Mal 3:14, serving God more generally is called "vain" (שוא).

31   כפי + [noun] + בְ + [first person singular verb] + ו.

32   Clines claims the word in Isaiah is "dubious" and thus this word in Job 9:30 is "probably *hapax*" (Clines, *Job*, 1:220), but it need not be since, if translated purity, it appears in Job 22:30; 2 Sam 22:21, 25; Ps 18:21, 25.

33   The same word בר ("pure") appears in Ps 73:1, though it is pointed בַּר and not בֹּר.

34   Good, *Job*, 112.

seems unlikely because Job's complaint of the vanity of such rituals would do little to contribute to the psalmist's confidence, but the latter is possible. Both Job
and the author of Psalm 73 are describing a similar experience of vainly attempting to prove their moral purity, so the direction of dependence is difficult to
determine, though the broader similarities between Job and the psalm and the
specificity of the connections here do suggest some sort of dependence between
them as opposed to a mere repetition of formulaic phraseology.[35] The indications
of the Job poet's dependence on the psalm in 22:13 suggest that Job is also the
later text here, as well, and the elaboration on the psalmic language corresponds
with several of Job's other allusions (e.g., Job 10:20–22; cf. Ps 39:14; Job 7:17–18;
cf. Ps 8:5).

8.5.3. The Friends: 15:27; 18:3, 11, 14; 20:8

Each of the friends also recalls distinctive imagery from Psalm 73. First, Eliphaz
draws on the psalmist's description of the prosperity of the wicked:[36]

Job 15:27

כִּי־כִסָּה פָנָיו בְּחֶלְבּוֹ וַיַּעַשׂ פִּימָה עֲלֵי־כָסֶל   ... because they have covered their faces
with their fat,
and gathered fat upon their loins ...

Ps 73:7

יָצָא מֵחֵלֶב עֵינֵמוֹ עָבְרוּ מַשְׂכִּיּוֹת לֵבָב   Their eyes swell out with fatness;
their hearts overflow with follies.

Then, Bildad repeats the psalmist's comparison of himself to an animal,[37] and his
threat of "terrors":[38]

---

35   Culley mentions the use of the shared phrase in Psalms 26 and 73 as a psalmic formula, but the
diametrically opposed meaning given the imagery in Psalm 73 is unique in the Psalms and unique
to Psalm 73 and Job in the HB, so the verse as a whole appears far from formulaic. See Culley,
Formulaic Language, 75.

36   For this parallel, see, e.g., Delitzsch, *Job*, 1:266; Andersen, *Job*, 178; Alonso Schökel and Sicre
Díaz, *Job*, 246. Ringgren and Smith argue on this basis against emending the text of the psalm, as
some, such as Dahood, have suggested. See H. Ringgren, "Einige Bemerkungen zum 73. Psalm,"
VT 3 (1953): 266; Smith, "Psalm 73," 173; cf. Dahood, *Psalms*, 2:189. Based on the common use
of שלום in Job 15:21 and Ps 73:3 and the blasphemous attitude of the wicked in both passages,
Baumgärtel concludes the exact same sort of evildoers are described (Baumgärtel, *Hiobdialog*, 88).

37   For this parallel, see, e.g., Fohrer, *Hiob*, 300; Pope, *Job*, 133; Alonso Schökel and Sicre Díaz, *Job*,
273.

38   For this parallel, see, e.g., Dahood, *Psalms*, 2:193; Marvin E. Tate, *Psalms 51–100* (WBC 20; Dallas: Word Books, 1990), 229. Alonso Schökel considers this parallel especially interesting in light
of the relationship between the book and this psalm (Alonso Schökel and Sicre Díaz, *Job*, 274).

Job 18:3

מַדּוּעַ נֶחְשַׁבְנוּ כַבְּהֵמָה נִטְמִינוּ בְּעֵינֵיכֶם

Why are we counted as cattle?
Why are we stupid in your sight?

Ps 73:22

וַאֲנִי־בַעַר וְלֹא אֵדָע בְּהֵמוֹת הָיִיתִי עִמָּךְ

I was stupid and ignorant;
I was like a brute beast toward you.

Job 18:11, 14

11 סָבִיב בִּעֲתֻהוּ בַלָּהוֹת וֶהֱפִיצֻהוּ לְרַגְלָיו

11 Terrors frighten them on every side,
and chase them at their heels. ...

14 יִנָּתֵק מֵאָהֳלוֹ מִבְטַחוֹ וְתַצְעִדֵהוּ לְמֶלֶךְ בַּלָּהוֹת

14 They are torn from the tent in which they
trusted,
and are brought to the king of terrors.

Ps 73:19

אֵיךְ הָיוּ לְשַׁמָּה כְרָגַע סָפוּ תַמּוּ מִן־בַּלָּהוֹת

How they are destroyed in a moment,
swept away utterly by terrors!

Finally, Zophar uses the same comparison of the wicked to a fleeting dream:[39]

Job 20:8

כַּחֲלוֹם יָעוּף וְלֹא יִמְצָאוּהוּ וְיֻדַּד כְּחֶזְיוֹן לָיְלָה

They will fly away like a dream, and not be
found;
they will be chased away like a vision of
the night.

Ps 73:20

כַּחֲלוֹם מֵהָקִיץ אֲדֹנָי בָּעִיר צַלְמָם תִּבְזֶה

They are like a dream when one awakes;
on awaking you despise their phantoms.

All of this shared imagery is relatively rare in the HB as a whole. "Fat" is used to represent wickedness and rebellion in three other passages (Deut 32:15; Jer 5:28; Ps 119:70), but Luyten claims that only in Job and Psalm 73 is the rare term בלהות used to describe the speedy demise of the wicked[40] and their existence compared to a dream.[41] The collection of this rare imagery suggests that the friends are drawing on the psalm, particularly vv. 18–20, where the destruction of the wicked is assured, to warn Job of a similar fate if he does not repent.[42]

---

39 For this parallel, see, e.g., Delitzsch, *Psalms*, 2:366; Gunkel, *Psalmen*, 315; Alonso Schökel and Sicre Díaz, *Job*, 305.

40 The term is used in Ezek 26:21; 27:36; 28:19; Isa 17:14 but not in the same active sense.

41 Luyten, "Psalm 73," 72. Isa 29:7 also employs חלום ("dream") and חזון לילה ("visions of the night") as similes for destruction, but the prophet is referring to the nations and not the wicked in general. The Job poet may be conflating the two passages.

42 Irsigler notes the similarity between the traditional view of the fate of the wicked in vv. 18–20 of the psalm and the friends' speeches in chs. 18 and 20 (Irsigler, *Adamssohn*, 91).

8.5.4. Job: 19:25–27

However, in the midst of this onslaught of threatening imagery, there appears a parallel in Job's words to the psalm's most hopeful section:

Job 19:25–27

וַאֲנִי יָדַעְתִּי גֹּאֲלִי חָי וְאַחֲרוֹן עַל־עָפָר יָקוּם 25 For I know that my Redeemer lives, and that at the last he will stand upon the earth;

וְאַחַר עוֹרִי נִקְּפוּ־זֹאת וּמִבְּשָׂרִי אֶחֱזֶה אֱלוֹהַּ 26 and after my skin has been thus destroyed, then in my flesh I shall see God,

אֲשֶׁר אֲנִי אֶחֱזֶה־לִּי וְעֵינַי רָאוּ וְלֹא־זָר כָּלוּ 27 whom I shall see on my side, כָלְיֹתַי בְּחֵקִי and my eyes shall behold, and not another. My heart faints within me!

Ps 73:23–26

וַאֲנִי תָמִיד עִמָּךְ אָחַזְתָּ בְּיַד־יְמִינִי 23 Nevertheless I am continually with you; you hold my right hand.

בַּעֲצָתְךָ תַנְחֵנִי וְאַחַר כָּבוֹד תִּקָּחֵנִי 24 You guide me with your counsel, and afterward you will receive me with honor.

מִי־לִי בַשָּׁמָיִם וְעִמְּךָ לֹא־חָפַצְתִּי בָאָרֶץ 25 Whom have I in heaven but you? And there is nothing on earth that I desire other than you.

כָּלָה שְׁאֵרִי וּלְבָבִי צוּר־לְבָבִי וְחֶלְקִי אֱלֹהִים 26 My flesh and my heart may fail, לְעוֹלָם but God is the strength of my heart and my portion forever.

Though the lexical connections are not striking since the shared words are all common, Luyten observes that "both texts are stylistically and thematically characterized by a strong cohesion and a climatic structure."[43] The four repeated words (אני, לי, אחר, כלה) appear in the same order and roughly the same distance apart. The first two of those words are both prefixed with a *waw* in both texts. The contrast between the certainty about God's presence in the future and the speaker's physical weakness expressed toward the end of both passages[44] is a further "strikingly common feature of both texts."[45] Job's reference to his heart (or "kidneys" [כליה]) failing may also have the same concessive meaning as the similar phrase in the psalm.[46] Similarly, Hengstenberg, who considers Ps 73:26 to be a

---

43   Luyten, "Psalm 73," 78.

44   Several commentators believe a half-line at the end of Job 19:27 is missing. See Gustav Hölscher, *Das Buch Hiob* (2nd ed.; HAT 17; Tübingen: Mohr, 1952), 48; Fohrer, *Hiob*, 309.

45   Luyten, "Psalm 73," 79. Hitzig notes this similarity between the texts (Hitzig, *Hiob*, 147).

46   Luyten, "Psalm 73," 79.

"compend of" Job 19:25–27, claims that the psalmist, like Job, is putting his trust in the power and love of God to deliver him even if his body should fail him.[47] Dahood goes even further to propose that both texts give expression to a "doctrine of the creation of a new body for the afterlife."[48]

Few scholars would now agree with Hengstenberg's claim, when comparing Psalm 73 to this passage of Job, that "the germ of the doctrine of the resurrection" in the psalm is "clear as day."[49] Terrien, for example, denies that the psalmist had resurrection or the immortality of the soul in view, but "was merely convinced that nothing could interrupt his present intimacy with God."[50] Though Crenshaw agrees that a new understanding of God's presence is primarily in view in these verses of Psalm 73, he notes how the psalmist, like Job, uses the adverb אחר ("afterward") but leaves the reader with the question, "After what?" Referring to Ps 73:25, he claims the psalmist has "opted for divine presence now and forever." Though mortality threatens to conclude that relationship, Crenshaw wonders with the psalmist, "But if death does not signal the end. . . ."[51] The scope of this study does not permit pursuing Crenshaw's pregnant ellipsis further, but, as Smith remarks, "Regardless of how one interprets the verse, the psalmist has received the faith to overcome his present difficulties."[52] For Job, however, the revelation does not appear to be so definitive because his argument with God rages on.

8.5.5. Job: 21:13–14

Job returns to the psalm once again in his next speech, setting the stage for a confrontation with Eliphaz:

Job 21:14

וַיֹּאמְרוּ לָאֵל סוּר מִמֶּנּוּ וְדַעַת דְּרָכֶיךָ לֹא חָפָצְנוּ They say to God, "Leave us alone!
We do not desire to know your ways."

---

47 Hengstenberg, *Psalms*, 2:414. Rankin discusses the similar view portrayed by these two passages on the afterlife. However, he does not address a possible literary connection between them. See O. S. Rankin, *Israel's Wisdom Literature: Its Bearing on Theology and the History of Religion* (Edinburgh: T&T Clark, 1936), 146–62. Heinrich Groß also claims Job, like the author of Psalm 73, is convinced he will encounter a gracious God after his earthly life is over (Heinrich Groß, *Ijob* [NEchtB 13; Würzburg: Echter, 1986], 10). Similarly, Briggs, *Psalms*, 2:147; Kittel, *Psalmen*, 273.

48 Dahood, *Psalms*, 2:196.

49 Hengstenberg, *Psalms*, 2:414.

50 Samuel L. Terrien, *The Elusive Presence: Toward a New Biblical Theology* (RP 26; San Francisco: Harper & Row, 1978), 318.

51 Crenshaw, *Whirlpool*, 107–8.

52 Smith, "Psalm 73," 182.

Ps 73:11

וְאָמְרוּ אֵיכָה יָדַע־אֵל וְיֵשׁ דֵּעָה בְעֶלְיוֹן   And they say, "How can God know?
Is there knowledge in the Most High?"

Here Job characterizes the attitude of the wicked by quoting words they might have said, which is a common poetic device (cf. Pss 10:4, 6, 11; 12:5; 14:1; 53:2; 94:7).[53] His depiction combines אל as the divine name for God with the theme of knowledge, just as in Psalm 73, and in no other hypothetical quotations of the wicked (with the possible exception of the words Eliphaz attributes to Job in 22:13).[54] Fohrer, who believes Job 21 contains a "Parodie eines Weisheitsliedes," gives Ps 73:11 as the prime example of the "Vorbild von Weisheitsliedern" for Job 21:14–15.[55] Similarly, Westermann claims 21:14–16 has "obvious parallels" in Ps 73:9, 11.[56] However, he observes, whereas the author of Psalm 73 extricates himself from acknowledging the ultimate good fortune of the wicked by opposing it with their eventual demise, Job questions precisely this solution to the problem by suggesting the end of the wicked is not always terrible (vv. 17–33).[57] Further, in Job's version, it is not God's ability to know, but the wicked's desire to know that is at issue. This heightens the arrogance of the wicked. They become the subjects, who can choose to know what they want, instead of the objects of God's knowledge. Unlike the righteous, who desire to know God's ways (Ps 25:4), the wicked reject such knowledge, and yet they still prosper, escaping the destruction Psalm 73 predicts for them (vv. 18–20).[58]

Luyten cites this common citation of the wicked's blasphemous speech among the many connections between Job 21:7–34 and Ps 73:1–12, which, he claims, are the most similar treatments of the theme of the prosperity of the wicked in biblical literature.[59] He also mentions the common use of the term רשעים ("wicked") (Ps 73:3, 12; Job 21:7, 17), allusions to their portliness (Ps 73:12; Job 21:23–24),[60] the durability of their happiness (Ps 73:12; Job 21:7), their success in gaining followers (Ps 73:10; Job 21:33), preceding expressions of

---

53   Newsom, "Job," 492.

54   Luyten finds it significant that in citing the wicked both passages avoid the name יהוה but instead use two other divine appellations, אל and עליון in Psalm 73 and אל and שדי (21:15) in Job, and that "knowledge" is a key element in both (Luyten, "Psalm 73," 74).

55   Fohrer, *Hiob*, 340.

56   Westermann, *Structure*, 95 n. 16. He argues that the common juxtaposition of the godlessness and good fortune of transgressors in Job 21 and Psalms 10, 54, and 73, offers "a sure confirmation of the thesis that the motifs of the individual lament psalm are presupposed in Job 21."

57   Westermann, *Structure*, 88.

58   Though Job himself has asked God to leave him alone (7:16, 19; 10:20), he repeatedly expresses a desire to know God's ways (e.g., 10:2; 23:3–5).

59   Luyten, "Psalm 73," 74.

60   Note the repeated use of the word שלו ("ease"), which only appears eight times in the HB.

unease about their prosperity by both speakers (Ps 73:2–3; Job 21:6–7), and a series of shared terms and roots: חיל (Ps 73:12; Job 21:7), שלום (Ps 73:3; Job 21:9), תמם (Ps 73:4;[61] Job 21:23), חלב (Ps 73:7; Job 21:24), מלא (Ps 73:10; Job 21:24), and שלו (Ps 73:12; Job 21:23). To this list could be added the word רגע ("moment"), which Job uses in the verse immediately preceding his allusion to the psalm's citation of the wicked (Ps 73:19; Job 21:13).[62]

Despite these similarities, Luyten claims, "In Job the prosperity of the wicked is presented in a much more concrete and detailed manner."[63] In contrast to the psalmist, Job also draws more on traditional descriptions of the doctrine of retribution, turning them upside down to describe the prosperous wicked instead (e.g., the parody of Ps 1:4 in v. 18[64]), so that, following Fohrer, Luyten claims the passage may best be characterized as "a parody of a wisdom song."[65]

8.5.6. Job: 23:11

In response, as noted above, Eliphaz, who has been listening closely to Job's speech (21:14; cf. 22:17; 21:16; cf. 22:18), puts the words of the wicked in Job's mouth (22:13; cf. 21:14; Ps 73:11), thereby suggesting that it is not the wicked, but Job, who rejects the knowledge of God. Job, however, will not stand to be slandered in such a way. He counters in the next chapter with yet another allusion to Psalm 73:

Job 23:11

בַּאֲשֻׁרוֹ אָחֲזָה רַגְלִי דַּרְכּוֹ שָׁמַרְתִּי וְלֹא־אָט   My foot has held fast to his steps;
                                                           I have kept his way and have not turned aside.

Ps 73:2

וַאֲנִי כִּמְעַט נָטוּי [נָטָיוּ] רַגְלָי כְּאַיִן שֻׁפְּכָה   But as for me, my feet had almost stumbled;
[שֻׁפְּכוּ] אֲשֻׁרָי   my steps had nearly slipped.

---

61   This depends on the emendation of the text from למותם ("to their death") to two words: למו ("to them") and תמם ("to be complete").

62   The positive connotation Job seems to give the word, in contrast with its threatening intimation when used by the psalmist, has led some to suggest that in Job it is actually an otherwise unattested noun form of the verb רגע II ("to be at rest") (see discussion in Clines, *Job*, 2:509). However, Job could be using the same word to parody the psalmist, since Job could be communicating, as Clines puts it, "Even the death of the wicked, its time and its manner, declares their good fortune … they suffer no lingering death but suddenly slip away, 'in a moment'" (2:526–27).

63   Luyten, "Psalm 73," 74.

64   See pp. 146–150.

65   Luyten, "Psalm 73," 74.

Clines notes that in 23:10–12, Job uses the most appropriate language to describe his upright life, that of "psalmic piety."[66] After the allusions to Psalm 73 in the previous two chapters, the lexical similarity between v. 11 and Ps 73:2, which seems too great to be mere coincidence, suggests the language of a specific psalm and not merely psalmic language informs Job's confession here. In itself, the word אשר ("step") is rare, only appearing nine times in the HB, but nowhere else does this combination of three words (נטה, רגל, אשר) appear together. The imagery of steps holding fast when in danger of slipping or departing from God's way appears several times in the Psalms (e.g., Pss 17:5; 37:31; 40:3; 44:19), but none are as close lexically to this passage from Job. In contrast to Eliphaz's implied accusation that Job is among the wicked in Psalm 73, Job uses this allusion to claim for himself a righteousness even greater than the psalmist's. Whereas the psalmist admits that he almost "stumbled" (נטה) and his feet had "nearly slipped," Job claims his foot has held fast to God's steps, and he has not "turned aside" or "stumbled" (נטה).[67] Clines thinks it unusual that Job uses the term אשר since elsewhere it "always refers to the steps of humans, not of God."[68] However, Job could be using the term in this way to accentuate his piety over the psalmist's—although his steps almost slipped, Job has held fast to *God's* steps.[69]

8.6. Holistic Interpretation

Both Job and his friends found a kindred spirit in the author of Psalm 73. Job identified with the psalmist's affliction (v. 14; cf. Job 7:18), frustration (v. 13; cf. Job 9:30), and even flights of hope (vv. 23–26; cf. Job 19:25–27), but he did not

---

66 Clines, *Job*, 2:598. Similarly, Newsom remarks that Job here "comes closest to speaking in the accents of traditional prayer and wisdom" (Newsom, "Job," 509), and Lindström claims these verses are "an example of the dialogues' caricatural use of the theological tradition of the psalms, like, e.g., Job 7:17–19" (Lindström, *Suffering*, 422 n. 6). For allusions to Ps 1:1, 6 and possibly Ps 139:23–24 in 23:10, see pp. 155–157, 117, respectively.

67 Alonso Schökel notes the contrast between this verse in Job and Ps 73:2, but claims Job is citing Ps 17:5 (Alonso Schökel and Sicre Díaz, *Job*, 356).

68 Clines, *Job*, 2:598.

69 Wolfers suggests one further allusion to Psalm 73. He claims Ps 73:17–19 and Job 27:20–23 are "virtually twin texts" that express "exactly the same sentiment" that "the avoidance of the agony of death in a state of alienation from God more than compensates for all the material advantages of an evil life" (Wolfers, *Job*, 166, 253). The only lexical connection between the passages is the shared combination of the word בלהה ("terror") in the plural with a word from the root סוף (Ps 73:19; Job 27:20). This is suggestive, since only one other passage combines these elements (Isa 17:13–14). However, because the speaker in this passage is disputed, I am reluctant to draw conclusions about the use of the psalm on the basis of this parallel. Job, to whom the passage is attributed, may be co-opting the friends' references to these verses to claim that retribution for the wicked, though not as immediate as they imagine, will eventually come.

think the psalmist pushed deeply enough into the problem of the prosperity of the wicked, and so he pressed further, drawing Psalm 73 into his parody of a sapiential solution (vv. 11, 19; cf. Job 21:13–14). Finally, he declared himself even more righteous than his predecessor (v. 2; cf. Job 23:11). The friends identified with the psalmist's derisive description of the wicked (v. 7; Job 15:27), his threat of "terrors" for them (v. 19; cf. Job 18:11, 14), and of the wicked's dreamlike ephemerality (v. 20; cf. Job 20:8). They were not willing, unlike the psalmist, to admit their ignorance (v. 22; cf. Job 18:3),[70] but were glad to use his words to accuse Job of making such a charge against God, just like the wicked (v. 11; cf. Job 22:12–13).[71]

8.7. Reciprocation

The Job poet's use of Psalm 73 enables it to be seen in a new light. Comparing Psalm 73 to Job, Newsom[72] observes that in the psalm both skeptical and traditional positions on retribution are presented monologically within the same consciousness, which resolves the tension between them as a chronological progression from error to enlightenment. As a result, the skeptical position "is perceived only through the lens of another position now deemed superior to it." The dialogue in Job, however, enables distinct characters to embody this tension without one serving self-evidently as the spokesperson for the author's view, allowing the contrasting positions to "address the reader with formally equivalent force." Newsom concludes, "The difference between the two modes is the difference between the didactic and the dialogic." Tracing the allusions to Psalm 73 in Job makes the distinction Newsom observes even more pronounced because not only do Job and his friends represent opposing sides of the tensions evident in the psalm, they interpret the psalm itself differently to support their arguments, thus creating a dialogue that is just as hermeneutical as it is theological. But the ability of both Job and the friends to find resources for their opposing arguments in the same psalm also demonstrates the psalm's dialogical potential, which enables the author of Job to put its conflicting ideas into conversation with one another.

---

70   Alonso Schökel claims that if they had, they could have advanced in their understanding like the author of Psalm 73 (Alonso Schökel and Sicre Díaz, *Job*, 273).

71   Thus, Jacques Vermeylen points to this final parallel, as well as v. 20; cf. Job 20:8, as indicators that Psalm 73 is one of the two psalms, along with Psalm 37 (see p. 42 n. 119), that presents the most characteristic affinities with the discourse of the friends and their conception of retribution (Jacques Vermeylen, *Job, ses amis et son Dieu: La légende de Job et ses relectures postexiliques* [StB 2; Leiden: Brill, 1986], 57–58).

72   Newsom, *Contest*, 86–87.

McCann further explores the play of genres in the psalm, proposing that the psalm's tension is reflected in the opposition between the two major form-critical classifications to which it is generally assigned.[73] The sapiential reading of the psalm generally corresponds with its interpretation as a *Problemgedicht*, in which the psalmist struggles with the problem of righteous suffering. Those who read the psalm as a song of thanksgiving, however, claim the psalmist is recounting his gratitude to God for his deliverance from suffering or for the solution to the problem of divine retribution he has obtained. The psalm holds both possibilities in a tension that reflects the tension Brueggemann has identified as the essence of Old Testament theology, the attempt "both *to legitimate structure* and *to embrace pain*."[74] The former appears in the psalmist's affirmation of his continuing loyalty to the community and its institutions (vv. 15, 28) and of the traditional definition of purity of heart (vv. 1, 13), while the latter is added through the rejection of the traditional presentation of the consequences of this purity (vv. 1, 28 as opposed to vv. 4–12). Thus, the psalmist suggests "the 'pure in heart' or 'Israel' are those who continue to obey, serve, and praise God even while stricken and troubled," and in this way, "the innocent psalmist continues to suffer (*Problemgedicht*) and yet simultaneously celebrates his victory over suffering (song of thanksgiving)."[75] In other words, the psalm depicts a battle between faith and experience,[76] which, as the vivid personal portrayal of the problem in vv. 1–3 indicates, is about the survival of the psalmist's faith and not just the resolution of a theological or intellectual problem.[77]

Because of this tension between legitimating structure and embracing pain in the psalm, both Job and the friends can use it for their own ends. Job refers to the psalmist's pain as well as the hope that could only arise in the midst of such anguish when nothing else was left. The friends appeal to the structure of retributive justice, which the psalmist reaffirms despite his struggles.

---

73   J. Clinton McCann, Jr., "Psalm 73: A Microcosm of Old Testament Theology," in *The Listening Heart* (eds. Kenneth G. Hoglund et al.; JSOTSup 58; Sheffield: JSOT Press, 1987).

74   Walter Brueggemann, "A Shape for Old Testament Theology, I: Structure Legitimation," *CBQ* 47 (1985): 30. Emphasis original. See also, Walter Brueggemann, "A Shape for Old Testament Theology, II: Embrace of Pain," *CBQ* 47 (1985): 395–415.

75   McCann, "Psalm 73," 251–52.

76   Several commentators have recognized this aspect of the psalm, e.g., W. O. E. Oesterley, *The Psalms* (2 vols.; London: Society for Promoting Christian Knowledge, 1939), 2:345; Schaefer, *Psalms*, 177.

77   Weiser, *Psalms*, 507. Similarly, Kraus claims the psalm is not "merely abstract wisdom" or a "theoretical doctrinal essay" but the personal account of how "a human being ... was under threat of losing confidence in the perfection of Yahweh's goodness vis-à-vis the צדקים" (Kraus, *Psalms*, 2:86, 87). See also, with an emphasis on the psalmist's victory in this conflict, Calvin, *Psalms,* 3:124; Anderson, *Psalms*, 2:529; Crenshaw, *Whirlpool*, 94.

8.8. Historical Implications

Job's interaction with the developing understanding of retribution as delayed and even eschatological in the Second Temple period is further substantiated in his use of Psalm 73.[78] However, the book's interaction with the Psalms also demonstrates a second development in conceptions of retribution. Though the friends are often said to represent the "traditional" view of retribution,[79] in their strict "mathematical equation" between deed and consequence they actually reflect a "*developed form* of the theory of reward and retribution."[80] The nuanced view of retribution in Psalms 1 and 73 to which Job appeals, however, is widespread in the HB. Even Proverbs, the text to which interpreters often envision the book of Job reacting, "*undermines* … a simplified moral calculus."[81] Texts that privilege the poor in that collection (e.g., Prov 14:31; 19:17; 22:2) contradict a direct equivalence between wealth and righteousness.[82] Proverbs does not proclaim the strict view of Job's friends, instead teaching only that "both the righteous and the wicked will *eventually* get what they deserve."[83] Van Leeuwen observes that the "widespread dogmatic misuse of retributive sayings or concepts … does not itself render the sayings dogmatic." This scholarly "oversimplification" overlooks the many proverbs which recognize the explanatory limits of retribution. Thus, he claims that, like the Psalms of lament, "the book of Job was inevitable, not because Proverbs was too simplistic, but because life's inequities, as reflected in Proverbs, drive faith to argue with the Deity."[84] Therefore, Job's plea for a broad understanding of retribution associates him with a view evident throughout the HB.[85] After all, as Rowley points out, "it is hard to suppose that the reader of the Bible is expected to conclude that Abel, Uriah the Hittite, and Naboth were murdered because they deserved to be."[86]

---

78 For the contribution of Psalm 73 to an evolving belief in the afterlife, see Adams, *Wisdom*, 150.

79 E.g., Roland E. Murphy, *The Tree of Life: An Exploration of Biblical Wisdom Literature* (3rd ed.; Grand Rapids, Mich.: Eerdmans, 2002), 34.

80 Rankin, *Wisdom*, 91. Emphasis original.

81 J. Clinton McCann, Jr., "Wisdom's Dilemma: The Book of Job, the Final Form of the Book of Psalms, and the Entire Bible," in *Wisdom, You Are My Sister: Studies in Honor of Roland E. Murphy, O. Carm., on the Occasion of his Eightieth Birthday* (ed. Michael L. Barré; CBQMS 29; Washington, DC: Catholic Biblical Association of America, 1997), 19. Emphasis original.

82 McCann, "Dilemma," 19–20.

83 Adams, *Wisdom*, 85. Emphasis original.

84 Raymond C. Van Leeuwen, "Wealth and Poverty: System and Contradiction in Proverbs," *HS* 33 (1992): 29, 34.

85 McCann, "Dilemma," 18.

86 Rowley, *Job*, 18.

Apparently, at the time Job was written, various proposals for understanding retribution were in conflict, with some arguing for a strict equivalence of deed and consequence in this life and others beginning to propose an eschatological judgment. The friends, representing the former view, are repudiated in Job's speeches, relegated to silence in the dialogue, reprimanded in Elihu's speeches (32:11–16), and rejected in the epilogue (42:7–8), while Job toys with the latter view (e.g., 19:25–27), but the author does not present a firm answer to the problem. Instead, like so many other aspects of the book, he allows the dialogue of ideas to speak for itself.[87] This may reflect the unresolved debates at the time, possibly initiated by the exile, or may result merely from the author's greater interest in the proper response to suffering rather than its theological explanation.

8.9. Conclusion

In the wisdom psalms, Dell claims, the proper response to injustice is to wait because in these texts "the hope that life will be just is thrown into the future and the psalmists look to the end time, even if this only means the moment when injustices will end rather than an afterlife."[88] She refers to Pss 37:37; 73:23–26, but the last chapter suggested that a similar future-oriented hope is evident in Ps 1:5, and Ps 49:15–20 could be mentioned, as well.[89] However, as Psalm 73 dramatically demonstrates, more than justice is at issue. The psalmist is undoubtedly encouraged that the wicked will get their just deserts (vv. 18–20, 27), but the ultimate source of his hope to face the present comes not from the future, but from the immediate presence of God (vv. 23–26). He reaffirms the proverb of v. 1, which proclaims that God is good to Israel, with a new nuance to its meaning, in which "divine goodness is not prosperity but presence,"[90] and therefore concludes, "The nearness of God is good" (v. 28).[91] For Job, the intensity of his suffering makes this good more difficult to grasp. Dell notes that the internal tension which plagues his thought involves "a desire both to affirm and deny God."[92] Yet, in the end, with the help of the psalmist's example (Job 19:25–27; cf. Ps 73:23–26) and God's appearance, and despite the friends' use of Psalm 73 to threaten and accuse, Job is able to affirm God's goodness while still on the ash heap and devoid of material prosperity because he has "seen" God (Job 42:5–6).

---

87   See Murphy, *Tree*, 34.

88   Dell, *Sceptical*, 80–81.

89   For the similarity of the solution provided by Psalms 37, 49, and 73 see, e.g., Delitzsch, *Psalms*, 2:355; Dahood, *Psalms*, 2:188; Irsigler, "Quest," 259.

90   Tate, *Psalms*, 232. Similarly, Crenshaw, *Whirlpool*, 96.

91   Tate's translation (Tate, *Psalms*, 232).

92   Dell, *Sceptical*, 81.

Though the meaning of the divine speeches in Job is debated, as a resolution to the book, the theophany appears to have the same function for Job as the psalmist's visit to the temple.[93] As Zenger observes, "Like Psalm 73, the book of Job also presents, as a way out of the existential crisis, a 'vision of God.'"[94] A new experience settles the battle between faith and experience in faith's favor. This vision convinces Job, like the psalmist, that life is not the supreme good; divine presence is.[95] Considering the repeated allusions to Psalm 73, it is little surprise that the book of Job should provide the same solution as this psalm that has influenced it profoundly.[96]

8.9.1. Psalms of Instruction in Job

By creating a dialogue with both Psalm 1 and Psalm 73, the author of Job also puts these two psalms in dialogue with each other. Though there may be a tension between these psalms "as theoretical competitors for the primary position in the Book of Psalms,"[97] the Job poet's allusions to them suggest that their messages may not actually be that different. Even though Psalm 73 may represent "a painful retreat from the naiveté of instant retribution,"[98] it also "finally has the character of a profession of faith."[99] Job's interaction with Psalm 1 had demonstrated the same nuance and faith in that psalm. Together, Job's use of Psalms 1 and 73 challenge the widespread characterization of the Job dialogue as a challenge to the doctrine of retribution. Though Job does hold the doctrine up to a caustic critique (e.g., ch. 21), he does not reject it wholesale, but only the strict application of it represented by the friends. To be vindicated, his driving desire, Job needs some form of retribution to be operative in the world, and he clings to this hope despite his experience to the contrary.

---

93 Luyten, "Psalm 73," 77. See also Kraus, *Psalms*, 2:89.

94 Frank-Lothar Hossfeld and Erich Zenger, *Psalms 2: A Commentary on Psalms 51–100* (trans. Linda M. Maloney; Hermeneia; Minneapolis: Fortress Press, 2005), 225. He is referring to Job 19:26, as well as 38:1 and 42:5. For this significance of the divine speeches in Job, see Rowley, *Job*, 20.

95 There are hints that Job knows this even before the theophany. Immediately before his allusion to Psalm 73 in ch. 23, he longs to see God but laments that he is unable to do so (vv. 8–9).

96 For the influence of Psalm 73 on Job, see Alonso Schökel and Sicre Díaz, *Job*, 305. For the similarity between the solutions offered by both texts in their emphasis on God's presence and faith see, respectively, Perdue, *Wisdom and Cult*, 290–91 and Bentzen, *Introduction*, 2:178.

97 Angel, "Differences," 164.

98 Leslie C. Allen, "Psalm 73: Pilgrimage from Doubt to Faith," *BBR* 7 (1997): 9.

99 McCann, "Psalms," 968.

9. Conclusion

And so at last the sailor lays firm hold,
Upon the rock on which he had been dashed.[1]

Like the book of Job, this study has drawn various voices together to create, through their dialogue, a whole that is greater than the sum of its parts. First, listening to the centuries-old critical conversation over the import of parallels between Job and the Psalms has led to my development of an intertextual method that attends to both their historical and hermeneutical significance. Second, this method has incorporated aspects from both traditional diachronic and progressive synchronic approaches to intertextuality to suggest a way forward given the uncertainty surrounding the relative dating of these texts. Third, I have gathered the sporadic and isolated comments from past scholarship into an extensive and coherent description of the use of particular psalms in Job. This has enabled an investigation not merely into the presence but also the purpose of allusions to the Psalms in Job, with implications for the interpretation of both texts and our understanding of Israel's history, thus filling significant scholarly lacunae.

9.1. The Psalms in the Dialogue

Considering the parallels between Job and the Psalms more broadly revealed that several of the psalms that have the strongest lexical connections are also alluded to several times. Both the particularly marked parallels and the repeated affinities suggested, when their internal and external coherence were considered, that these psalms were sources for the Joban dialogue. The recurring allusions to these psalms, in most cases by both Job and the friends, made them subtexts for the dispute between Job, his friends, and God, creating a rich tapestry of textual resonance and allusion.

The six psalms for which this phenomenon is the most pronounced are spread across three general psalmic categories. In the first category, praise, Job

---

1   Goethe's *Tasso*. Cited in Karl Barth, *Church Dogmatics IV: The Doctrine of Reconciliation, Part 3.1* (trans. G. W. Bromiley; London: T&T Clark International, 2004), 424.

and the friends both appeal to Psalms 8 and 107. For the former psalm, they exploit the tension between human hubris and humility in relation to God found in the question "What are humans?" at the center of Psalm 8, which presents humanity in a lowly and yet exalted place in God's creation. Through Job's parody of this question (7:17–18), he charges God with replacing the "care" (פקד; Ps 8:5) he deserves with oppressive investigation, using the same verb but giving it a different meaning. Job continues in this vein as he accuses God of stripping him of his "glory" and tearing the "crown" from his head (19:9; cf. Ps 8:6). The friends, however, object to Job's high view of himself and use the psalm's contrast of humanity with heavenly beings and the heavens (Ps 8:4–6) to try to silence Job's accusations by arguing that he is ontologically, and thus morally, inferior and therefore has no right to accuse God (15:14–16; 25:5–6).

Though the most marked allusion between Job and Psalm 107 comes in Job's fourth speech (12:21, 24; cf. Ps 107:40), it is Eliphaz who initially draws the psalm into the dialogue through his emphasis on its promises of deliverance from distress in ch. 5. Job, however, responds in 12:13–13:2 by using selective citation and parody to indicate that the afflictions in the psalm are also God's doing. This parodic hymn to the God who destroys, like Job's parodies of Psalm 8, both expresses his frustration at his current state and implicitly calls on God to remedy it. Though Eliphaz concedes some ground to Job's implicit accusation in ch. 15 (e.g., vv. 22–23), he maintains that Job should cry out to the Lord to find deliverance as the psalm's refrain declares (15:24). When Job responds with a further parody of the blessing the psalm promises (21:11; cf. Ps 107:41), Eliphaz draws psalmic parody and citation together to reject Job's words and suggest he is actually among the wicked (22:19; cf. Ps 107:42). In the psalm's underlying tension between the threatening and beneficent sides of divine sovereignty, Job's experience forces him to challenge Eliphaz's emphasis on God's certain blessing for the righteous since it does not accord with what he has seen and heard (13:1–2). The polemic setting of Job's interpretation pushes it in a strongly negative direction as a response to Eliphaz's rosy reading, but Job intends to use the psalm to convince God to intervene on his behalf, so he cannot dismiss it altogether.

Job's intent to motivate God is evident in his allusions to two psalms of supplication, 139 and 39, which also have this purpose, though each pursues it very differently. Psalm 139, which Job engages with throughout ch. 10, attempts to move God through praise, lauding his omniscience and omnipresence before concluding with a request for vindication (vv. 19–24). Job mixes this acclamation with accusation, most notably by taking the psalmist's poignant image of God's care for him from the womb (Ps 139:13–16) and using it to charge God with destroying his creation (10:8–12). In response, Zophar threatens Job with the same divine attributes that inspired the psalmist's praise (11:7–9; cf. Ps 139:7–10), revealing the ambiguity of the psalm's depiction of God. Job then uses that same imagery to again accuse God, now of avoiding him (23:8–9), because God knows Job is in the right (23:10; cf. Ps 139:23–34).

Instead of appealing to God's greatness and the way things should be, the author of Psalm 39, uses his own afflicted insignificance and the sorrowful way things are to attempt to move God to intervene. Job can employ that technique as well, and he exchanges parody for intensification to outdo the psalmist in his lament. His repeated allusions to the psalm in his second speech (chs. 6–7), particularly to the psalmist's desire for his end and yet affirmation of his hope (Ps 39:5, 8), the latter of which Job denies, reach a climax in his nearly verbatim, yet even more pathetic, repetition of the psalmist's demand that God leave him alone (10:20–21; cf. Ps 39:14). Though he returns to imagery from the psalm again in 13:28–14:6, the friends let Job's use of Psalm 39 go without a response, possibly because, while surpassing one of the most dismal psalms in the Psalter serves Job well to express the depth of his sorrow, the friends would gain little in their evident desire to silence Job's complaints by legitimizing similar lamentation.

The friends are much more comfortable with psalms of instruction. As with Psalm 107, which also accords closely with their message of blessing for the repentant, it is Eliphaz and not Job who introduces Psalm 1 into the debate (5:13–14). Like Zophar's allusion to Psalm 139, Eliphaz takes the implicit threat of Ps 1:1–2 and makes it explicit. Whereas the psalm promises happiness to the righteous, Eliphaz declares misery for the wicked. As with his response to Eliphaz's allusions to Psalm 107, Job replies by indicating that this has not been his experience. Instead, he has seen God favor the plans of the wicked (10:3), something Job would never do himself (21:16), as God treats him (13:25), and not the wicked (21:18), like windblown chaff (Ps 1:4). Though he rejects Eliphaz's appeal to the psalm, even though Eliphaz tries to reinstate it (22:18), Job does not reject the doctrine of retribution it presents, instead relying once again on the hope of eventually finding vindication through God's judgment (23:10–11).

Eliphaz's naive understanding of retribution is something the author of Psalm 73 himself struggles with. As the psalmist attempts to reconcile his faith in God's justice with the prosperity of the wicked, he offers resources for both Job and the friends. Job appeals to the psalmist's description of his affliction (7:18; cf. Ps 73:14) and the apparent vanity of his purity (9:30; cf. Ps 73:13). Though Job alludes to the psalmist's declaration of hope (19:25–27; cf. Ps 73:23–26), he follows it with a scathing parody of a wisdom song that draws heavily on the psalm (21:7–34). Then, Job draws a contrast with the psalmist's admission of nearly stumbling into his demand for vindication (23:11; cf. Ps 73:2). The friends each refer to a different image from the psalm that threatens or denigrates the wicked (15:27; 18:11, 14; 20:8) before Eliphaz associates Job with them by attributing to him the words the psalm ascribes to the wicked (22:12–13; cf. Ps 73:11). Demonstrating the friends' affinity for this psalm of instruction, this is the only time the most marked allusion to a psalm is made by one of them and not Job.

9.2. The Interpretive Conflict

Previous research on allusions to the Psalms in Job has tended either to address each allusion separately among the many intertextual references in the book or to consider the sustained interaction with only one psalm. Combining a more extensive approach that was able to identify the psalms that play the most prominent role in the dialogue with a thorough examination of how those psalms contributed to the debate has revealed the sophistication of the author's interpretation of earlier texts. The author does not simply repeat the odd word or phrase from the Psalms but engages broadly with each psalm, interpreting it as he alludes to it, identifying its central tension and interacting with it. To do so, he interprets the psalms through his characters, as Job reads the Psalms differently than the friends. Adroitly employing a dialogical style, the author embodies in the assorted characters not merely different theological ideas but contrasting interpretive perspectives, as well. Thus, this study has revealed a new depth to the dialogue between Job and the friends, in which the interpretation of earlier texts is a means by which the author develops his characters and their dispute.

Because Job and the friends appeal to the Psalms in different ways and for contrasting purposes, and the author provides little beyond their voices, his own interpretive approach is complex and difficult to pinpoint. It defies general classification as skeptical parody or scriptural piety, but mixes elements of both. To understand the author's interpretation, one must understand his characters' readings of the Psalms and how they interact. The recurrent references to the Psalms, filled with their anguished or adoring address to God, testify to the book's existential emphasis, and demonstrates its great, if not primary, interest in the proper response to suffering in the context of relationship with God.[2] Job and the friends, however, have very different views on what that response should be.

9.2.1. Job: Piety through Parody

The book of Job seems to depict two Jobs: the pious Job of the frame narrative[3] and the rebellious Job of the dialogue.[4] In turn, Job appears to refer to two Gods: one, his tormentor (16:9), and the other, his deliverer (19:25–27). Job's allusions

---

2   For other proponents of this understanding of the book, see p. 11.

3   For the preference for this Job in traditional readings, see Nahum N. Glatzer, "Introduction: A Study of Job," in *The Dimensions of Job: A Study and Selected Readings* (ed. Nahum N. Glatzer; New York: Schocken Books, 1969). See also, Michael V. Fox, "Job the Pious," *ZAW* 117 (2005): 351–66. Fox rejects the skeptical interpretation of the book (364), but still considers the character Job to have rebelled against God (360–61).

4   See, e.g. Dell, *Sceptical.*

to the Psalms offer a means for explaining both of these tensions without eradi-
cating them.

The pious Job appears to transform into the rebellious one when, in the dialogue, he exchanges his earlier submissive attitude (1:21; 2:10) for accusation
against God for wrongdoing. Though he blames God and no other cause for his
suffering, he also appeals to God for the vindication he craves, thereby confronting the God of his experience with the God of his faith. Job's predominantly
parodic allusions to the Psalms, which express the frustration he has with the dis-
connect between these two views of God, make Job appear to be a skeptical rebel
lashing out against a God who has disappointed him and become unrecognizable.
And yet, in these same psalmic allusions, Job appeals to the God they describe,
one who cares for (Psalms 8, 107, 139) and is present with (Psalms 73, 139)
God's people and acts with justice (Psalms 1, 73, 107), thereby inspiring hope in
the midst of despair (Psalm 39); the appeal itself suggesting he knows God is
capable, and could be willing, should the deity be so moved, to right the wrong
Job feels he is enduring.[5] By turning the psalmic depictions of divine-human relationship upside-down, Job communicates that things are not the way they should
be, but he does so by appealing to texts that present that relationship right-side-
up. Only because he has such faith in the God of justice does he employ the
Psalms to rebel against the God of violence he is currently experiencing, for he
knows these conflicting Gods are not two but one.[6] And only because he believes
what the Psalms teach does he twist their meaning in his accusations. His piety
expresses itself through parody. Therefore, the book also depicts not two Jobs
but one, who expresses two types of piety, submission and challenge.[7] Though
Job's "psalm has turned into weeping" (Job 30:31 LXX), to cite the title of this
book, in his psalmic tears, he hopes for vindication.

Thus, by using the Psalms as paradigms to challenge God, Job reflects a central theological principle in Israelite religion, perhaps even, considering the
meaning given the nation's name in Gen 32:29, the defining principle—struggling
with God. Job joins the heroes of Israelite faith, Abraham (Gen 18:25), Jacob
(Gen 32:24–32), and Moses (Exod 32:12), the psalmists who dare to cry "Why?"

---

5   Norman Whybray notes this similarity between Job and the complaints in the Psalms (R. N.
     Whybray, "'Shall not the Judge of All the Earth Do What is Just?': God's Oppression of the
     Innocent in the Old Testament," in *Shall Not the Judge of All the Earth Do What is Right?: Studies on
     the Nature of God in Tribute to James L. Crenshaw* [eds. D. Penchansky and P. L. Redditt; Winona
     Lake, Ind.: Eisenbrauns, 2000], 13). Similarly, Volz claims Job's "Anklage gegen Gott ist doch
     ein Zeichen der fortdauernden Gottverbundenheit" (Volz, *Weisheit*, 62).

6   See Gordis, *Job*, 526–27.

7   For submission and challenge as two non-mutually exclusive forms of piety, see Lennart
     Boström, "Patriarchal Models for Piety," in *Shall Not the Judge of All the Earth Do What Is Right?:
     Studies on the Nature of God in Tribute to James L. Crenshaw* (eds. David Penchansky and Paul L. Red-
     ditt; Winona Lake, Ind.: Eisenbrauns, 2000), 57–72.

and "How long?" and prophets such as Jeremiah and Habakkuk, in confronting God and demanding that the deity make things right.[8] This broad tradition suggests that this was not considered an act of rebellion, but was fully consonant with great faith, apparently because these challenges were motivated by a belief that God is good, powerful, and loving enough to act justly. Confronting God on the basis of divine character may even be the consummate act of piety because it expresses faith in God even when God's current actions seem to militate against it.[9]

Therefore, when read in light of the broader testimony of the HB, Job's rebellion in the dialogue against the apparent injustice of God may be interpreted as evidence of courageous faith in God despite his experience of divine antagonism.[10] It would then demonstrate a vision of God for which Job deems it worth fighting God. The friends, however, as their allusions to the Psalms indicate, have a much smaller understanding of God for which they are only willing to fight Job.

9.2.2. The Friends: Pious Proof-texting

Allusions to these six psalms show Eliphaz to be the leader in responding to Job. His repeated allusions include the initiation of the debate over two of the psalms (Psalms 1, 107) and the most marked allusion to another (Psalm 73), while the other friends only have one substantial allusion each (Bildad to Psalm 8 and Zophar to Psalm 139). Thus, Eliphaz is "a well-defined, major character, who from both the artistic and the ideological aspect fulfills the role of constituting a clear antithesis to Job," while Bildad and Zophar merely fill in the background.[11]

---

8   See Robert Davidson, *The Courage to Doubt: Exploring an Old Testament Theme* (London: SCM Press, 1983). Roland Murphy also associates Job with this tradition, which he claims is "at the heart of Israel's faith" (Murphy, *Tree*, 34), as does Patrick Miller in his study of petitionary prayer as an attempt to coax God into acting according to God's character (Patrick D. Miller, "Prayer and Divine Action," in *God in the Fray: A Tribute to Walter Brueggemann* [eds. Tod Linafelt and Timothy K. Beal; Minneapolis: Fortress Press, 1998], 211–32). Additionally, Crenshaw includes Job among those who refuse to abandon God in the midst of divine testing (Crenshaw, *Whirlpool*, 117).

9   This mix of faith and doubt is evident in ANE texts that reproach deities, as well. See Dorothea Sitzler, *"Vorwurf gegen Gott": Ein religiöses Motiv im Alten Orient (Ägypten und Mesopotamien)* (StOR 32; Wiesbaden: Harrassowitz, 1995), 231–32. Heckl observes that these texts, like Job, present a pious person, who, in spite of his charge against his god, holds fast to the relationship with him (Heckl, *Hiob*, 213).

10 For this interpretation of Job's accusations against God as a means of addressing the difficulties Christian interpreters have had with reconciling them with God's approval of Job's words in 42:7–8, see Will Kynes, "The Trials of Job: Re-litigating Job's 'Good Case' in Christian Interpretation," *SJT* (forthcoming).

11 Hoffman, *Blemished*, 134. This corresponds with God's address to Eliphaz and his "two friends" (42:7).

Eliphaz leads the friends in manipulating the Psalms to make their arguments, but their negative distortion does not depend on the positive message of the psalm to be effective. Instead of implicitly appealing to the right-side-up message of the Psalms, they erase it. Instead of arguing against the way things are based on the way they should be, they claim things are the way they should be, and attempt to use the Psalms as support. If the distance between Job's experience and the psalm leaves them with some discomfort, particularly as it threatens their own confidence in their strict retributory worldview, they try to shape the psalm to fit his experience instead of appealing to the psalm to change it. Therefore, they transform the positive messages of the Psalms into negative ones that denigrate humanity (Psalm 8), suggest guilt (Psalm 107), threaten with unavoidable judgment (Psalm 139), ignore lament (Psalm 39), warn of retribution (Psalm 1), and accuse of wickedness (Psalm 73).

This suggests, *contra* James Sanders, that it is Job, and not the friends, who depends on the "static" meaning of the text, at least in his use of the Psalms, since, if the Psalms do not represent an enduring standard, he cannot use them to accuse God. Job is the one trying to "make the present look and act like the past,"[12] as he desires an exchange of his present suffering and distance from God for the past ideal of the Psalms. It is the friends who dynamically transform the Psalms as they attempt to make the past look like the present. With a "consuming passion" for self-justification,[13] they read these psalms through Job's experience, devising meanings for them that can explain both their prosperity and his pain, and thus using them as "prooftexts," citing them "in support of previously determined conclusions."[14] In fact, Cheney claims "simple proof-texting" is the friends' predominate approach to the HB.[15] However, he contrasts this with Job's "subverting" of the text, when it actually appears that the friends' interpretations do more to undermine the plain meaning of these psalms. This adds nuance to Dell's claim that all the "misuse of forms" in the dialogue occurs exclusively in Job's speeches.[16] Though Job does use parody to emphasize the difference between his representation of the Psalms and their original meaning while the friends generally present their position as consistent with the Psalms, the friends are actually manipulating the Psalms just as much as Job is.

Therefore, if God's judgment of the friends' arguments in the epilogue (42:7–8) is indeed a response to what they have said in the dialogue (and whether written by the same author or not, it certainly seems to play this role in the book

---

12   James A. Sanders, "The Book of Job and the Origins of Judaism," *BTB* 39 (2009): 67.

13   Crenshaw, *Whirlpool*, 70.

14   Boyarin, *Intertextuality*, 22.

15   Cheney, *Dust*, 135.

16   Dell, *Sceptical*, 136.

as it has been edited together), then the friends draw God's ire for their apparently pious defense of God against Job's attack because it demonstrates a lack of faith in God to make things right, to live up to the psalmic descriptions of the deity, which they must twist to support their arguments. Thus, when comparing Job with the friends, Robert Davidson remarks, "There was more faith in such deeply questioning protests and scepticism than in the pious affirmation of untroubled, but blind, certainty."[17]

9.3. The Interpretation of the Psalms in Job

The author of Job's dialogic interpretation of these six psalms testifies to the complexity of interpreting them. He draws out the ambiguity and tension in each psalm, demonstrating how different interpreters can capitalize on these portions of each psalm's message to make the psalms say what they want by resolving the ambiguity in favor of their view. God's commendation of Job and denunciation of the friends in 42:7–8, if it does take the dialogue into account, may even include a judgment on their respective interpretive approaches to these psalms, thereby endorsing Job's interpretation of their tensions over those of the friends, and suggesting that, for example, Psalm 8 does present humanity as exalted and not insignificant.[18] Either way, these allusions to the Psalms in a debate over the proper response to suffering demonstrate that even in the Second Temple period they had relevance beyond the cult. How far their influence spread is a topic for further study.

Through the dialogue of his book with the Psalms, the author of Job also creates an inter-psalmic intertextuality, which anticipates the tensions in the collected Psalter. Most notable are the allusions to both Psalm 1 and Psalm 73, which present contrasting positions on retribution, the first confident and the second unsettled. Through drawing both into the dialogue, the author of Job suggests they can be held together, though not without difficulty. The same can be said for the unabashed praise of Psalm 8 and anguished complaint of Psalm 39. This juxtaposition of psalms and the Job poet's choice of psalms that span the Psalter and include the opening psalms of its first, third, and fifth books, may

---

17   Davidson, *Doubt*, 183.

18   Job's "confession" in 42:6 might be suggested as an objection to considering his interpretive approach exemplary, but the ambiguity of those words leaves open the real possibility that they are not a confession of wrongdoing. See, e.g., Clines's translation: "So I submit, and I accept consolation for my dust and ashes" (Clines, *Job,* 3:1205). Even if Job is repenting, because, as I have argued, he relies on the positive side of the tensive presentation of God's relationship with humanity in these Psalms, it is unlikely that this is what he is repudiating.

shed light on the shaping of the collection, though this is another subject for another time.

9.4. Historical Implications

These allusions to the Psalms also have historical implications. The disputes over their meaning actually testify to their authority in the community, as well as anticipating the debating style of midrashic interpretation. In the sustained interaction with each psalm and occasional verbatim repetition, these allusions suggest these psalms were in written (though not necessarily complete) form when Job was composed and that the book itself was a written composition. Not only had the psalms likely reached a written form by this time, but they also seem to have taken on the status of "scripture," even as the text-infused nature of Job's address to God corresponds to the "scripturalization" of prayer in the Second Temple period. The reevaluation of the nature of retribution, as Job hopes for at least a delayed, if not yet eschatological, vindication of the righteous, also agrees with a transition in thought on this question at that time, but the friends' development of a strict form of retribution suggests it was disputed. Though the date of Job will continue to be debated, this study has shown that its intertextual method and theological message fit well in the early Second Temple period. If this is the case, then, since I have also argued that the psalms studied were likely written before Job, these psalms originated no later than that period. And though the dates of the psalms are similarly disputed, this direction of dependence would at least exclude the patriarchal date given Job in traditional interpretation.

9.5. Broader Relevance and Further Research

This study also has relevance beyond Job and the Psalms, particularly in the interpretive insight provided by the intertextual method used, which puts synchronic and diachronic intertextualities in dialogue by combining aspects from both types and adapting them to apply to the HB, where the relative dates of texts are often unknown. This method offers a way forward given the historical impasse regarding the relative dates of Job and most of the psalms by using a synchronic simultaneous comparison of the purposes the purported allusions would have in the respective texts to suggest the text most likely to be alluding to the other. For example, Job was deemed later than Psalm 8 because parody of praise seems much more likely than a hymn incorporating accusation against God. The synchronic perspective also provides a means for pursuing the current of recurring allusions coursing between the texts once one marked allusion solders them together and the reciprocal implications of allusions for the interpretation of the source text. However, diachronic intertextuality channels that hermeneutical voltage by providing historical and authorial limits on its potential significance through reading the texts sequentially and interpreting the allusions as a later author's intentional references to earlier texts, thus offering insight into their plausible meaning within history and building a foundation for further historical conclusions. As the intertextual method used here was developed by refining earlier approaches to address the difficulties of pursuing literary connections between Job and the Psalms, so this method could itself be fine-tuned for exploring connections between other texts.

Additionally, the intertextual approach helps move the discussion beyond the use of common forms and formulas, which had dominated much of the earlier research on connections between Job and the Psalms, to the role specific texts play in the Job dialogue. Though I acknowledged the possibility of influence from formulaic language, by considering connections primarily between texts, the sustained dialogue with those texts and the tensions within them became evident. Therefore, this study is a further endorsement for the current trend moving from form criticism toward intertextuality in the analysis of parallels between biblical texts, even as it suggests the relationship between these two approaches needs further research. This relationship is delicate, since either could be the explanation for many textual connections, and yet neither is the explanation for all. The balance between them is not yet established. Form criticism still has a great deal to offer in the interpretation of both Job and the Psalms, particularly for the resonance of larger forms between the texts, which are better explained by formal comparison. However, form-critical attempts to identify literary genres with particular historical settings and corresponding circles of authors need to be treated with care, as they can create overly strict boundaries between texts associated with different forms.[19]

The dialogical nature of the book of Job also comes to the fore in this study. This appears not only in Job's dialogue with the friends and God, which takes up much of the book, but in the dialogue created between the book and the Psalms through the psalmic allusions and the Job poet's dialogical embodiment of contrasting ideas, and even interpretive approaches, in Job and the friends. Though aspects of Bakhtinian dialogism have been found in many texts in the HB, this dialogical interplay of interpretive perspectives on earlier texts has seldom been investigated. This and other interpretive techniques in the Second Temple period deserve more systematic and comprehensive study.

---

19   See, e.g., Rolf Knierim, "Old Testament Form Criticism Reconsidered," *Int* 27 (1973): 435–68, and more recently, Dell, *Proverbs*, 184–85; Stuart Weeks, *An Introduction to the Study of Wisdom Literature* (New York: T&T Clark, 2010), 21, 128, 136.

The close connections between Job and the Psalms also pose significant questions for the classification of both texts. For Job, this sustained dialogue with psalms of all types may draw the book's common wisdom classification into question, as it endorses Kuhl's observation that the book stands as close to the Psalms as to wisdom[20] and invites further research into the genre categorization of Job. At the same time, it suggests the classification of the individual psalms should also be reconsidered. Some have attempted to classify all these psalms as "wisdom psalms," basing their arguments for all but Psalm 1 in large part on their connections with Job. But these arguments are considerably weaker if those similarities are the result of the Job poet alluding to the psalms and if doubts remain about Job being a "wisdom" text itself.

Finally, the detailed and sophisticated interaction with these psalms in the Job dialogue invites further research into allusions in Job. This could include allusions to these and other psalms, such as Psalm 37, elsewhere in the work,[21] but also intertextual connections with other books in Job.[22] Having shown himself capable of this type of intertextual interpretation with the Psalms, the author of Job is likely to have interacted with other texts in this way. Some research into this issue has already been done, but rarely with sustained attention to Job's interaction with a single text, leaving the depths of the interpretive significance of the author's use of intertextuality yet to be plumbed. As these connections continue to be investigated, they may further challenge the classification of Job as "wisdom," demonstrating instead that it is a much more eclectic work. They will also, like the Job poet's integration of material from the Psalms into Job's fight of faith, further demonstrate the artistic skill and theological complexity of his work.[23]

---

20   See p. 2.

21   See p. 33 for the possible implications of such studies.

22   For a broad investigation of intertextuality in Job, not merely restricted to intentional allusions nor to texts in the HB, see Katharine Dell and Will Kynes, eds. *Reading Job Intertextually* (LHBOTS; New York: T&T Clark, forthcoming).

23   See Henning Graf Reventlow, *Gebet im Alten Testament* (Stuttgart: Kohlhammer, 1986), 268–69.

Bibliography

Adams, Samuel L. *Wisdom in Transition: Act and Consequence in Second Temple Instructions.* Supplements to the Journal for the Study of Judaism 125. Leiden: Brill, 2008.

Aichele, George and Gary A. Philips. "Exegesis, Eisegesis, Intergesis." *Semeia* 69/70 (1995): 7–18.

Akenson, Donald Harman. *Surpassing Wonder: The Invention of the Bible and the Talmuds.* Chicago: University of Chicago Press, 1998.

Albertson, R. G. "Job and Ancient Near Eastern Wisdom Literature." Pages 213–30 in *Scripture in Context II: More Essays on the Comparative Method.* Edited by William W. Hallo, James C. Moyer, and Leo G. Perdue. Winona Lake, Ind.: Eisenbrauns, 1983.

Alkier, Stefan. "Intertextuality and the Semiotics of Biblical Texts." Pages 3–21 in *Reading the Bible Intertextually.* Edited by Richard B. Hays, Stefan Alkier, and Leroy A. Huizenga. Waco, Tex.: Baylor University Press, 2009.

———. "New Testament Studies on the Basis of Categorical Semiotics." Pages 223–48 in *Reading the Bible Intertextually.* Edited by Richard B. Hays, Stefan Alkier, and Leroy A. Huizenga. Waco, Tex.: Baylor University Press, 2009.

Allen, Graham. *Intertextuality.* London: Routledge, 2000.

Allen, Leslie C. "Faith on Trial: An Analysis of Psalm 139." *Vox evangelica* 10 (1977): 5–23.

———. "Psalm 73: Pilgrimage from Doubt to Faith." *Bulletin of Biblical Research* 7 (1997): 1–9.

———. *Psalms 101–150.* Word Biblical Commentary 21. Nashville: Thomas Nelson, 2002.

Alonso Schökel, Luis. "Todo Adán es Abel: Salmo 39." *Estudios bíblicos* 46 (1988): 269–81.

Alonso Schökel, Luis and José Luis Sicre Díaz. *Job: Comentario teológico y literario.* Nueva Biblia Española. Madrid: Ediciones Cristiandad, 1983.

Alster, Bendt. *Studies in Sumerian Proverbs.* Copenhagen Studies in Assyriology 3. Copenhagen: Akademisk Forlag, 1975.

Alter, Robert. *The Art of Biblical Poetry.* Edinburgh: T&T Clark, 1990.

———. *The Pleasures of Reading in an Ideological Age.* New York: W. W. Norton, 1996.

Ambrose. "The Prayer of Job and David." Pages 325-420 in *Saint Ambrose: Seven Exegetical Works.* Translated by Michael P. McHugh. Fathers of the Church 65. Washington, D.C.: Catholic University of America Press, 1971.

Andersen, Francis I. *Job.* London: Inter-Varsity Press, 1976.

Anderson, A. A. *The Book of Psalms.* 2 vols. New Century Bible. Grand Rapids, Mich.: Eerdmans, 1981.

Anderson, G. W. "A Note on Psalm i 1." *Vetus Testamentum* 24 (1974): 231–33.

Angel, Hayyim. "The Differences Between the Wise and the Foolish in Psalms: Theodicy, Understanding Providence, and Religious Responses." *Jewish Bible Quarterly* 38 (2010): 157–65.

Aquinas, Thomas. *The Literal Exposition on Job: A Scriptural Commentary Concerning Providence.* Edited by Martin D. Yaffe. Translated by Anthony Damico. Classics in Religious Studies 7. Atlanta: Scholars Press, 1989.

Auvray, P. "Le Psaume 1. Notes de grammaire et d'exégèse." *Revue biblique* 53 (1946): 365–71.

Bakhtin, Mikhail M. "From the Prehistory of Novelistic Discourse." Pages 41–83 in *The Dialogic Imagination: Four Essays.* Edited by Michael Holquist. Translated by Caryl Emerson and Michael Holquist. Austin: University of Texas Press, 1981.

———. *Problems of Dostoevsky's Poetics.* Translated by Caryl Emerson. Theory and History of Literature 8. Manchester: Manchester University Press, 1984.

Balentine, Samuel E. *Job.* Macon, Ga.: Smyth & Helwys, 2006.

———. "'What are Human Beings, That You Make So Much of Them?': Divine Disclosure from the Whirlwind: 'Look at the Behemoth.'" Pages 259-78 in *God in the Fray: A Tribute to Walter Brueggemann.* Edited by Tod Linafelt and Timothy K. Beal. Minneapolis: Fortress Press, 1998.

Ball, C. J. *The Book of Job.* Oxford: Clarendon Press, 1922.

Baron, Scarlett. *"Strandentwining Cable": Joyce, Flaubert, and Intertextuality.* Oxford English Monographs. Oxford: Oxford University Press, 2012.

Barr, James. "The Book of Job and its Modern Interpreters." *Bulletin of the John Rylands Library* 54 (1971–1972): 28–46.

———. *The Semantics of Biblical Language.* Oxford: Oxford University Press, 1961.

———. "The Synchronic, the Diachronic and the Historical: A Triangular Relationship?" Pages 1–14 in *Synchronic or Diachronic?: A Debate on Method in Old Testament Exegesis.* Edited by Johannes C. de Moor. Oudtestamentische Studiën 34. Leiden: Brill, 1995.

Barth, J. *Beiträge zur Erklärung des Buches Hiob.* Leipzig: J.C. Hinrichs'sche Buchhandlung, 1878.

Barth, Karl. *Church Dogmatics IV: The Doctrine of Reconciliation, Part 3.1.* Translated by G. W. Bromiley. London: T&T Clark International, 2004.

Barthes, Roland. "The Death of the Author." Pages 142–48 in *Image-Music-Text.* Translated by Stephen Heath. New York: Hill and Wang, 1977.

Barton, John. *"Déjà lu*: Intertextuality, Method or Theory?" in *Reading Job Intertextually.* Edited by Katharine Dell and Will Kynes. Library of Hebrew Bible/Old Testament Studies. New York: T&T Clark, forthcoming.

———. "Intertextuality and the 'Final Form' of the Text." Pages 33–37 in *Congress Volume Oslo 1998.* Edited by A. Lemaire and M. Sæbø. Supplements to Vetus Testamentum. Leiden: Brill, 2000.

———. *The Nature of Biblical Criticism.* Louisville, Ky.: Westminster John Knox, 2007.

———. *Reading the Old Testament: Method in Biblical Study.* 2nd ed. London: Darton, Longman & Todd, 1996.

Bauks, Michaela. *Die Feinde des Psalmisten und die Freunde Ijobs: Untersuchungen zur Freund-Klage im Alten Testament am Beispiel von Ps 22.* Stuttgarter Bibelstudien 203. Stuttgart: Katholisches Bibelwerk, 2004.

———. "Was ist der Mensch, dass du ihn großziehst? (Hiob 7,17)." Pages 1–13 in *Was ist der Mensch, dass du seiner gedenkst? (Psalm 8,5): Aspekte einer theologischen Anthropologie.* Edited by Michaela Bauks. Neukirchen-Vluyn: Neukirchener Verlag, 2008.

Baumann, E. "Struktur-untersuchungen im Psalter I." *Zeitschrift für die alttestamentliche Wissenschaft* 61 (1945–1948): 114–76.

Baumgärtel, Friedrich. *Der Hiobdialog: Aufriss und Deutung.* Beiträge zur Wissenschaft vom Alten und Neuen Testament 61. Stuttgart: W. Kohlhammer, 1933.

Baxandall, Michael. *Patterns of Intention: On the Historical Explanation of Pictures.* New Haven, Conn.: Yale University Press, 1985.

Beal, Timothy K. "Glossary." Pages 21–24 in *Reading Between Texts: Intertextuality and the Hebrew Bible.* Edited by Danna Nolan Fewell. Literary Currents in Biblical Interpretation. Louisville, Ky.: Westminster John Knox, 1992.

———. "Ideology and Intertextuality: Surplus of Meaning and Controlling the Means of Production." Pages 27–39 in *Reading Between Texts: Intertextuality and the Hebrew Bible.* Edited by Danna Nolan Fewell. Literary Currents in Biblical Interpretation. Louisville, Ky.: Westminster John Knox, 1992.

Ben-Porat, Ziva. "The Poetics of Literary Allusion." *PTL: A Journal for Descriptive Poetics and Theory of Literature* 1 (1976): 105–28.

Bentzen, Aage. *Introduction to the Old Testament.* 2 vols. Copenhagen: G. E. C. Gad, 1948–1949.

Bergmeier, Roland. "Zum Ausdruck עצת רשעים in Ps 1:1, Hi 10:3, 21:16 und 22:18." *Zeitschrift für die alttestamentliche Wissenschaft* 79 (1967): 229–32.

Beyerlin, Walter. "Psalm 8: Chancen der Überlieferungskritik." *Zeitschrift für Theologie und Kirche* 73 (1976): 1–22.

———. *Werden und Wesen des 107. Psalms.* Beihefte zur Zeitschrift für die alttestamentliche Wissenschaft 151. Berlin: Walter de Gruyter, 1979.

Bloch, Renée. "Midrash." Pages 1263–81 in vol. 5 of *Supplément au Dictionnaire de la Bible.* Edited by H. Cazelles and A. Feuillet. Paris: Le Touzey, 1950.

Bloom, Harold. *The Anxiety of Influence: A Theory of Poetry.* 2nd ed. Oxford: Oxford University Press, 1997.

———. *A Map of Misreading.* Oxford: Oxford University Press, 1975.

Bolducius, Jacobus. *Commentaria in librum Job.* 2 vols. Paris: 1637.

Booij, T. "Psalm cxxxix." *Vetus Testamentum* 55 (2005): 1–19.

Boström, Lennart. "Patriarchal Models for Piety." Pages 57–72 in *Shall Not the Judge of All the Earth Do What Is Right?: Studies on the Nature of God in Tribute to James L. Crenshaw.* Edited by David Penchansky and Paul L. Redditt. Winona Lake, Ind.: Eisenbrauns, 2000.

Botha, Phil J. "Intertextuality and the Interpretation of Psalm 1." Pages 58–76 in *Psalms and Mythology.* Edited by Dirk J. Human. Journal for the Study of the Old Testament: Supplement Series 462. New York: T&T Clark, 2007.

Boyarin, Daniel. *Intertextuality and the Reading of Midrash.* Indiana Studies in Biblical Literature. Bloomington: Indiana University Press, 1990.

Braude, William Gordon. *The Midrash on Psalms.* 2 vols. Yale Judaica Series 13. New Haven: Yale University Press, 1959.

Briggs, Charles Augustus. *The Book of Psalms.* 2 vols. International Critical Commentary. Edinburgh: T&T Clark, 1906–1909.

Brown, William P. *Character in Crisis: A Fresh Approach to the Wisdom Literature of the Old Testament.* Grand Rapids, Mich.: Eerdmans, 1996.

——. "*Creatio Corporis* and the Rhetoric of Defense in Job 10 and Psalm 139." Pages 107–24 in *God Who Creates: Essays in Honor of Sibley Turner*. Edited by William P. Brown and S. Dean McBride, Jr. Grand Rapids, Mich.: Eerdmans, 2000.

Broyles, Craig C. *The Conflict of Faith and Experience in the Psalms: A Form-Critical and Theological Study*. Journal for the Study of the Old Testament: Supplement Series 52. Sheffield: JSOT Press, 1989.

——. *Psalms*. New International Biblical Commentary on the Old Testament 11. Peabody, Mass.: Hendrickson, 1999.

Brueggemann, Walter. *The Message of the Psalms: A Theological Commentary*. Augsburg Old Testament Studies. Minneapolis: Augsburg, 1984.

——. "A Shape for Old Testament Theology, I: Structure Legitimation." *Catholic Biblical Quarterly* 47 (1985): 28–46.

——. "A Shape for Old Testament Theology, II: Embrace of Pain." *Catholic Biblical Quarterly* 47 (1985): 395–415.

——. "Voice as Counter to Violence." *Calvin Theological Journal* 36 (2001): 22–33.

Buss, Martin J. *Biblical Form Criticism in its Context*. Journal for the Study of the Old Testament: Supplement Series 274. Sheffield: Sheffield Academic Press, 1999.

——. *The Changing Shape of Form Criticism: A Relational Approach*. Hebrew Bible Monographs 18. Sheffield: Sheffield Phoenix Press, 2010.

Buttenwieser, Moses. *The Psalms: Chronologically Treated with a New Translation*. Library of Biblical Studies. New York: Ktav, 1969.

Calvin, John. *Sermons on Job*. Edinburgh: The Banner of Truth Trust, 1993. Reprint of *Sermons on Job*. Translated by Arthur Golding. London: George Bishop, 1574.

——. *Commentary on the Book of Psalms*. Translated by James Anderson. 5 vols. Grand Rapids, Mich.: Baker Book House, 1993.

Campbell, Anthony F. "Form Criticism's Future." Pages 13–31 in *The Changing Face of Form Criticism for the Twenty-First Century*. Edited by Marvin A. Sweeney and Ehud Ben Zvi. Grand Rapids, Mich.: Eerdmans, 2003.

Caquot, Andre. "Traits royaux dans le personnage de Job." Pages 32–45 in *Maqqel shaqedh: La branche d'amandier: Hommage à Wilhelm Vischer*. Edited by Daniel Lys. Montpelier: Cause Graille Castelnau, 1960.

Carbajosa, I. "Salmo 107: Unidad, Organización y Teología." *Estudios bíblicos* 59 (2001): 451–85.

Carr, David M. "The Many Uses of Intertextuality in Biblical Studies: Actual and Potential." Pages 505–35 in *International Organization for the Study of the Old Testament Congress Volume: Helsinki 2010*. Edited by Martti Nissinen. Supplements to Vetus Testamentum 148. Leiden: Brill, 2012.

——. "Method in Determination of Direction of Dependence: An Empirical Test of Criteria Applied to Exodus 34,11–26 and Its Parallels." Pages 107–40 in *Gottes Volk am Sinai: Untersuchungen zu Ex 32–34 und Dtn 9–10*. Edited by Matthias Köckert and Erhard Blum. Gütersloh: Chr. Kaiser, Gütersloher Verlaghaus, 2001.

——. *Writing on the Tablet of the Heart: Origins of Scripture and Literature*. Oxford: Oxford University Press, 2005.

Carroll, Robert P. *Jeremiah: A Commentary*. Old Testament Library. London: SCM Press, 1986.

Chandler, James K. "Romantic Allusiveness." *Critical Inquiry* 8 (1982): 461–87.

Chappelow, Leonard. *A Commentary on the Book of Job.* 2 vols. Cambridge: J. Bentham, 1752.

Cheney, Michael. *Dust, Wind and Agony: Character, Speech and Genre in Job.* Coniectanea biblica, Old Testament 36. Stockholm: Almqvist & Wiksell International, 1994.

Cheyne, T. K. *The Book of Psalms.* 2 vols. London: Kegan Paul, Trench, Trübner & Co., 1904.

———. *Job and Solomon: Or, The Wisdom of the Old Testament.* New York: T. Whittaker, 1887.

Childs, Brevard S. *Introduction to the Old Testament as Scripture.* Philadelphia: Fortress Press, 1979.

———. "Psalm 8 in the Context of the Christian Canon." *Interpretation* 23 (1969): 20–31.

Chrysostom, John. *Kommentar zu Hiob.* Edited by U. Hagedorn and D. Hagedorn. Patristische Texte und Studien 35. Edited by K. Aland and E. Mühlenberg. Berlin: de Gruyter, 1990.

Clayton, Jay. "The Alphabet of Suffering: Effie Deans, Tess Durbeyfield, Martha Ray, and Hetty Sorrel." Pages 37–60 in *Influence and Intertextuality in Literary History.* Edited by Jay Clayton and Eric Rothstein. Madison, Wisc.: University of Wisconsin Press, 1991.

Clayton, Jay and Eric Rothstein. "Figures in the Corpus: Theories of Influence and Intertextuality." Pages 3–36 in *Influence and Intertextuality in Literary History.* Edited by Jay Clayton and Eric Rothstein. Madison: University of Wisconsin Press, 1991.

———, eds. *Influence and Intertextuality in Literary History.* Madison: University of Wisconsin Press, 1991.

Clements, R. E. *Wisdom in Theology.* The Didsbury Lectures. Carlisle: Paternoster, 1992.

Clifford, Richard J. "What Does the Psalmist Ask for in Psalms 39:5 and 90:12?" *Journal of Biblical Literature* 119 (2000): 59–66.

Clines, David J. A. *Job.* 3 vols. Word Biblical Commentary 17–18B. Nashville: Thomas Nelson, 1989, 2006, 2011.

Collins, John J. "Wisdom Reconsidered, in Light of the Dead Sea Scrolls." *Dead Sea Discoveries* 4 (1997): 265–81.

Craigie, Peter C. *Psalms 1–50.* Word Biblical Commentary 19. Nashville: Thomas Nelson, 2004.

Crashaw, Richard. "Dies iræ, dies illa." in *The English Poems of Richard Crashaw.* Edited by Edward Hutton. London: Methuen, 1901.

Creach, Jerome F. "Like a Tree Planted by the Temple Stream: The Portrait of the Righteous in Ps 1:3." *Catholic Biblical Quarterly* 61 (1999): 34–46.

Crenshaw, James L. "The Journey from Voluntary to Obligatory Silence (Reflections on Psalm 39 and Qoheleth)." Forthcoming in a Festschrift for Douglas A. Knight.

———. *A Whirlpool of Torment: Israelite Traditions of God as an Oppressive Presence.* Overtures to Biblical Theology 12. Philadelphia: Fortress Press, 1984.

Culler, Jonathan. "Presupposition and Intertextuality." Pages 100–118 in *The Pursuit of Signs: Semiotics, Literature, Deconstruction.* London: Routledge & Kegan Paul, 1981.

Culley, Robert C. *Oral Formulaic Language in the Biblical Psalms.* Toronto: University of Toronto Press, 1967.

Dahood, Mitchell J. *Psalms.* 3 vols. Anchor Bible 16–17A. Garden City, N.Y.: Doubleday, 1966–1970.

Dalman, Gustaf Hermann. *Arbeit und Sitte in Palästina.* 7 vols. Schriften des Deutschen Palästina-Instituts. Hildesheim: Georg Olms, 1964.

Danell, G. A. "Psalm 139." *Uppsala Universitets Årsskrift* 1 (1951): 1–37.

Dathe, Johann August. *Jobus Proverbia Salomonis Ecclesiastes Canticum Canticorum ex recensione textus hebraei et versionum antiquarum latine versi notisque philologicis et criticis illustrati.* Halle: Sumtibus Orphanotrophei, 1789.

Davidson, A. B. *The Book of Job.* Cambridge Bible for Schools and Colleges. Cambridge: Cambridge University Press, 1889.

Davidson, H. T. S. *Eliot and Hermeneutics: Absence and Interpretation in the Waste Land.* Baton Rouge: Louisiana State University Press, 1985.

Davidson, Robert. *The Courage to Doubt: Exploring an Old Testament Theme.* London: SCM Press, 1983.

Davis, Ellen F. "Job and Jacob: The Integrity of Faith." Pages 203–24 in *Reading Between Texts: Intertextuality and the Hebrew Bible.* Edited by Danna Nolan Fewell. Literary Currents in Biblical Interpretation. Louisville, Ky.: Westminster John Knox, 1992.

Deissler, Alfons. "Zur Datierung und Studierung der 'Kosmischen Hymnen' Pss 8, 19, 29." Pages 47–58 in *Lex tua veritas.* Edited by Heinrich Groß and Franz Mußner. Trier: Paulinus-Verlag, 1961.

Delitzsch, Franz. *Biblical Commentary on the Book of Job.* Translated by Francis Bolton. 2 vols. Clark's Foreign Theological Library 10–11. Edinburgh: T&T Clark, 1866.

———. *Biblical Commentary on the Psalms.* Translated by David Eaton. 3 vols. Clark's Foreign Theological Library 29–31. Edinburgh: T&T Clark, 1887–1889.

Dell, Katharine J. *The Book of Job as Sceptical Literature.* Beihefte zur Zeitschrift für die alttestamentliche Wissenschaft 197. Berlin: de Gruyter, 1991.

———. *The Book of Proverbs in Social and Theological Context.* Cambridge: Cambridge University Press, 2006.

———. "On the Development of Wisdom in Israel." Pages 135–51 in *Congress Volume: Cambridge 1995.* Edited by J. A. Emerton. Supplements to Vetus Testamentum 66. Leiden: Brill, 1997.

Dell, Katharine and Will Kynes, eds. *Reading Job Intertextually.* Library of Hebrew Bible/Old Testament Studies. New York: T&T Clark, forthcoming.

Dhorme, Edouard. *A Commentary on the Book of Job.* Translated by Harold Knight. London: Thomas Nelson and Sons, 1967. Translation of *Le livre de Job.* Paris: V. Lecoffre, 1926.

Dillmann, August. *Hiob.* 4th ed. Kurzgefasstes exegetisches Handbuch zum Alten Testament 2. Leipzig: S. Hirzel, 1891.

Dion, Paul-Eugène. "Formulaic Language in the Book of Job: International Background and Ironical Distortions." *Studies in Religion* 16 (1987): 187–93.

Döderlein, Johann Christoph. *Scholia in libros Veteris Testamenti poeticos: Iobum, Psalmos et tres Salomonis.* Halle: Io.Iac. Curt, 1779.

Dozeman, Thomas. "Inner-Biblical Interpretation of Yahweh's Gracious and Compassionate Character." *Journal of Biblical Literature* 108 (1989): 207–23.

Driver, S. R. *An Introduction to the Literature of the Old Testament.* 9th ed. International Theological Library. Edinburgh: T&T Clark, 1929.

Driver, Samuel Rolles and George Buchanan Gray. *A Critical and Exegetical Commentary on the Book of Job.* International Critical Commentary. Edinburgh: T&T Clark, 1921.

Duhm, Bernhard. *Das Buch Hiob.* Freiburg: Mohr, 1897.

———. *Die Psalmen.* KHC 14. Leipzig: Mohr, 1899.

Eaton, J. H. *The Psalms.* London: Continuum, 2005.

Edenburg, Cynthia. "Intertextuality, Literary Competence and the Question of Readership: Some Preliminary Observations." *Journal for the Study of the Old Testament* 35 (2010): 131–48.

Eliot, T. S. "Tradition and the Individual Talent." Pages 47–59 in *The Sacred Wood: Essays on Poetry and Criticism.* London: Methuen, 1920.

Empson, William. *Seven Types of Ambiguity.* 3rd ed. Harmondsworth: Penguin, 1960.

Engnell, Ivan. "The Figurative Language of the Old Testament." Pages 242–90 in *Critical Essays on the Old Testament.* Edited and translated by John T. Willis. London: SPCK, 1970.

Eslinger, Lyle. "Inner-Biblical Exegesis and Inner-Biblical Allusion: The Question of Category." *Vetus Testamentum* 42 (1992): 47–58.

Ewald, Heinrich A. *Commentary on the Book of Job.* Translated by J. Frederick Smith. Theological Translation Fund Library 28. London: Williams & Norgate, 1882.

———. *Commentary on the Psalms.* Translated by E. Johnson. 2 vols. Theological Translation Fund Library 23–24. London: Williams and Norgate, 1880–1881.

Fishbane, Michael. *Biblical Interpretation in Ancient Israel.* Oxford: Clarendon Press, 1985.

———. "The Book of Job and Inner-Biblical Discourse." Pages 86–98 in *The Voice From the Whirlwind.* Edited by Leo G. Perdue and W. Clark Gilpin. Nashville: Abingdon, 1992.

———. "Inner-Biblical Exegesis: Types and Strategies of Interpretation in Ancient Israel." Pages 19–37 in *Midrash and Literature.* Edited by Geoffrey H. Hartman and Sanford Budick. New Haven: Yale University Press, 1986.

Fohrer, Georg. *Das Buch Hiob.* Kommentar zum Alten Testament 16. Gütersloh: Gütersloher Verlagshaus Gerd Mohn, 1963.

———. Review of Claus Westermann, *Der Aufbau des Buches Hiob. Vetus Testamentum* 7 (1957): 107–11.

———. "Form und Funktion in der Hiobdichtung." Pages 60–77 in *Studien zum Buche Hiob (1956–1979).* Beihefte zur Zeitschrift für die alttestamentliche Wissenschaft 159. Berlin: de Gruyter, 1983.

Forster, Christine. *Begrenztes Leben als Herausforderung: Das Vergänglichkeitsmotiv in weisheitlichen Psalmen.* Zürich: Pano, 2000.

Fox, Michael V. "Job the Pious." *Zeitschrift für die alttestamentliche Wissenschaft* 117 (2005): 351–66.

Frevel, Christian. "'Eine kleine Theologie der Menschenwürde': Ps 8 und seine Rezeption im Buch Ijob." Pages 244–72 in *Das Manna fällt auch heute noch: Beiträge zur Geschichte und Theologie des Alten, Ersten Testaments.* Edited by Frank-Lothar Hossfeld and Ludger Schwienhorst-Schönberger. Herders Biblische Studien 44. Freiburg: Herder, 2004.

———. "Dann wär' ich nicht mehr da: Der Todeswunsch Ijobs als Element der Klagerhetorik." Pages 25–41 in *Tod und Jenseits im alten Israel und in seiner Umwelt.* Edited by Angelika Berlejung and Bernd Janowski. Tübingen: Mohr Siebeck, 2009.

―――. "Schöpfungsglaube und Menschenwürde im Hiobbuch: Anmerkungen zur Anthropologie der Hiob-Reden." Pages 467–97 in *Das Buch Hiob und seine Interpretationen: Beiträge zum Hiob-Symposium auf dem Monte Verità vom 14.-19. August 2005*. Edited by Thomas Krüger, Manfred Oeming, Konrad Schmid, and Christoph Uehlinger. Abhandlungen zur Theologie des Alten und Neuen Testaments 88. Zürich: Theologischer Verlag, 2007.

Friedländer, Moriz. *Griechische Philosophie im Alten Testament: Eine Einleitung in die Psalmen- und Weisheitsliteratur: Psalmen, Proverbien, Hiob, Koheleth, Sirach, Pseudo-Salomo, und Anhang der Bücher Jona und Ruth*. Amsterdam: Philo Press, 1904.

Friedman, Susan Stanford. "Weavings: Intertextuality and the (Re)Birth of the Author." Pages 146–80 in *Influence and Intertextuality in Literary History*. Edited by Jay Clayton and Eric Rothstein. Madison: University of Wisconsin Press, 1991.

Frost, Stanley Brice. "Psalm 139: An Exposition." *Canadian Journal of Theology* 6 (1960): 113–22.

Genette, Gérard. *Palimpsests: Literature in the Second Degree*. Translated by C. Newman and C. Doubinsky. Stages 8. Lincoln: University of Nebraska Press, 1997.

Gerstenberger, Erhard S. *Psalms and Lamentations*. 2 vols. Forms of the Old Testament Literature 14–15. Grand Rapids, Mich.: Eerdmans, 1988, 2001.

Gibson, Edgar C. S. *The Book of Job*. 3rd ed. London: Methuen & Co., 1919.

Gillingham, Susan E. *The Poems and Psalms of the Hebrew Bible*. Oxford Bible Series. Oxford: Oxford University Press, 1994.

Ginzberg, Louis. *The Legends of the Jews*. 7 vols. Baltimore: John Hopkins University Press, 1998.

Glatzer, Nahum N. "Introduction: A Study of Job." Pages 1–48 in *The Dimensions of Job: A Study and Selected Readings*. Edited by Nahum N. Glatzer. New York: Schocken Books, 1969.

Goldingay, John. *Psalms*. 3 vols. Baker Commentary on the Old Testament Wisdom and Psalms. Grand Rapids, Mich.: Baker Academic, 2006–2008.

Good, Edwin M. *In Turns of Tempest: A Reading of Job*. Stanford, Calif.: Stanford University Press, 1990.

Good, John Mason. *The Book of Job*. London: Black, Parry & Co., 1812.

Gordis, Robert. *The Book of God and Man: A Study of Job*. Chicago: University of Chicago Press, 1978.

―――. *The Book of Job: Commentary, New Translation, and Special Studies*. Moreshet 2. New York: Jewish Theological Seminary of America, 1978.

Goulder, Michael D. *The Psalms of the Return: Book 5, Psalms 107–150*. Journal for the Study of the Old Testament: Supplement Series 258. Sheffield: Sheffield Academic Press, 1998.

Gray, John. *The Book of Job*. Edited by David J. A. Clines. The Text of the Hebrew Bible 1. Sheffield: Sheffield Phoenix Press, 2010.

Green, Barbara. *Mikhail Bakhtin and Biblical Scholarship: An Introduction*. Atlanta: Society of Biblical Literature, 2000.

Green, Douglas J. "The Good, the Bad and the Better: Psalm 23 and Job." Pages 69–83 in *The Whirlwind: Essays on Job, Hermeneutics and Theology in Memory of Jane Morse*. Edited by Stephen L. Cook, Corrine L. Patton, and James W. Watts. Journal for the Study of the Old Testament: Supplement Series 336. London: Sheffield Academic Press, 2001.

Greene, Thomas M. *The Light in Troy: Imitation and Discovery in Renaissance Poetry*. New Haven: Yale University Press, 1982.

Greenspahn, Frederick E. "A Mesopotamian Proverb and Its Biblical Reverberations." *Journal of the American Oriental Society* 114 (1994): 33–38.

Greenstein, Edward L. "Jeremiah as an Inspiration to the Poet of Job." Pages 98–110 in *Inspired Speech: Prophecy in the Ancient Near East: Essays in Honor of Herbert B. Huffmon*. Edited by John Kaltner and Louis Stulman. Journal for the Study of the Old Testament: Supplement Series 378. London: T&T Clark International, 2004.

———. "The Language of Job and its Poetic Function." *Journal of Biblical Literature* 122 (2003): 651–66.

———. "Misquotation of Scripture in the Dead Sea Scrolls." Pages 71–83 in vol. 1 of *The Frank Talmage Memorial Volume*. Edited by Barry Walfish. 2 vols. Haifa: Haifa University Press, 1993.

———. Review of Yohan Pyeon, *You Have Not Spoken What Is Right About Me: Intertextuality and the Book of Job*. *Review of Biblical Literature* 11 [http://www.bookreviews.org] (2003).

Grill, Julius. *Zur Kritik der Komposition des Buchs Hiob*. Tübingen: Fuesi, 1890.

Grohmann, Marianne. "Psalm 113 and the Song of Hannah (1 Samuel 2:1–10): A Paradigm for Intertextual Reading?" Pages 119–35 in *Reading the Bible Intertextually*. Edited by Richard B. Hays, Stefan Alkier, and Leroy A. Huizenga. Waco, Tex.: Baylor University Press, 2009.

Groß, Heinrich. *Ijob*. Neue Echter Bibel 13. Würzburg: Echter, 1986.

Grotius, Hugo. *Hugonis Grotii Annotata ad Vetus Testamentum*. Paris: Sebastiani Cramoisy, Regis & Reginae Architypographi, et Gabrielis Cramoisy, 1644.

Gruber, Mayer I. *Rashi's Commentary on Psalms*. Brill Reference Library of Judaism 18. Leiden: Brill, 2004.

Gunkel, Hermann. *Die Psalmen*. Göttingen: Vandenhoeck & Ruprecht, 1926.

———. "Die Psalmen." Pages 19–54 in *Zur Neueren Psalmenforschung*. Edited by Peter H. A. Neumann. Wege der Forschung 192. Darmstadt: Wissenschaftliche Buchgesellschaft, 1976.

Gunkel, Hermann and Joachim Begrich. *Introduction to Psalms: The Genres of the Religious Lyric of Israel*. Mercer Library of Biblical Studies. Macon, Ga.: Mercer University Press, 1998.

Habel, Norman C. "'Naked I Came …': Humanness in the Book of Job." Pages 373–92 in *Die Botschaft und die Boten*. Edited by Jörg Jeremias and Lothar Perlitt. Neukirchen-Vluyn: Neukirchener Verlag, 1981.

———. *The Book of Job: A Commentary*. Old Testament Library. Philadelphia: Westminster Press, 1985.

Hare, Francis. *Psalmorum liber: in versiculos metrice divisus*. Ugolini's Thesaurus antiquitatum sacrarum 31. Venice: 1766.

Hartley, John E. *The Book of Job*. New International Commentary on the Old Testament. Grand Rapids, Mich.: Eerdmans, 1988.

Hatina, Thomas R. "Intertextuality and Historical Criticism in New Testament Studies: Is There a Relationship?" *Biblical Interpretation* 7 (1999): 28–43.

Hays, Christopher B. "Echoes of the Ancient Near East? Intertextuality and the Comparative Study of the Old Testament." Pages 20-43 in *The Word Leaps the Gap: Essays on Scripture and Theology in Honor of Richard B. Hays*. Edited by J. Ross Wagner, C. Kavin Rowe, and A. Katherine Grieb. Grand Rapids, Mich.: Eerdmans, 2008.

Hays, Richard B. *The Conversion of the Imagination: Paul as Interpreter of Israel's Scripture*. Grand Rapids, Mich.: Eerdmans, 2005.

——. *Echoes of Scripture in the Letters of Paul*. New Haven: Yale University Press, 1989.

——. "On the Rebound: A Response to Critiques of *Echoes of Scripture in the Letters of Paul*." Pages 70–96 in *Paul and the Scriptures of Israel*. Edited by Craig A. Evans and James A. Sanders. Journal for the Study of the New Testament: Supplement Series 83. Sheffield: JSOT Press, 1993.

Hays, Richard B., Stefan Alkier, and Leroy A. Huizenga, eds. *Reading the Bible Intertextually*. Waco, Tex.: Baylor University Press, 2009.

Hebel, Udo J. "Towards a Descriptive Poetics of *Allusion*." Pages 135–64 in *Intertextuality*. Edited by Heinrich F. Plett. Research in Text Theory 15. Berlin: de Gruyter, 1991.

Heckl, Raik. *Hiob: Vom Gottesfürchtigen zum Repräsentanten Israels*. Forschungen zum Alten Testament 70. Tübingen: Mohr Siebeck, 2010.

Hempel, Johannes. "Mensch und König: Studie zu Psalm 8 und Hiob." *Forschungen und Fortschritte* 35 (1961): 119–23.

Hengstenberg, Ernst Wilhelm. *Commentary on the Psalms*. Translated by Patrick Fairbairn and John Thomson. 3 vols. Clark's Foreign Theological Library 1–2, 12. Edinburgh: T&T Clark, 1845–1848.

Hesse, Franz. *Hiob*. Züricher Bibelkommentare 14. Zürich: Theologischer Verlag, 1978.

Hitzig, Ferdinand. *Das Buch Hiob*. Leipzig: C.F. Winter'sche Verlagshandlung, 1874.

Hoffer, Victoria. "Illusion, Allusion, and Literary Artifice in the Frame Narrative of Job." Pages 84–99 in *The Whirlwind: Essays on Job, Hermeneutics and Theology in Memory of Jane Morse*. Edited by Stephen L. Cook, Corrine L. Patton, and James W. Watts. Journal for the Study of the Old Testament: Supplement Series 336. London: Sheffield Academic Press, 2001.

Hoffman, Yair. *A Blemished Perfection: The Book of Job in Context*. Journal for the Study of the Old Testament: Supplement Series 213. Sheffield: Sheffield Academic Press, 1996.

——. "The Technique of Quotation and Citation as an Interpretive Device." Pages 71–79 in *Creative Biblical Exegesis: Christian and Jewish Hermeneutics through the Centuries*. Edited by Benjamin Uffenheimer and Henning Graf Reventlow. Journal for the Study of the Old Testament: Supplement Series 59. Sheffield: JSOT Press, 1988.

Holladay, William L. *Jeremiah*. 2 vols. Hermeneia. Philadelphia: Fortress Press, 1986–1989.

Hollander, John. *The Figure of Echo: A Mode of Allusion in Milton and After*. Berkeley, Calif.: University of California Press, 1981.

Holm-Nielsen, Svend. *Hodayot: Psalms from Qumran*. Acta theologica danica 2. Aarhus: Universitetsforlaget, 1960.

Holman, J. C. M. "Analysis of the Text of Ps. 139." *Biblische Zeitschrift* 14 (1970): 37–71; 198–227.

Hölscher, Gustav. *Das Buch Hiob*. 2nd ed. Handbuch zum Alten Testament 17. Tübingen: Mohr, 1952.

Horst, Friedrich. *Hiob 1–19*. Biblischer Kommentar: Altes Testament 16/1. Neukirchen-Vluyn: Neukirchener Verlag, 1968.

Hossfeld, Frank-Lothar and Erich Zenger. *Die Psalmen*. 2 vols. Neue Echter Bibel 29, 40. Würzburg: Echter, 1993, 2002.

———. *Psalmen 101–150*. Herders theologischer Kommentar zum Alten Testament. Freiburg: Herder, 2008.

———. *Psalms 2: A Commentary on Psalms 51–100*. Translated by Linda M. Maloney. Hermeneia. Minneapolis: Fortress Press, 2005.

Hurvitz, Avi. "The Date of the Prose-Tale of Job Linguistically Reconsidered." *Harvard Theological Review* 67 (1974): 17–34.

———. *A Linguistic Study of the Relationship between the Priestly Source and the Book of Ezekiel*. Cahiers de la Revue biblique 20. Paris: J. Gabalda, 1982.

———. "Originals and Imitations in Biblical Poetry: A Comparative Examination of 1 Sam 2:1–10 and Ps 113:5–9." Pages 115–22 in *Biblical and Related Studies Presented to Samuel Iwry*. Edited by Ann Kort and Scott Morschauser. Winona Lake, Ind.: Eisenbrauns, 1985.

Irsigler, Hubert. "Quest for Justice as Reconciliation for the Poor and the Righteous in Psalms 37, 49 and 73." *Zeitschrift für altorientalische und biblische Rechtsgeschichte* 5 (1999): 258–76.

———. *Vom Adamssohn zum Immanuel*. Arbeiten zu Text und Sprache im Alten Testament 58. St. Ottilien: EOS, 1997.

Irwin, William. "Against Intertextuality." *Philosophy and Literature* 28 (2004): 227-42.

———. "What is an Allusion?" *The Journal of Aesthetics and Art Criticism* 59 (2001): 287–97.

Jameson, Fredric. *The Political Unconscious: Narrative as a Socially Symbolic Act*. Ithaca, N.Y.: Cornell University Press, 1981.

Jamieson-Drake, D. W. "Literary Structure, Genre and Interpretation in Job 38." Pages 217–35 in *The Listening Heart: Essays in Wisdom and Psalms in Honor of Roland E. Murphy*. Edited by Kenneth G. Hoglund, E. F. Huwiler, J. T. Glass, and R. W. Lee. Journal for the Study of the Old Testament: Supplement Series 85. Sheffield: JSOT Press, 1987.

Janzen, J. Gerald. *Job*. Interpretation. Atlanta: John Knox Press, 1985.

Jenny, Laurent. "The Strategy of Form." Pages 34–63 in *French Literary Theory Today*. Edited by T. Todorov. Cambridge: Cambridge University Press, 1982.

Johnson, Anthony. "Allusion in Poetry." *PTL: A Journal for Descriptive Poetics and Theory of Literature* 1 (1976): 579–87.

Joüon, Paul and T. Muraoka. *A Grammar of Biblical Hebrew*. 2 vols. Subsidia Biblica 14/1–2. Rome: Editrice Pontificio Istituto Biblico, 2005.

Julian the Arian. *Der Hiobkommentar des Arianers Julian*. Edited by Dieter Hagedorn. Patristische Texte und Studien 14. Berlin: de Gruyter, 1973.

Kaiser, Otto. "Psalm 39." Pages 133–45 in *Von Gott reden: Beiträge zur Theologie und Exegese des Alten Testament*. Neukirchen-Vluyn: Neukirchener Verlag, 1995.

Kierkegaard, Søren. *Repetition.* Translated by W. Lowrie. Princeton: Princeton University Press, 1941.

Kirkpatrick, A. F. *The Book of Psalms.* 3 vols. Cambridge: Cambridge University Press, 1892–1901.

Kissane, Edward J. *The Book of Job.* Dublin: Brown and Nolan Ltd., 1939.

———. *The Book of Psalms.* 2 vols. Dublin: Browne and Nolan Ltd., the Richview Press, 1953–1954.

Kittel, D. Rudolph. *Die Psalmen.* Kommentar zum Alten Testament 13. Leipzig: A. Deichertsche Verlagsbuchhandlung, 1914.

Klein, Hans. "Zur Wirkungsgeschichte von Psalm 8." Pages 183–98 in *Konsequente Traditionsgeschichte.* Edited by Rüdiger Bartelmus, Thomas Krüger, and Helmut Utzschneider. Orbis biblicus et orientalis. Göttingen: Vandenhoeck & Ruprecht, 1993.

Klein, J. "'The Ballad about Early Rulers' in Eastern and Western Traditions." Pages 203–16 in *Languages and Cultures in Contact: At the Crossroads of Civilizations in the Syro-Mesopotamian Realm.* Edited by Karel van Lerberghe and Gabriella Voet. Orientalia lovaniensia analecta 96. Leuven: Uitgeverij Peeters, 2000.

Knierim, Rolf. "Old Testament Form Criticism Reconsidered." *Interpretation* 27 (1973): 435–68.

Knudtzon, J. A. *Die El-Amarna-Tafeln.* 2 vols. Aalen: Otto Zeller, 1964.

Köhlmoos, Melanie. *Das Auge Gottes: Textstrategie im Hiobbuch.* Forschungen zum Alten Testament 25. Tübingen: Mohr Siebeck, 1999.

Koole, J. L. "Quelques remarques sur Psaume 139." Pages 176–80 in *Studia Biblica et Semitica.* Edited by W. C. van Unnik. Wageningen: H. Veenman & Zonen N.V., 1966.

Krašovec, J. "Die polare Ausdruckweise im Psalm 139." *Biblische Zeitschrift* 18 (1974): 224–48.

Kraus, Hans-Joachim. *Psalms: A Continental Commentary.* Translated by Hilton C. Oswald. 2 vols. Minneapolis: Fortress Press, 1993.

Kristeva, Julia. "Bakhtine, le mot, le dialogue et le roman." *Critique* 23 (1967): 438–65.

———. *Revolution in Poetic Language.* Translated by Margaret Waller. New York: Columbia University Press, 1984.

———. "Word, Dialogue, and Novel." Pages 64–91 in *Desire in Language: A Semiotic Approach to Literature and Art.* Edited by Leon S. Roudiez. Oxford: Basil Blackwell, 1980.

Kugel, James L. "The Bible's Earliest Interpreters." *Prooftexts: A Journal of Jewish Literary History* 7 (1987): 269–83.

———. *The Idea of Biblical Poetry: Parallelism and its History.* New Haven: Yale University Press, 1981.

———. "Topics in the History of the Spirituality of the Psalms." Pages 113–44 in vol. 1 of *Jewish Spirituality: From the Bible through the Middle Ages.* Edited by Arthur Green. 3 vols. New York: SCM Press, 1985.

Kuhl, Curt. "Neuere Literarkritik des Buches Hiob." *Theologische Rundschau* 21 (1953): 163–204; 257–317.

Kuntz, J. Kenneth. "Continuing the Engagement: Psalms Research Since the Early 1990s." *Currents in Biblical Research* 10 (2012): 321–78.

————. "Reclaiming Biblical Wisdom Psalms: A Response to Crenshaw." *Currents in Biblical Research* 1 (2003): 145–54.

Kynes, Will. "Beat Your Parodies into Swords, and Your Parodied Books into Spears: A New Paradigm for Parody in the Hebrew Bible." *Biblical Interpretation* 19 (2011): 276–310.

————. "Intertextuality: Method and Theory in Job and Psalm 119." in *Biblical Interpretation and Method: Essays in Honour of Professor John Barton*. Edited by K. J. Dell and P. M. Joyce. Oxford: Oxford University Press, forthcoming.

————. "Reading Job Following the Psalms." in *The Shape of the Ketuvim: History, Contoured Intertextuality, and Canon*. Edited by Julius Steinberg and Tim Stone. Siphrut. Winona Lake: Eisenbrauns, forthcoming.

————. "The Trials of Job: Re-litigating Job's 'Good Case' in Christian Interpretation." *Scottish Journal of Theology* (forthcoming).

Lambert, W. G. *Babylonian Wisdom Literature*. Oxford: Clarendon Press, 1960.

Le Clerc, Jean. *Sentimens de quelques theologiens de Hollande sur l'Histoire critique du Vieux Testament*. Amsterdam: Chez Henri Desbordes, 1685.

Lee, Samuel. *The Book of the Patriarch Job*. London: Duncan, 1837.

Leonard, Jeffery M. "Identifying Inner-Biblical Allusions: Psalm 78 as a Test Case." *Journal of Biblical Literature* 127 (2008): 241–65.

Lindström, Fredrik. *Suffering and Sin: Interpretations of Illness in the Individual Complaint Psalms*. Coniectanea biblica, Old Testament 37. Stockholm: Almqvist & Wiksell International, 1994.

Lipinski, E. "Macarismes et psaumes de congratulation." *Revue biblique* 75 (1968): 321–67.

Lombaard, C. J. S. "By Implication: Didactical Strategy in Psalm 1." *Old Testament Essays* 12 (1999): 506–14.

Luther, Martin. *Selected Psalms*. 3 vols. Luther's Works 12–14. St. Louis: Concordia, 1955–1958.

Luyten, Jos. "Psalm 73 and Wisdom." Pages 59–81 in *La Sagesse de l'Ancien Testament*. Edited by Maurice Gilbert. Gembloux: J. Duculot, 1979.

Lyons, Michael A. *From Law to Prophecy: Ezekiel's Use of the Holiness Code*. Library of Hebrew Bible/Old Testament Studies 507. New York: T&T Clark, 2009.

MacLaren, Alexander. "The Psalms." Pages 4–343 in *Psalms–Isaiah*. An Exposition of the Bible 3. Hartford, Conn.: S. S. Scranton Co., 1904.

Mai, Hans-Peter. "Bypassing Intertextuality: Hermeneutics, Textual Practice, Hypertext." Pages 30–59 in *Intertextuality*. Edited by Heinrich F. Plett. Research in Text Theory 15. Berlin: de Gruyter, 1991.

Mandolfo, Carleen. "A Generic Renegade: A Dialogic Reading of Job and Lament Psalms." Pages 45–63 in *Diachronic and Synchronic: Reading the Psalms in Real Time*. Edited by Joel S. Burnett, W. H. Bellinger, and W. Dennis Tucker. New York: T&T Clark, 2007.

Mathewson, Dan. *Death and Survival in the Book of Job: Desymbolization and Traumatic Experience*. Library of Hebrew Bible/Old Testament Studies 450. New York: T&T Clark, 2006.

Mays, James Luther. *Psalms*. Interpretation. Louisville, Ky.: Westminster John Knox, 1994.

Mazor, Yair. "When Aesthetics is Harnessed to Psychological Characterization–'Ars Poetica' in Psalm 139." *Zeitschrift für die alttestamentliche Wissenschaft* 109 (1997): 260–71.

McCann, J. Clinton, Jr. "The Book of Psalms." Pages 639–1280 in *1 & 2 Maccabees, Introduction to Hebrew Poetry, Job, Psalms*. The New Interpreter's Bible 4. Nashville: Abingdon Press, 1996.

———. "Psalm 73: A Microcosm of Old Testament Theology." Pages 247–57 in *The Listening Heart*. Edited by Kenneth G. Hoglund, Elizabeth F. Huwiler, Jonathan T. Glass, and Roger W. Lee. Journal for the Study of the Old Testament: Supplement Series 58. Sheffield: JSOT Press, 1987.

———. "Wisdom's Dilemma: The Book of Job, the Final Form of the Book of Psalms, and the Entire Bible." Pages 18–30 in *Wisdom, You Are My Sister: Studies in Honor of Roland E. Murphy, O. Carm., on the Occasion of his Eightieth Birthday*. Edited by Michael L. Barré. Catholic Biblical Quarterly Monograph Series 29. Washington, D.C.: Catholic Biblical Association of America, 1997.

Mejía, J. "Some Observations on Psalm 107." *Biblical Theology Bulletin* 5 (1975): 56-66.

Mettinger, Tryggve N. D. "The Enigma of Job: The Deconstruction of God in Intertextual Perspective." *Journal of Northwest Semitic Languages* 23 (1997): 1–19.

———. "Intertextuality: Allusion and Vertical Context Systems in Some Job Passages." Pages 257–80 in *Of Prophets' Visions and the Wisdom of Sages*. Edited by Heather A. McKay and D. J. A. Clines. Journal for the Study of the Old Testament: Supplement Series 162. Sheffield: JSOT Press, 1993.

Miller, Geoffrey D. "Intertextuality in Old Testament Research." *Currents in Biblical Research* 9 (2011): 283–309.

Miller, Patrick D. "Prayer and Divine Action." Pages 211–32 in *God in the Fray: A Tribute to Walter Brueggemann*. Edited by Tod Linafelt and Timothy K. Beal. Minneapolis: Fortress Press, 1998.

Miner, Earl. "Allusion." Pages 10–11 in *The Princeton Handbook of Poetic Terms*. Edited by A. Preminger. Princeton, N.J.: Princeton University Press, 1986.

Miscall, Peter D. "Isaiah: New Heavens, New Earth, New Book." Pages 41–56 in *Reading Between Texts: Intertextuality and the Hebrew Bible*. Edited by Danna Nolan Fewell. Literary Currents in Biblical Interpretation. Louisville, Ky.: Westminster John Knox, 1992.

———. "Texts, More Texts, a Textual Reader and a Textual Writer." *Semeia* 69/70 (1995): 247–60.

Moi, Toril. "Introduction." Pages 1–22 in *The Kristeva Reader*. Edited by Toril Moi. Oxford: Basil Blackwell, 1986.

Moore, Stephen D. and Yvonne Sherwood. *The Invention of the Biblical Scholar: A Critical Manifesto*. Minneapolis: Fortress Press, 2011.

Morawski, Stefan. "The Basic Functions of Quotation." Pages 690–705 in *Sign, Language, Culture*. Edited by A. J. Greimas. The Hague: Mouton, 1970.

Morgan, Thaïs. "The Space of Intertextuality." Pages 239–79 in *Intertextuality and Contemporary American Fiction*. Edited by P. O'Donnell and R.C. Davis. Baltimore, Md.: Johns Hopkins University Press, 1989.

Morrow, William S. *Protest against God: The Eclipse of a Biblical Tradition*. Hebrew Bible Monographs 4. Sheffield: Sheffield Phoenix Press, 2006.

Morson, Gary S. "Parody, History and Metaparody." Pages 63–86 in *Rethinking Bakhtin: Extensions and Challenges*. Edited by Gary S. Morson and C. Emmerson. Evanston: Northwestern University Press, 1989.

Moyise, Steve. "Intertextuality and Biblical Studies: A Review." *Verbum et Ecclesia* 23 (2002): 418–31.

———. "Intertextuality and Historical Approaches to the Use of Scripture in the New Testament." Pages 23–32 in *Reading the Bible Intertextually*. Edited by Richard B. Hays, Stefan Alkier, and Leroy A. Huizenga. Waco, Tex.: Baylor University Press, 2009.

Muilenburg, James. "The Book of Isaiah: Chapters 40–66." Pages 381–773 in *Ecclesiastes; Song of Songs; Isaiah; Jeremiah*. Interpreter's Bible 5. New York: Abingdon, 1956.

———. "Form Criticism and Beyond." *Journal of Biblical Literature* 88 (1969): 1–28.

Müller, Hans-Peter. *Das Hiobproblem: Seine Stellung und Entstehung im alten Orient und im Alten Testament*. 3rd ed. Erträge der Forschung 84. Darmstadt: Wissenschaftliche Buchgesellschaft, 1995.

Murphy, Roland E. *The Tree of Life: An Exploration of Biblical Wisdom Literature*. 3rd ed. Grand Rapids, Mich.: Eerdmans, 2002.

Neumann-Gorsolke, Ute. "'Mit Ehre und Hoheit hast Du ihn gekrönt' (Ps 8,6b): Alttestamentliche Aspekte zum Thema Menschenwürde." *Jahrbuch für Biblische Theologie* 15 (2000): 39–65.

Neusner, Jacob. *Canon and Connection: Intertextuality in Judaism*. Studies in Judaism. Lanham, Md.: University Press of America, 1987.

Newman, Judith H. *Praying by the Book: The Scripturalization of Prayer in Second Temple Judaism*. Society of Biblical Literature Early Judaism and Its Literature 14. Atlanta: Scholars Press, 1999.

Newsom, Carol A. "Bakhtin, the Bible, and Dialogic Truth." *Journal of Religion* 76 (1996): 290–306.

———. "The Book of Job." Pages 317–637 in *1 & 2 Maccabees, Introduction to Hebrew Poetry, Job, Psalms*. The New Interpreter's Bible 4. Nashville: Abingdon Press, 1996.

———. "The Book of Job as Polyphonic Text." *Journal for the Study of the Old Testament* 97 (2002): 87–108.

———. *The Book of Job: A Contest of Moral Imaginations*. Oxford: Oxford University Press, 2003.

Niditch, Susan. *Oral World and Written Word: Ancient Israelite Literature*. Library of Ancient Israel. Louisville, Ky.: Westminster John Knox, 1996.

Nogalski, J. D. "Intertextuality and the Twelve." Pages 102–24 in *Forming Prophetic Literature*. Edited by James W. Watts and P. R. House. Sheffield: Sheffield Academic Press, 1996.

Nurmela, Risto. *The Mouth of the Lord Has Spoken: Inner-Biblical Allusions in Second and Third Isaiah*. Studies in Judaism. Lanham, Md.: University Press of America, 2006.

———. *Prophets in Dialogue: Inner-Biblical Allusions in Zechariah 9–14*. Åbo: Åbo Akademi University Press, 1996.

Oeming, Manfred. *Das Buch der Psalmen: Psalm 1–41*. Neuer Stuttgarter Kommentar, Altes Testament 13/1. Stuttgart: Verlag Katholisches Bibelwerk GmbH, 2000.

Oesterley, W. O. E. *The Psalms.* 2 vols. London: Society for Promoting Christian Knowledge, 1939.

Olympiodorus, Deacon of Alexandria. *Kommentar zu Hiob.* Edited by U. Hagedorn and C. Hagedorn. Patristische Texte und Studien 24. Berlin: de Gruyter, 1984.

Oorschot, Jürgen van. "Die Entstehung des Hiobbuches." Pages 165–84 in *Das Buch Hiob und seine Interpretationen: Beiträge zum Hiob-Symposium auf dem Monte Verità vom 14.–19. August 2005.* Edited by Thomas Krüger, Manfred Oeming, Konrad Schmid, and Christoph Uehlinger. Abhandlungen zur Theologie des Alten und Neuen Testaments 88. Zürich: Theologischer Verlag, 2007.

Orr, Mary. *Intertextuality: Debates and Contexts.* Cambridge: Polity, 2003.

Patrologia latina. 217 vols. Edited by J.-P. Migne. Paris: 1844–1864.

Pascal, Blaise. *The Thoughts, Letters and Opuscules of Blaise Pascal.* Translated by O. W. Wight. New York: Derby & Jackson, 1859.

Patrick, Dale. "Job's Address of God." *Zeitschrift für die alttestamentliche Wissenschaft* 91 (1979): 268–82.

Perdue, Leo G. *Wisdom and Cult: A Critical Analysis of the Views of Cult in the Wisdom Literatures of Israel and the Ancient Near East.* Society of Biblical Literature Dissertation Series 30. Missoula, Mont.: Scholars Press, 1976.

Perri, Carmela. "On Alluding." *Poetics* 7 (1978): 289–307.

Peters, Charles. *A Critical Dissertation on the Book of Job.* London: E. Owen, 1751.

Pineda, Ioannis de. *Commentariorum in Iob libri tredecim, adiuncta singulis capitibus sua paraphrasi, quae et longioris commentarii summam continet.* Cologne: A. Hierat, 1605.

Piscator, Johannes. *In Librum Jobi commentarius: In quo, praeter novam versionem, versioni Tremellio-Junianae è regione adjectam, ordine & distincte proponuntur. I. Analysis logica singulorum capitum. II. Scholia in singula capita. III. Observationes locorum doctrinae è singulis capitibus depromtae.* Herborn: Officina Typographica Christophori Corvini, 1612.

Plett, Heinrich F. "Intertextualities." Pages 3–29 in *Intertextuality.* Edited by Heinrich F. Plett. New York: de Gruyter, 1991.

Polaski, Donald C. *Authorizing an End: The Isaiah Apocalypse and Intertextuality.* Biblical Interpretation Series 50. Leiden: Brill, 2001.

Polliack, Meira. "Deutero-Isaiah's Typological Use of Jacob in the Portrayal of Israel's National Renewal." Pages 72–110 in *Creation in Jewish and Christian Tradition.* Journal for the Study of the Old Testament: Supplement Series 319. London: Sheffield Academic Press, 2002.

Pope, Marvin H. *Job.* 3rd ed. Anchor Bible 15. Garden City, N.Y.: Doubleday, 1973.

Prinsloo, Gert T. "Polarity as Dominant Textual Strategy in Psalm 8." *Old Testament Essays* 8 (1995): 370–87.

Pury, Roland de. *Job ou l'homme révolté.* Cahiers du renouveau 12. Geneva: Éditions labor et fides, 1958.

Pyeon, Yohan. *You Have Not Spoken What Is Right About Me: Intertextuality and the Book of Job.* Studies in Biblical Literature 45. New York: Lang, 2003.

Raabe, Paul R. "Deliberate Ambiguity in the Psalter." *Journal of Biblical Literature* 110 (1991): 213–27.

Rad, Gerhard von. *Wisdom in Israel*. Translated by James D. Martin. Harrisburg, Pa.: Trinity Press International, 1993.

Rankin, O. S. *Israel's Wisdom Literature: Its Bearing on Theology and the History of Religion*. Edinburgh: T&T Clark, 1936.

Reed, Walter L. *Dialogues of the Word: The Bible as Literature According to Bakhtin*. Oxford: Oxford University Press, 1993.

Rendsburg, Gary A. *Linguistic Evidence for the Northern Origin of Selected Psalms*. Society of Biblical Literature Monograph Series 43. Atlanta: Scholars Press, 1990.

Reventlow, Henning Graf. *Gebet im Alten Testament*. Stuttgart: Kohlhammer, 1986.

———. "Skepsis und Klage: Zur Komposition des Hiobbuches." Pages 281–94 in *Verbindungslinien*. Edited by Axel Graupner, Holger Delkurt, and Alexander B. Ernst. Neukirchen-Vluyn: Neukirchener, 2000.

Ricoeur, Paul. *Interpretation Theory: Discourse and the Surplus of Meaning*. Fort Worth, Tex.: Texas Christian University Press, 1976.

Ringgren, H. "Einige Bemerkungen zum 73. Psalm." *Vetus Testamentum* 3 (1953): 265–72.

Roberts, J. J. M. "Job and the Israelite Religious Tradition." *Zeitschrift für die alttestamentliche Wissenschaft* 89 (1977): 107–14.

Robertson, David A. *Linguistic Evidence in Dating Early Hebrew poetry*. Missoula, Mont.: Society of Biblical Literature, 1972.

Roffey, J. W. "Beyond Reality: Poetic Discourse and Psalm 107." Pages 60–76 in *A Biblical Itinerary: In Search of Method, Form and Content: Essays in Honor of George W. Coats*. Journal for the Study of the Old Testament: Supplement Series 240. Sheffield: Sheffield Academic Press, 1997.

Rosenmüller, C. *Iobus*. 2nd ed. Scholia in Vetus Testamentum 5. Edited by C. Rosenmüller. Leipzig: Ioh. Ambros. Barthii, 1824.

———. *Psalmi*. 3 vols. Scholia in Vetus Testamentum 4. Leipzig: Ioh. Ambros. Barthii, 1821–1823.

Roudiez, Leon S. "Introduction." Pages 1–22 in *Desire in Language: A Semiotic Approach to Literature and Art*. Edited by Leon S. Roudiez. Oxford: Basil Blackwell, 1980.

Rowley, Harold Henry. "The Book of Job and its Meaning." Pages 141–83 in *From Moses to Qumran: Studies in the Old Testament*. London: Lutterworth Press, 1963.

———. *Job*. New Century Bible. Grand Rapids, Mich.: Eerdmans, 1980.

Rubin, Aaron D. "The Form and Meaning of Hebrew 'ašrê." *Vetus Testamentum* 60 (2010): 366–72.

Saadiah Ben Joseph Al-Fayyumi. *The Book of Theodicy: Translation and Commentary on the Book of Job*. Edited by Lenn Evan Goodman. Yale Judaica Series 25. New Haven: Yale University Press, 1988.

Sanders, James A. "The Book of Job and the Origins of Judaism." *Biblical Theology Bulletin* 39 (2009): 60–70.

———. "Intertextuality and Canon." Pages 316–33 in *On the Way to Nineveh: Studies in Honor of George M. Landes*. Edited by Stephen L. Cook and S. C. Winter. Atlanta: Scholars Press, 1999.

Sarrazin, Bernard. "Du rire dans la Bible: La théophanie de Job comme parodie." *Recherches de science religieuse* 76 (1988): 39–56.

Saussure, Ferdinand de. *Course in General Linguistics.* Translated by Roy Harris. Edited by C. Bally and A. Sechehaye. London: Duckworth, 1983.

Savran, George. "Seeing is Believing: On the Relative Priority of Visual and Verbal Perception of the Divine." *Biblical Interpretation* 17 (2009): 320–61.

Schaefer, Konrad. *Psalms.* Berit Olam. Collegeville, Minn.: Liturgical Press, 2001.

Schmid, Konrad. "Innerbiblische Schriftdiskussion im Hiobbuch." Pages 241–61 in *Das Buch Hiob und seine Interpretationen: Beiträge zum Hiob-Symposium auf dem Monte Verità vom 14.–19. August 2005.* Edited by Thomas Krüger, Manfred Oeming, Konrad Schmid, and Christoph Uehlinger. Abhandlungen zur Theologie des Alten und Neuen Testaments 88. Zürich: Theologisher Verlag Zürich, 2007.

Schmidt, Hans. *Das Gebet der Angeklagten im Alten Testament.* Beihefte zur Zeitschrift für die alttestamentliche Wissenschaft 49. Giessen: Töpelmann, 1928.

Schmidt, W. H. "Gott und Mensch in Ps. 8: Form- und überlieferungsgeschichtliche Erwägungen." *Theologische Zeitschrift* 25 (1969): 1–15.

Schnieringer, Helmut. *Psalm 8: Text – Gestalt – Bedeutung.* Ägypten und Altes Testament 59. Wiesbaden: Harrassowitz, 2004.

Schnurrer, Christian Friedrich. *Disputatio philologica ad Psalmum centesimum septimum.* Tübingen: Litteris Sigmundianis, 1789.

Schreiner, Susan Elizabeth. "'Why Do the Wicked Live?' Job and David in Calvin's Sermons on Job." Pages 129–43 in *The Voice from the Whirlwind: Interpreting the Book of Job.* Edited by Leo G. Perdue and W. Clark Gilpin. Nashville: Abingdon, 1992.

Schultens, Albert. *Opera minora, animadversiones ejus in Jobum, et ad varia loca V.T. nec non varias dissertationes et orationes, complectentia, antehae seorsum in lucem emissa, nunc in unum corpus collecta et conjunctim edita, una cum indicibus necessariis.* Leiden: Joh. le Mair & H. A. de Chalmot, 1769.

Schultz, Richard L. *The Search for Quotation: Verbal Parallels in the Prophets.* Journal for the Study of the Old Testament: Supplement Series 180. Sheffield: Sheffield Academic Press, 1999.

Schüngel-Straumann, Helen. "Zur Gattung und Theologie des 139. Psalms." *Biblische Zeitschrift* 17 (1973): 46–51.

Seeligmann, I. L. "Voraussetzungen der Midraschexegese." Pages 150–81 in *Congress Volume. Copenhagen 1953.* Edited by G. W. Anderson, Aage Bentzen, P. A. H. De Boer, Millar Burrows, Henri Cazelles, and Martin Noth. Supplements to Vetus Testamentum 1. Leiden: Brill, 1953.

Seybold, Klaus. *Die Psalmen.* Tübingen: Mohr, 1996.

———. "Psalmen im Buch Hiob." Pages 270–87 in *Studien zur Psalmenauslegung.* Edited by Klaus Seybold. Stuttgart: Kohlhammer, 1998.

Sherwood, Yvonne. *A Biblical Text and its Afterlives: The Survival of Jonah in Western Culture.* Cambridge: Cambridge University Press, 2000.

Silva, Moisés. *Has the Church Misread the Bible?: The History of Interpretation in the Light of Current Issues.* Leicester: Apollos, 1987.

Sitzler, Dorothea. *"Vorwurf gegen Gott": Ein religiöses Motiv im Alten Orient (Ägypten und Mesopotamien).* Studies in Oriental Religions 32. Wiesbaden: Harrassowitz, 1995.

Smend, Rudolf. "Baruch Spinoza." Pages 282–84 in vol. 15 of *Encyclopaedia Judaica.* 16 vols. Jerusalem: Keter, 1972.

Smick, Elmer B. *Job*. The Expositor's Bible Commentary 4. Edited by Frank Gaebelein and Richard P. Polcyn. Grand Rapids, Mich.: Zondervan, 1988.

Smith, Terry L. "A Crisis in Faith: An Exegesis of Psalm 73." *Restoration Quarterly* 17 (1974): 162–84.

Snaith, Norman Henry. "The Language of the Old Testament." Pages 220–32 in *General Articles on the Old Testament*. Interpreter's Bible 1. New York: Abingdon Press, 1952.

Snyman, Gerrie. "Who Is Speaking? Intertextuality and Textual Influence." *Neotestamentica* 30 (1996): 427–49.

Sommer, Benjamin D. "Exegesis, Allusion and Intertextuality in the Hebrew Bible: A Response to Lyle Eslinger." *Vetus Testamentum* 46 (1996): 479–89.

———. *A Prophet Reads Scripture: Allusion in Isaiah 40–66*. Stanford, Calif.: Stanford University Press, 1998.

Spieckermann, Hermann. *Heilsgegenwart: Eine Theologie der Psalmen*. Forschungen zur Religion und Literatur des Alten und Neuen Testaments 148. Göttingen: Vandenhoeck & Ruprecht, 1989.

Stead, Michael R. *The Intertextuality of Zechariah 1–8*. Library of Hebrew Bible/Old Testament Studies 506. New York: T&T Clark International, 2009.

Stec, David M. *The Targum of Psalms*. The Aramaic Bible 16. Collegeville, Minn.: Liturgical Press, 2004.

Stolz, F. "Der 39. Psalm." *Wort und Dienst* 13 (1975): 23–34.

Strahan, James. *The Book of Job Interpreted*. Edinburgh: T&T Clark, 1913.

Strazicich, John. *Joel's Use of Scripture and the Scripture's Use of Joel: Appropriation and Resignification in Second Temple Judaism and Early Christianity*. Biblical Interpretation Series 82. Leiden: Brill, 2007.

Tanner, Beth LaNeel. *The Book of Psalms Through the Lens of Intertextuality*. Studies in Biblical Literature 26. New York: Lang, 2001.

Tate, Marvin E. *Psalms 51–100*. Word Biblical Commentary 20. Dallas: Word Books, 1990.

Templeton, D. A. "A 'Farced Epistol' to a Sinking Sun of David. *Ecclesiastes* and *Finnegan's Wake*: The Sinoptic [*sic*] View." Pages 282–90 in *Text as Pretext: Essays in Honour of Robert Davidson*. Edited by R. Carroll. Journal for the Study of the Old Testament: Supplement Series 138. Sheffield: JSOT Press, 1992.

Terentius, Johannes. *Liber Ijobi Chaldaice et Latine, cum notis, item Graece* στιχηρως, *cum variantibus lectionibus*. Franeker: Johann Wellens, 1663.

Terrien, Samuel L. *The Elusive Presence: Toward a New Biblical Theology*. Religious Perspectives 26. San Francisco: Harper & Row, 1978.

———. *Job*. 2nd ed. Commentaire de l'Ancien Testament 13. Geneva: Labor et Fides, 2005.

———. *The Psalms: Strophic Structure and Theological Commentary*. The Eerdmans Critical Commentary. Grand Rapids, Mich.: Eerdmans, 2003.

Thomas, D. Winton. "Some Observations on the Hebrew Root חדל." Pages 8–16 in *Volume du Congrès*. Supplements to Vetus Testamentum 4. Leiden: Brill, 1957.

Torczyner, Harry. *Das Buch Hiob: Eine kritische Analyse des überlieferten Hiobtextes*. Wien: R. Löwit, 1920.

Tromp, Nicholas J. *Primitive Conceptions of Death and the Nether World in the Old Testament*. Biblica et orientalia 21. Rome: Pontifical Biblical Institute, 1969.

Tull, Patricia K. "Intertextuality and the Hebrew Scriptures." *Currents in Research: Biblical Studies* 9 (2000): 59–90.

———. "Rhetorical Criticism and Intertextuality." Pages 156–80 in *To Each Its Own Meaning: An Introduction to Biblical Criticisms and Their Application.* Edited by Steven L. McKenzie and Stephen R. Haynes. Louisville, Ky.: Westminster John Knox, 1999.

Tur-Sinai, N. H. (H. Torczyner). *The Book of Job: A New Commentary.* Revised ed. Jerusalem: Kiryath Sepher, 1967.

Umbreit, Friedrich. *Das Buch Hiob.* 2nd ed. Heidelberg: Mohr, 1832.

Van Leeuwen, Raymond C. "The Background of Proverbs 30:4aα." Pages 102–21 in *Wisdom, You Are My Sister: Studies in Honor of Roland E. Murphy, O. Carm., on the Occasion of His Eightieth Birthday.* Edited by Michael L. Barré. Catholic Biblical Quarterly Monograph Series 29. Washington, D.C.: Catholic Biblical Association of America, 1997.

———. "Psalm 8.5 and Job 7.17-18: A Mistaken Scholarly Commonplace?" Pages 205–15 in *The World of the Aramaeans I: Biblical Studies in Honour of Paul-Eugène Dion.* Edited by P. M. Michèle Daviau, John W. Wevers, and Michael Weigl. Journal for the Study of the Old Testament: Supplement Series 324. Sheffield: Sheffield Academic Press, 2001.

———. "Wealth and Poverty: System and Contradiction in Proverbs." *Hebrew Studies* 33 (1992): 25–36.

Vassar, John S. *Recalling a Story Once Told: An Intertextual Reading of the Psalter and the Pentateuch.* Macon, Ga.: Mercer University Press, 2007.

Vermeylen, Jacques. *Job, ses amis et son Dieu: La légende de Job et ses relectures postexiliques.* Studia biblica 2. Leiden: Brill, 1986.

Volz, Paul. *Weisheit: (Das Buch Hiob, Sprüche und Jesus Sirach, Prediger).* Die Schriften des Alten Testaments. Göttingen: Vandenhoeck & Ruprecht, 1911.

Wagner, Siegfried. "Zur Theologie des Psalms 139." Pages 357–76 in *Congress Volume Göttingen 1977.* Supplements to Vetus Testamentum 29. Leiden: Brill, 1978.

Warburton, William. *The Divine Legation of Moses Demonstrated.* The Works of the Right Reverend William Warburton, Lord Bishop of Gloucester 5. London: John Nichols, 1765.

Waschke, E.-J. "'Was ist der Mensch, daß du seiner gedenkst?' (Ps 8,5): Theologische und anthropologische Koordinaten für die Frage nach dem Menschen im Kontext alttestamentlicher Aussagen." *Theologische Literaturzeitung* 116 (1991): 801–11.

Watson, Wilfred G. E. *Classical Hebrew Poetry.* Journal for the Study of the Old Testament: Supplement Series 26. Sheffield: JSOT Press, 1984.

Weeks, Stuart. *An Introduction to the Study of Wisdom Literature.* New York: T&T Clark, 2010.

Weinfeld, Moshe. "Job and its Mesopotamian Parallels–A Typological Analysis." Pages 217–26 in *Text and Context: Old Testament and Semitic Studies for F. C. Fensham.* Edited by W. Claasen. Journal for the Study of the Old Testament: Supplement Series 48. Sheffield: Sheffield Academic Press, 1988.

Weiser, Artur. *Das Buch Hiob.* 8th ed. Das Alte Testament Deutsch 13. Göttingen: Vandenhoeck & Ruprecht, 1988.

———. *The Psalms: A Commentary.* Old Testament Library. Philadelphia: Westminster Press, 1962.

Westermann, Claus. "The Complaint Against God." Pages 233–41 in *God in the Fray: A Tribute to Walter Brueggemann.* Edited by Tod Linafelt and Timothy K. Beal. Minneapolis: Fortress Press, 1998.

———. *The Structure of the Book of Job: A Form-Critical Analysis.* Translated by Charles A. Muenchow. Philadelphia: Fortress Press, 1981.

Whybray, R. N. "'Shall not the Judge of All the Earth Do What is Just?': God's Oppression of the Innocent in the Old Testament." Pages 1–19 in *Shall Not the Judge of All the Earth Do What is Right?: Studies on the Nature of God in Tribute to James L. Crenshaw.* Edited by D. Penchansky and P. L. Redditt. Winona Lake, Ind.: Eisenbrauns, 2000.

Willey, Patricia Tull. *Remember the Former Things: The Recollection of Previous Texts in Second Isaiah.* Society of Biblical Literature Dissertation Series 161. Atlanta: Scholars Press, 1997.

Williamson, H. G. M. Review of Marvin A. Sweeney and Ehud Ben Zvi, *The Changing Face of Form Criticism. Journal of Jewish Studies* 56 (2005): 138–39.

Wilson, Gerald Henry. *Job.* New International Biblical Commentary on the Old Testament. Peabody, Mass.: Hendrickson, 2007.

Wilson, Leslie S. *The Book of Job: Judaism in the 2nd Century BCE: An Intertextual Reading.* Studies in Judaism. Lanham, Md.: University Press of America, 2006.

Witte, Markus. "Die dritte Rede Bildads (Hiob 25) und die Redaktionsgeschichte des Hiobbuches." Pages 349–55 in *The Book of Job.* Edited by W. A. M. Beuken. Bibliotheca ephemeridum theologicarum lovaniensium 114. Leuven: Leuven University Press, 1994.

Wolde, Ellen van. "Trendy Intertextuality?" Pages 43–49 in *Intertextuality in Biblical Writings: Essays in Honour of Bas van Iersel.* Edited by Sipke Draisma. Kampen: Kok, 1989.

Wolfers, David. *Deep Things out of Darkness: The Book of Job.* Kampen: Kok Pharos, 1995.

Wright, G. H. Bateson. *The Book of Job.* London: Williams and Norgate, 1883.

Würthwein, Ernst. "Erwägungen zu Psalm 73." Pages 161–78 in *Wort und Existenz: Studien zum Alten Testament.* Göttingen: Vandenhoeck & Ruprecht, 1970.

———. "Erwägungen zu Psalm 139." *Vetus Testamentum* 7 (1957): 165–82.

Young, Ian. *Diversity in Pre-Exilic Hebrew.* Forschungen zum Alten Testament 5. Tübingen: Mohr, 1993.

———. "Is the Prose Tale of Job in Late Biblical Hebrew?" *Vetus Testamentum* 59 (2009): 606–29.

Zachman, Randall C. "Gathering Meaning From Context: Calvin's Exegetical Method." *Journal of Religion* 82 (2002): 1–26.

Zenger, Erich. "'Was ist das Menschlein, daß du seiner gedenkst.?' (Ps 8,5). Die Sorge für den Menschen in Theologie und Verkündigung." Pages 127–45 in *Der Dienst für den Menschen in Theologie und Verkündigung.* Edited by Reinhard M. Hübner, Bernhard Mayer, and Ernst Reiter. Regensburg: Friedrich Pustet, 1981.

Ziegler, Joseph. *Iob.* Septuaginta: Vetus Testamentum Graecum XI, 4. Göttingen: Vandenhoeck & Ruprecht, 1982.

Zimmerli, Walther. *Man and His Hope in the Old Testament.* Studies in Biblical Theology. Second Series 20. London: SCM Press, 1971.

————. "Was ist der Mensch?" Pages 311–24 in *Studien zur alttestamentlichen Theologie und Prophetie: Gesammelte Aufsätze Band II*. Edited by Walther Zimmerli. Theologische Bücherei 51. Munich: Chr. Kaiser Verlag, 1974.

Zuckerman, Bruce. *Job the Silent: A Study in Historical Counterpoint*. Oxford: Oxford University Press, 1991.

Zuniga, Didacus. *In Job commentaria*. Rome: 1591.

Index of Ancient Sources

119:11	4	144:3	12, 67, 73
119:28	9	144:3-4	67
119:50	9	144:4	67
119:69	9	145:18	5
119:70	169	147	15
119:73	103	147:3	40
119:103	9	147:8	8
125:3	4	147:9	8
126	35		
126:2	35, 39	*Job*	
126:5	40	1:2-3	160
135:6	113	1:9	151
138:8	103	1:11-12	122
139:1	113	1:21	184
139:1-4	111	1:22	122
139:1-5	109	2:5-6	122
139:1-18	101	2:10	122, 184
139:2	114-15	2:20	122
139:5	116, 119, 156	3	89, 122, 137
139:5-7	120	3:1	122
139:6	110	3:1-12	45
139:7	112	3:5	86, 90
139:7-9	119	3:23	122
139:7-10	111-13, 116, 156, 181	4	11
		4:3-4	166
139:7-12	43, 114, 116	4:7	42
139:8	116	4:8	40
139:8-9	113	4:17-19	71
139:10	110, 114	4:18	73
139:11	109, 119	4:19	9, 136, 138
139:11-12	108	5	11, 87, 89, 91-93, 97, 181
139:12	109	5:2	42
139:13	102, 106	5:2-3	87
139:13-16	101-2, 104, 110-11, 181	5:2-5	87
		5:6	4
139:13-18	106-8	5:8-9	87
139:14	109-110	5:9	88
139:15	102, 106	5:9-16	11, 39, 42, 88-89
139:16	111	5:10	8, 88, 90, 93, 95
139:17-18	107	5:11	86, 88
139:19-22	109-110	5:12-13	88
139:19-24	101, 109	5:12-14	92
139:20	114	5:13	90, 152
139:21	109, 111, 118	5:13-14	151, 182
139:22	113	5:14	88
139:23	113, 119	5:16	4-5, 7, 9, 11, 80, 85-86, 88, 93, 94-95
139:23-24	111, 117, 156, 174, 182	5:17	86, 152
139:24	111		
144	65, 67-68		

Index of Subjects

Index of Authors

Williamson 42
Wilson, G. H. 147, 150-51, 155
Wilson, L. S. 14, 48
Witte 72
Wolde, van 23, 26
Wolfers 75, 167, 174
Wright 8, 42
Würthwein 109, 113, 120

Young 50

Zachman 5-6
Zenger 68, 79, 82-83, 87-88, 90, 95, 126,
    131, 136, 179
Ziegler 124
Zimmerli 77, 132, 137, 141
Zuckerman 1, 45, 137-38
Zuniga 6